Public Policy and Aboriginal

N.B.

1965-1992

Volume 2

Summaries of Reports by Federal Bodies and Aboriginal Organizations

Produced by the
Centre for Policy and Program Assessment
School of Public Administration
Carleton University

Royal Commission on Aboriginal Peoples

Canadian Cataloguing in Publication Data
Main entry under title:
Summaries of reports by federal bodies and Aboriginal organizations
Vol. 2
At head of title: *Public policy and Aboriginal peoples 1965-1992*

Also issued in French under the title:
Résumés de rapports d'organismes fédéraux et d'organisations autochtones.

ISBN 0-660-15413-7
Cat. no. Z1-1991/1-41-1-2E

1. Native people – Canada – Government relations.
2. Native peoples – Canada – Politics and government.
I. Canada. Royal Commission on Aboriginal Peoples.
II. Title: Public policy and Aboriginal peoples 1965-1992.

E78.C2S85 1994   323.1'197071   C94-980090-2

Public Policy and Aboriginal Peoples, 1965-1992

Volume 1
Overview of major trends in public policy relating
to Aboriginal peoples *(forthcoming, 1994)*

Volume 2
Summaries of reports by federal bodies and
Aboriginal organizations *(1994)*

Volume 3
Summaries of reports by provincial/territorial bodies
and other organizations *(1994)*

Volume 4
Bibliography (1993)

Available in Canada through
your local bookseller
or by mail from
Canada Communication Group – Publishing
Ottawa, Canada K1A 0S9

Cat. no. Z1-1991/1-41-1-2E
ISBN 0-660-15413-7

Canada	Groupe
Communication	Communication
Group	Canada
Publishing	Édition

Contents

Summaries of Reports by Aboriginal Organizations

Preface

When the Royal Commission on Aboriginal Peoples was established in the fall of 1991, it was advised by the Honourable Brian Dickson, former Chief Justice of the Supreme Court of Canada, to build on what work had already been done in the field of Aboriginal affairs. One way the Royal Commission followed this advice was to examine the major reports and studies by federal, provincial, territorial and municipal governments, by Aboriginal organizations, and by other non-government organizations on public policy in this field.

The project, conducted for the Commission by the Centre for Policy and Program Assessment of the School of Public Administration, Carleton University, examined reports by royal commissions, inquiries, parliamentary and legislative committees, and task forces, as well as commissioned studies. The focus was on reports that involved public input and that recommended changes in government policy relating to Aboriginal peoples.

Almost 900 such reports were identified for the period since 1965, when the landmark Hawthorn report provided the last benchmark analysis of government policy in this field. These reports are listed in Volume 4 of the overall project, the Bibliography, published in August 1993.

Volume 1 will be published in the summer of 1994 and will provide a thematic overview of major trends in public policy relating to Aboriginal peoples since 1965.

Volumes 2 and 3 provide the following descriptive information on more than 200 of the most significant documents described above:

• Background
• Purpose
• Issues and Findings
• Recommendations

Volume 2 contains summaries of reports by the federal government and by Aboriginal organizations. Volume 3 includes summaries of reports and studies by provincial, territorial and municipal governments, as well as non-governmental organizations. For each government and organization, the summaries are arranged in chronological order according to date of publication. This enables the reader to trace the evolution of public policy thinking in each government and organization over time. Both volumes include subject and author indexes.

The Royal Commission is using this information to inform itself as it develops its thinking regarding public policy recommendations. When completed, the collection of four volumes will provide a comprehensive overview of public policy development in the field of Aboriginal affairs. It will also comprise a significant series of reference documents for those interested in the field and will set a new benchmark in terms of public policy analysis and Aboriginal peoples.

Marlene Brant Castellano and David C. Hawkes
Co-Directors of Research

Acknowledgements

Preparation of the material in this volume occurred between March 1992 and June 1993. Many people assisted in the work. Gail Bradshaw, Carolyn Dittburner and Alex Ker, at different times, acted as logistics co-ordinator for the project, acquiring documents, distributing them to research assistants and editing draft summaries. All three did the job with the necessary mix of good humour, evenhandedness and attention to detail. The summaries themselves were prepared by a host of people, most of whom were students in the School of Public Administration at Carleton University. Our thanks go to Michael Allen, Kelly Ann Beaton, Trevor Bhupsingh, Michelle Bishop, Stéphane Gagnon, David Hennes, Melanie Jeffs, Daniel Jost, David Kravitz, Chris Lee, Julie Mugford, Aideen Nabigon, Elizabeth Peace, Gordon Quaiattini and Dan Stevenson. In addition, Martha Clark and Amanda Begbie of the School of Public Administration provided administrative support to the project.

The research team would like to thank the staff of the Royal Commission on Aboriginal Peoples and the organizations that submitted documents and/or participated in on-site reviews. It would have been impossible to prepare this volume without their assistance.

Finally, I would like to thank two faculty colleagues who served as co-investigators in the early phases of this project. Leigh Anderson was heavily involved in the original conception of the project and in setting up the data base that is one of its foundations. She continued to offer support for the work after her formal involvement had ended. Frances Abele was also involved in the early stages of the project and then assumed a somewhat different role as she went to the Royal Commission to become Director of its Northern Research Program. Her work on the project continues as it enters its final stage.

Katherine A. Graham
Principal Investigator

Note

This research project was launched during the Canada round of constitutional negotiations that led to the Charlottetown Accord of August 28, 1992. As such, the lists and summaries of reports prepared by governments and Aboriginal organizations and contained in volumes 2, 3 and 4 of this series are not comprehensive of all documents published during the Canada round. However, Volume 1, the overview of public policy discourse during the period 1965-1992, does take into account additional documents from the Canada round that are not included in the other volumes.

Summaries of Reports
by Federal Bodies

1966

▲ Report of the Advisory Commission on the Development of Government in the Northwest Territories

AUTHOR: Advisory Commission on the Development of Government in the Northwest Territories, Chair, A.W.R. Carrothers
YEAR: 1966
ABORIGINAL GROUP: Inuit, All Aboriginal Peoples
TOPICS: Constitution, Constitutional Development, Communications/Transportation, Economic/Social Development
SUB-TOPIC: development
SOURCE: Federal Commission

BACKGROUND

At its first meeting in 1965, the Commission determined it they should attend the meeting of the Council of the Northwest Territories (N.W.T.), travel throughout the N.W.T. in order to hold meetings and observe the lifestyle, and commission professional studies on the economic prospects and nature of the people. The Commission would present the views of the N.W.T. residents as well as the residents of the rest of Canada, much of which would be heard through public hearings as well as through mailed submissions requested by the Commission.

PURPOSE

The purpose of this report was to advise the minister of Northern Affairs and National Resources on matters related to the political development of the N.W.T. The Commission was to recommend the form of government most appropriate and consistent with the area's political, economic and social development, giving special attention to the following matters:

1. the views of N.W.T. and of Canadian residents;
2. the nature of the federal government's responsibility for the N.W.T.;
3. consideration of its political development and the cost involved;
4. the present forms of government;
5. the subject matter of the previous proposals affecting the constitutional structure; and
6. other desirable recommendations.

ISSUES AND FINDINGS

The issues raised by the report may be categorized as follows:

1. **The characteristics of development of government in the N.W.T. since Confederation.** Canada's claim to the area of the N.W.T. was not clarified until 1925, when it asserted its supremacy over the area. Its first interest was economic, as it was increased private economic activity which stimulated the growth of government in order to provide law and order. The post-Confederation era vested power in the lieutenant-governor. After this period, the Yukon became a separate territory, and the government of the remaining lands consisted of a commissioner and an appointed council. Federal statute formed the constitution of the N.W.T. In 1951, the legislative and executive functions were separated, and in 1966, council members were first elected; the result was essentially a colonial form of government. The Commission found itself faced with the question of whether or not responsible government should be implemented.

2. **A functional review of government activity in the N.W.T.** The report identifies several federal government departments and agencies whose operation directly affected the residents of the N.W.T., the most prominent of which was the Department of Northern Affairs and National Resources, which acted largely as a civil service for the territorial government. Other key federal government departments involved in activities in the N.W.T. included the Department of Health and Welfare, the Department of Transport, the Department of Public Works, the Department of National Defence, the Department of Justice, the Department of Mines and Technical Surveys, the Department of Fisheries, the Department of Agriculture, the Department of Forestry, Post Office Department, Department of National Revenue, Department of Labour, the Royal Canadian Mounted Police (which is the only law enforcement agency in the N.W.T.), and the Canadian Broadcasting Corporation.

The Commission also examined the development of the territorial government. The report notes that the Council of the N.W.T. met twice annually and had responsibility for most of the same jurisdictions as provincial governments, with the most notable exception being natural resources.

The structure of local government was dependent on the type of community: (1) administrative, which lacks any developed economic base other than government; (2) defence service, which is established to fulfil a specific defence requirement; (3) traditional resource base, which relies on renewable resources; (4) non-renewable resource base, which relies on a single non-renewable resources (e.g., a single mine), and (5) complex, which contains elements of each of the previous types.

The forms of local government recognized by the territorial governments were (1) unorganized settlements, in which there was no need for controls to promote orderly development other than those applied by the area administrator; (2) development areas, which were created by the Commissioner when controls are required to ensure orderly development; (3) local improvement districts, where conditions supported local financial contributions toward the provision of services within the community; (4) villages, which had a degree of self-sufficiency and could be seen as the first form of local government; and (5) towns, which were the senior level of local government.

There were also non-governmental institutions related to the operation of government. These included religious institutions, co-operatives, and commercial and labour organizations.

3. **The relationships showing the qualities of the residents and the problems they faced.** The Commission examined social and economic problems faced by the residents. The report identifies hostility between the Aboriginal and non-Aboriginal people in the North, based on the irresolution of land claims disputes and also on the lack of economic opportunity available. A related problem among the Aboriginal people was the division among treaty and non-treaty Indians and Métis.

The Commission report also examines the effect of the physical environment on the form of government in the North. Its geographic factors, its vast size, its global, international and national position, its geology and mineral resources, its physiography, its climate, its flora and fauna, and its people, were all factors in deciding the form of government that was most appropriate. What was observed was an inverse relationship between the importance of the physical and biological characteristics of the land and the level of government.

4. **Alternative programs for political development and issues that were unique to the government of the N.W.T.** The fourth issue recognized by the Commission was that of alternative forms of government. The report notes that traditional political structures employ the federal principle, and may adopt the form of the present territorial government, full provincial status, or quasi-provincial status. The constitution of the Yukon was such that it more closely resembles provincial status than does the N.W.T. The non-traditional forms of government employ the unitary principle, which allows for all federal departments and agencies with establishments in the N.W.T., all federal powers, all territorial powers and agencies, and all powers that are

elsewhere provincial, to be vested in one territorial government, which would be headed by a representative appointed by the federal government. Whichever form of political development was chosen would involve the further choice of internal structures, with consideration given to the British parliamentary system and the American presidential system. These choices reflected concern with style, composition, and powers of the executive and legislative branches of government and their relationship with one another and to the federal government.

The issue of alternative geographical areas was also raised in regard to the best form of government. The choices were the maintenance of the status quo, division of the territories into two or more parts, annexation of the territories or parts of them to the provinces, and the union of the Yukon and N.W.T.

5. **The Commission's postulates, or statements of values fundamental to the political development.** The following constitute the postulates of the Commission on which its recommendations are based: (1) political development cannot be considered independently from the economic and social future of the N.W.T.; (2) an "optimum" number of residents should participate in government; (3) the form of government must be able to deal effectively with the unique social and economic problems of its people; (4) the type of government chosen must not be foreign to the political traditions of Canada; (5) the residents should be afforded economic opportunity roughly equivalent to other Canadians without having to relocate, and therefore, economic opportunity must be created in the north; (6) being a political unit separate from the provinces, the federal government has responsibility for the economic development of the N.W.T.; (7) and the Indigenous peoples should be free to maintain their ethnic and cultural identities.

RECOMMENDATIONS

The Commission limits its recommendations to those relating to the forms of government and procedures of administration.

1. Political Status

With regard to the issue of political status, the Commission recommends against the division of the N.W.T. into two or more political units, proposing that the territories be divided for the purposes of planning and co-ordination only. It also addresses the matter of provincehood, suggesting that it is not provincehood that is presently required, but rather the means to grow toward provincehood. The report recommends that the capital of the N.W.T. be located in Yellowknife.

2. Structure and Function of Territorial Government

Regarding the structure of the territorial government, it is recommended that there be a commissioner, a deputy commissioner, an executive council, a legislative assembly, departments of economic development, finance, local government, education, welfare and social services, public works, justice, and lands and resources, a N.W.T. Development Board, and a N.W.T. Development Corporation, all of which have specific roles, obligations, and structures. It recommends that the Department of Northern Affairs make an agreement with the government of the N.W.T. for the administration of Indian and Inuit affairs by the N.W.T. and that the territorial government be represented at federal-provincial and inter-provincial conferences. The Commission further recommends that surface rights to lands be transferred to the territorial government and that there be a public review (in not more than ten years) of the political, social and economic development of the N.W.T. Finally, the Commission recommends that postal services to outlying areas should be studied and that the number of political constituencies should be increased.

▲ Survey of the Contemporary Indians of Canada

AUTHOR: Department of Indian Affairs and Northern Development, Indian Affairs Branch, Director of Research and Editor, H.B. Hawthorn

YEAR: 1966

ABORIGINAL GROUP: All Aboriginal Peoples

TOPICS: Self-Government, Federal Government/Aboriginal Relations, Provincial Government/Aboriginal Relations

SUB-TOPICS: structures and institutions, policy, jurisdiction, economic development

SOURCE: Federal Department

BACKGROUND

The *Survey of the Contemporary Indians of Canada* (the Hawthorn Report) was written at a time when the unequal distribution of power between Indian and non-Indian peoples was being challenged at an international level. In Canada, the Aboriginal population was beginning to assert its rights and expressed a desire for independence from the special controls of the federal government.

The material poverty of Aboriginal peoples, compared to the rest of the Canadian population, had become a public issue and could no longer be tolerated in a new era of egalitarianism. To address these issues, more information on the state of Aboriginal affairs was needed and a comprehensive survey was commissioned.

PURPOSE

The general goal of the report was to consider and recommend courses of action that would improve the position of Aboriginal peoples in society, with the underlying principle that those affected must be in a position to choose among alternatives.

ISSUES AND FINDINGS

The Report was divided into two volumes. Volume one addresses primarily economic development, legal status and local government issues; volume two deals with education and band councils.

Economic development: It was noted that the Indian Affairs Branch was attempting to formulate a program to encourage more rapid economic development for Indians. The author recognized the interrelatedness of economic and social factors and equated the Branch's long-range program of balanced economic and social development with that of developing countries.

A large part of volume one was devoted to examining theories of economic development and commenting on their appropriateness in the Aboriginal context. Issues of note:

1. The report emphasized the use of real income from gainful employment as a measure of economic development.

2. There should be a balance between economic development and social development, with a shift away from the economics of exploitation to the economics of human investment; i.e., in education.

3. Contrary to the usual tenets of economic development, the survey did not find evidence that over-population was any more of a problem for Aboriginal peoples than it was for the rest of Canada.

4. It was believed that the ready provision of welfare led to apathy and could have been averted by a well-designed economic development program. The Indian Affairs Branch's new community development program was expected to address this problem.

5. The success of economic development would be fundamentally linked with the relationship that Aboriginal peoples developed with the rest of Canadian society; that is, their ability to participate in all aspects of society as equals.

The report contains a survey on the economic status of Indians in Canada. Findings were:

1. The economically depressed and under-employed status of Native people could be explained by their occupational distribution in the traditional fields of primary, resource-based industries.

2. Factors contributing to economic underdevelopment included distance and isolation from job centres, and social, cultural and psychological factors. The accumulation of capital was also not considered as important as elsewhere in society. Indian Affairs Branch had fostered dependency by playing an administrative rather than developmental role in its relations with Aboriginal peoples. Contact and relations with white society emphasized the weak bargaining position and growing dependency of Indians.

The survey also contains a comparative study of economic factors thought to affect development at the band level. The report found that:

1. ownership or access to resources, both on-reserve and off, had little if any correlation to the level of development;

2. ownership or availability of capital showed no consistent relationship to development;

3. geographic and social isolation were found to have a long-term effect on work incentives since there was little access to public facilities;

4. the existence of a professional or entrepreneurial middle-class in the band membership did little to raise aspirations since most professionals lived off-reserve;

5. although it was found that higher income bands had a higher percentage of their populations in the upper age group and lower percentages of the under-16 age group, this was felt to be a by-product rather than a determinant of economic growth.

Socio-economic factors thought to influence the level of economic development included:

1. Educational levels, seen as central to economic development and integration into Canadian society, were not as highly correlated with achievement as expected. It was also found that more than half the population was under 16, unskilled and unemployed.

2. There was a high degree of correlation between mobility and economic development, in that Aboriginal people fared better economically off-reserve. The report suggested more funds be used toward resettlement and off-reserve programs, without detracting from reserve programs.

Socio-cultural aspects of economic development were examined. It was found that:

1. Cultural revival may be necessary for rehabilitation and economic development by facilitating new pride and a sense of identity. The report recognized that cultural revival was viewed by some as an act of defeatism or retreat.

2. Kinship ties on-reserve had tended to encourage relationships of dependency between successful and unsuccessful relatives.

3. The higher the income of an Aboriginal person, the more organizations he/she belongs to, both on- and off-reserve.

The legal status of Indians and their relationship with the federal government were examined. Some issues were:

1. Although treaties were insubstantial, they seemed of great importance to the Aboriginal people, and this complicated Indian/government relations.

2. The federal government had historically limited its policies to on-reserve issues. In general it was felt that the federal government had much more discretion over jurisdictional matters than it exercised.

3. The budget of the Indian Affairs Branch was far from adequate.

4. Indian Affairs staffing requirements needed to stress expertise in special functions rather than administrative capabilities.

5. The Branch should cease its historical tendency of encouraging Native people to remain on-reserve.

6. There should be more provincial responsibility for Aboriginal peoples. The report pointed out that since the welfare activities of the Indian Affairs Branch were not statutory obligations, the provinces had no reason not to extend to Indians the benefits they would extend to any Canadian citizen.

Local self-government: Factors found to inhibit the proliferation of local self-government were:

1. the distribution of band members on- and off-reserve;

2. the inadequate amount of funds generated by local bands for local government purposes. The report stressed that revenues should be raised independently of government and that a local civil service was needed.

The Hawthorn Report noted that there were two possible frameworks for local self-government: the municipal/provincial framework, or the federal framework; it suggested a blending of the two. Although provinces were recognized as having obligations to Aboriginal people, it was felt there were many instances where federal involvement was still required.

It was also considered important that Aboriginal people vigorously pursue their goals through political avenues, as would any member of a free society.

Education: The report indicated that learning had meaning to an Indian child only if he/she were to receive responsibility and a fuller place in Canadian society. Hawthorn therefore advocated the integration of Indian children into provincial systems, with the provision of special services. The difficulties involved in integrating minorities into the dominant culture were recognized, as was the propensity for higher education to undermine cultural identity.

The education policies of the federal government and joint agreements with provincial governments were examined. Some inconsistency in federal education policy was found. Although the integration of Aboriginal peoples into Canadian society rather than assimilation was professed as the long-term goal of the federal government, it made no provision for the preservation of language and cultural traditions. It was also noted that the new philosophy on integrated education was not being implemented fully by subordinates. This led to a questioning of the federal government's policy as rhetoric aimed at appeasing the public.

With regard to joint agreements, it was found that there was a need for more parental involvement. The consultation process was inadequate, with many parents feeling forced to make decisions about their children's education without proper knowledge. It had been discovered there was great interest in education within the Aboriginal community as demonstrated by Indian School Committees.

Band councils: Increase in the activities of band councils was seen as evidence that Aboriginal peoples were very interested in their own affairs. It was felt there was a pressing need for bands to broaden their perspectives and be exposed to experiences transcending the strictly local.

RECOMMENDATIONS

The report contained myriad recommendations, some of which are:

Indians should be regarded as "citizens plus"; they possess certain rights as charter members of the Canadian community. The Indian Affairs Branch should have special responsibility for ensuring that this is recognized and that the Canadian people are educated in the acceptance of their existence.

Attempts to deny Indian access to basic public programs at any level of government on the grounds of an alleged incompatibility between Indian status and the program in question should be critically investigated.

The main emphasis on economic development should be on education, vocational training and techniques of mobility to enable Indians to take wage and salaried jobs.

More funding was needed for the Indian Affairs Branch. An adequate program for economic development required a much larger budget and staff. Staff should be specially trained in relevant services rather than strictly administratively competent. In addition, the Indian Affairs branch should act as an advocate for Indian rights.

The general policy of extending provincial services to Indians was strongly encouraged where applicable. Both levels of government were advised to pool their resources to overcome the poverty and isolation of Aboriginal peoples.

Local government was to be encouraged and not treated in the either/or terms of the *Indian Act* or the provincial framework of local government.

The integration of Indian children into the public school system was highly endorsed. All authorities were given the responsibility to recognize the special and remedial program needs of these children, while recognizing that the intellectual capacity of Aboriginal children was the same as other children.

Joint agreements should not be signed without lengthy consultation with parents, and contact between school officials and parents should be ongoing.

Band councils should be encouraged to seek professional legal, economic and social advice from other sources as well as official ones.

1969

▲ Statement of the Government of Canada on Indian Policy

AUTHOR: Minister of Indian Affairs and Northern Development
YEAR: 1969
ABORIGINAL GROUP: First Nations
TOPICS: Federal/Aboriginal Relations, Provincial/Aboriginal Relations

SUB-TOPICS: policy, institutions, legislation, program and service delivery

SOURCE: Federal Government

BACKGROUND

This White Paper on Indian policy was a response to consultations with Indian leaders. The preceding two years and conferences with such organizations as the National Indian Brotherhood (NIB) had shown the federal government that there was a forceful and articulate Indian leadership, dissatisfied with the impoverished situation of most Native people. It became apparent to the government that its traditional, paternalistic relationship with Indian peoples was in need of restructuring. It was felt that the differential treatment of Indians on the basis of race was no longer tolerable.

PURPOSE

The purpose of the White Paper was to change long-standing policies which separated Indian people from Canadian society and thereby denied them equal opportunity.

ISSUES AND FINDINGS

The new policy, as outlined in the White Paper references six issues:

1. legal structure;
2. Indian cultural heritage;
3. programs and services;
4. enriched services;
5. claims and treaties; and
6. Indian lands.

The report concludes with a section on implementation.

With regard to the legal structure, it was felt that the legislative and constitutional sources of discrimination needed to be removed.

Indian cultural heritage would be preserved and enhanced in order to recognize the unique contribution of Indian culture to Canadian society. It was felt that the enrichment of Canadian society through the celebration of cultural diversity was central to the policy.

Programs and services were the third aspect of the new policy. It was believed that services should be delivered through the same mechanisms and by the same government agencies for all Canadians. It was underlined that because the *Indian Act* was federal, Indians were not treated within their province as full and equal citizens and that most social remedies were available only under provincial jurisdiction.

The issue of enriched services dealt with the fact that the social and economic conditions of Indians were unsatisfactory compared with the rest of society, and that special services would be needed for some time. In relation to economic services more specifically, the federal government noted that Indian people have been unable to develop resources on-reserve lands, lacking adequate social and risk capital as well as managerial and technical experience.

With respect to claims and treaties, the report downplayed their significance and suggested they would become anomalies once the new policy had been in place for awhile. In the interim, lawful obligations needed to be recognized. The report noted that the government intended to introduce legislation to establish an Indian Claims Commission, but that it had serious doubts as to whether such a commission, as conceived in the 1965 proposal to Parliament, would be effective.

The report stated that control of Indian lands should be transferred to the Indian people in order to foster both financial freedom and self-determination.

Implementation of the policy would require the further development of a close working relationship with Indian peoples and communities. It was hoped that, for the most part, the policy would be in effect within five years.

RECOMMENDATIONS

On the question of legal structure, the report stated that the ultimate goal would be the eventual removal of specific references to Indians in the Constitution. The short-term goal would be to repeal the Indian Act.

With regard to Indian cultural heritage, the government made two recommendations:

1. Through Secretary of State the federal government would support associations and groups in developing a greater appreciation of their cultural heritage;
2. the support of provincial governments would be enlisted.

In order to improve the delivery of programs and services to Indian people and communities, the government made three recommendations:

1. negotiate with the provinces and conclude agreements (with Indian participation) for program and service delivery;

2. transfer federal disbursements for Indian programs in each province to that province; and

3. transfer of all remaining federal responsibilities for Indians from the Department of Indian Affairs and Northern Development to other federal departments.

In respect of enriched social programs, the government recommended that existing programs throughout the federal government be reviewed and new ones established with the objective of breaking patterns of deprivation. The termination of programs deemed no longer necessary under the new policy was noted as a way to free up funds for other uses. Eventually, it is hoped there will no longer be separate agencies for Indians, with associated administrative savings benefiting all Canadians.

For enriched economic programs, the government recommended that substantial additional funds be made available for investment in the economic progress of Indian people, and that all federal and provincial programs and advisory services be made readily available to Indians.

The government recommended further study of claims and treaty issues by both Indians and government, as well as the appointment of a Claims Commissioner.

It proposed the *Indian Lands Act*, which would transfer full control of reserve lands to Indians, including the determination of who shares in ownership. This would involve agreements between bands and provincial governments.

To implement the new policy, the government made two recommendations:

1. invite executives of NIB and various provincial associations to discuss their potential role and the financial resources that would be needed; and

2. national/regional associations act as principal agencies in consultations and negotiations.

▲ Terms of Reference of the Indian Claims Commission

AUTHOR: Privy Council Office
YEAR: 1969
ABORIGINAL GROUP: All Aboriginal Peoples

TOPIC: Claims
SUB-TOPIC: commission/institutions
SOURCE: Federal Department

BACKGROUND

The origin of the Indian Claims Commission stemmed from Crown recognition that many Indian people felt aggrieved about "matters arising out of the transaction between them and the other people of Canada during the settlement of Canada and the administration of certain of the Indians' affairs by the Government of Canada". These grievances were in the form of claims focusing on land occupation by non-Indians, non-fulfilment of treaty terms and agreements, and the administration of legislated Indian benefits.

It is noted that the first mentioned assertion of grievances is general and undefined and requires a policy " ... to enable Indians to participate fully as members of the Canadian community." With respect to the second and third classes of grievances, it is mentioned that adjudication might be in order.

The committee appointed Dr. Lloyd Barber as Commissioner and charged him with the task of receiving and studying grievances arising in respect of

(i) The performance of the terms of treaties and agreements formally entered into by representatives of the Indians and the Crown, and

(ii) the administration of moneys and lands pursuant to schemes established by legislation for the benefit of the Indians".

The Commissioner was also instructed to recommend measures the government could take for the resolution of claims and to advise as to categories of claims that ought to be referred to the courts (or any special quasi-judicial or administrative bodies) for adjudication.

1971

▲ **Minutes of Proceedings and Evidence of the Standing Committee on the Annual Reports of the Department of Indian Affairs and Northern Development (1967-68 and 1968-69),** Including: Fifth Report to the House
(re: the status of Indian and Eskimo education in Canada)

AUTHOR: Standing Committee on Indian Affairs and Northern Development

YEAR: 1971

ABORIGINAL GROUP: All Aboriginal Peoples

TOPIC: Education

SUB-TOPICS: pre-school/daycare, primary and secondary education, post-secondary, adult, vocational/training, curriculum, fiscal relations/responsibilities, professionals/educators.

SOURCE: House of Commons Committee

BACKGROUND

The Standing Committee on Indian Affairs decided to direct special attention to the issue of Indian and Inuit education because of the shared concern among Committee members that there were profound deficiencies in an education system as indicated by the school drop-out rate, the unemployment or underemployment rate, and the percentage of young people who were unemployed for most of the year.

The Committee heard testimony from a cross-section of witnesses concerned with Indian and Inuit education, including students, representatives of Aboriginal organizations, and government officials. The testimony was supplemented by visits to Indian and Inuit communities and by discussions with community leaders, parents, young people and students in those communities.

PURPOSE

The purpose of the report of the Standing Committee is to provide recommendations that would allow federal schools under the control of the Education Branch of the Department of Indian Affairs and Northern Development (DIAND) to furnish Indian and Inuit youth with an education which will provide equality of opportunity and the ability to be employed at every level of the economy of the regions in which they live. The model education program envisioned by the Committee is to have the following goals:

1. the elimination of obstacles which have condemned Indian students to a disadvantaged status within the school system as well as in the adult society into which they graduate;

2. the elimination of the gap between the average Canadian unemployment rate and that of the Indian people;

3. the elimination of the differences in the high school drop-out rate;

4. the elimination of negative parental and community attitudes toward education in many Indian and Inuit communities; and

5. the elimination of the problem of acculturation which faces most Indian and Inuit young people.

ISSUES AND FINDINGS

The Committee found there to be many deficiencies in the response of the education system to the needs of Indian and Inuit communities. Some concerns raised include:

1. neglect of the education system on the part of the federal government;

2. curriculum and language instruction unresponsive to the special needs of Indian and Inuit children;

3. disregard of pre-school instruction;

4. an insensitive system of student residences which distanced children from their parents and communities;

5. inflexible vacation timing which conflicted with traditional occupations such as hunting and trapping;

6. vocational training that was not responsive to the needs of the communities in which Indian and Inuit young people lived;

7. ineffective use of education committees and school boards;

8. a paucity of higher education programs related to Indian studies;

9. negative community and parental attitudes to education;

10. the failure to realize the potential of television and technology in educational programming for Indian, Inuit and Métis youth; and

11. the lack of provincial teacher training institutions which provide special training for those involved in the teaching of Indian and Inuit children.

RECOMMENDATIONS

It is the Committee's view that in light of the poor record of the federal school and the provincial systems, that the government must immediately and in full consultation and partnership with the Indian peoples and Inuit of Canada, develop a federal education system as free from the deficiencies afflicting the present program as is possible, and to this end, the Committee makes the following recommendations:

1. Transfer to Provinces

The Committee recommends that the government continue its policy that no transfers of education programs from the federal level to the provincial systems take place without the express and clear approval of the majority of the parents in each community concerned.

2. Culture

The Committee recommends that all curriculums within the federal program be revised to include more Indian history and culture.

3. Language Instruction

The Committee recommends that the language of instruction at the pre-school level and up to the first or second year of primary school should be in the language of the local Indian or Inuit community, with secondary and tertiary languages (English and/or French) being introduced gradually through the pre-school and primary period. It is further recommended that courses linked to the local Indian or Inuit culture continue to be taught in the local language through the primary level.

The report also suggests that decisions regarding the initial languages of instruction and the timing of introduction of secondary and tertiary languages should only be made after consultation with, and clear approval from a majority of parents in the community.

4. Pre-School Instruction

The Committee recommends that pre-school instruction be made available to all Indian and Inuit children, starting with the three-year-old category. This instruction is to be phased in over a period of five years.

5. Student Residences

The Committee endorses the present DIAND policy of phasing out elementary student residences and encouraging local day schools in order to end a system which sees children as young as five and six separated from their parents for eight or nine months of the year.

The Committee also recommends that the existing secondary level student resident system for Indian and Inuit children be phased out where the establishment of local high schools or use of non-reserve facilities at closer proximity to the reserve or local communities is possible and is desired by a majority of local parents.

6. Vacations

The Committee recommends that the timing of vacation periods be flexible and that they be planned in consultation with individual communities. The Committee members also suggest that the federal government consider setting aside funds for the transport of students to their homes at Christmas.

7. Vocational Training

The Committee recommends that vocational training programs be reviewed and revised in consultation with local Indian and Inuit communities, provincial Indian associations, employers, provincial labour departments, and the federal Department of Manpower to achieve a vocational training program which will properly reflect the employment opportunities and employment requirements in the areas in which Indian and Inuit young people live.

8. Education Committee and School Board Participation

The Committee encourages establishment of education committees, and the broadening of their scope and function to include a role in improving local community attitudes toward education. The Committee also recommends consideration of the idea to establish school board to administer all schools located on Indian reserves or within Indian and Inuit communities.

9. Higher Education

The Committee recommends that Canadian universities and colleges be encouraged to initiate university and college courses both at the under-graduate and post-graduate levels in Indian studies, including Indian history, culture, language, anthropology, guidance counselling, and community and social work studies. The Committee also suggests that the government widen its support for experimental teaching approaches and training programs designed for Indian, Inuit and Métis people at the secondary, post-secondary and university levels.

10. Community and Parental Attitudes to Education

The Committee recommends that consideration be given to providing additional resources to Indian and Inuit organizations for the encouragement of parental involvement in education and of more positive community and home attitudes toward education.

11. Television

The Committee recommends that, in collaboration with the Canadian Broadcasting Corporation, educational programming be developed aimed specifically at the Indian and Métis peoples and Inuit of Canada, including educational programming aimed at the all levels of education.

12. Teacher Training Program

The Committee recommends the establishment of additional teacher training and teacher assistant training programs designed to meet the special needs of Indian and Inuit children.

1973

▲ Report of the Task Force on Policing on Reserves

AUTHOR: Department of Indian Affairs and Northern Development, Task Force on Policing on Reserves, Chair, S.C.H. Nutting
YEAR: 1973
ABORIGINAL GROUP: All Aboriginal Peoples
TOPIC: Administration of Justice
SUB-TOPIC: law enforcement system
SOURCE: Federal Departmental Task Force

BACKGROUND

This Task Force was established in response to evidence, as obtained from Native peoples and from surveys such as "Indians and the Law" (1967), that there was a pressing need for improved policing services on-reserve. The survey was undertaken at the request of the Indian Affairs program. The Special Indian Constables (3b) program was established as a result of this Task Force report.

PURPOSE

The objective of the Task Force was to examine on-reserve policing at all levels in an effort to identify fundamental problems and, after consultation with all

21

concerned parties at appropriate levels, to make recommendations on this subject.

ISSUES AND FINDINGS

The work of the Task Force was undertaken in three phases. The first phase dealt with the current state of policing on-reserve for which the commissioners prepared relevant charts of statistical data, short papers on jurisdictional issues, guidelines and identified current policy problems. The Task Force then prepared a paper on various policing options, to be presented to Native peoples and co-ordinating committees in each region. Regional Committees would comprise provincial Attorneys General, provincial police forces, regional officers and Indian associations.

In the second phase, the Task Force prepared an interim report and identified a number of options in the form of a paper entitled "Development of Alternative Methods for Policing on Reserves" (Annex 6). An effort was made to fit all available options within a spectrum, divided on the basis of institutional authority in policing functions. The options in each area were:

1. Band Council Policing

   (a) Civil by-law enforcement only constables;

   (b) supernumerary special constables for enforcing by-laws and federal and provincial laws with respect to minor offences; and

   (c) supernumerary special constables with the authority to enforce all federal and provincial laws.

2. Municipal Policing

   (a) purchase of policing services from existing services;

   (b) band is considered a municipality by the province, for purposes of policing; and

   (c) use of existing police services.

3. Other

   (a) a separate Indian police force; and

   (b) an Indian branch or contingent of an existing police force, of which it would be an integral part.

The third or consultative phase involved regional offices in consultations with Native associations to determine the wishes of bands. The regions were urged to establish Regional Committees as an instrument of implementation. A number of meetings were held between the RCMP and the Task Force when it was apparent that 3(b) was a strong preference among the Native groups. The object of these meetings was to determine the national acceptability of option 3(b) and to develop a national basis for the proposed Indian regional contingents.

RECOMMENDATIONS

The Task Force concluded that the Native peoples on-reserve required better quality policing services and that much greater emphasis needed to be placed on preventive policing. They further concluded that a new broad and flexible system of policing was needed to meet the particular needs of evolving communities in different regions. Furthermore, any system offered to Native peoples should include the opportunity to police themselves within the structure of an existing police force such as in option 3(b).

Moreover, it was recognized that the federal government, in co-operation with the provinces, should offer a program which would enable option 3(b) to be implemented and that Regional Policing Committees be established in all regions. Finally, the Task Force recommended that special (3b) constables be located on-reserve wherever possible.

1975

▲ Indian Claims in Canada: An Essay and Bibliography

AUTHOR: Indian Claims Commission, Research and Resource Centre
YEAR: 1975
ABORIGINAL GROUP: All Aboriginal Peoples
TOPICS: Treaty Land Entitlement, Claims
SUB-TOPICS: comprehensive claims, specific claims
SOURCE: Federal Agency

BACKGROUND

The Indian Claims Commission set up a Research Resource Centre in Ottawa to assist researchers of Indian, Métis, and Inuit claims in identifying and accessing requisite published and unpublished documents. The Centre's library collection pertains mostly to Canada, but also includes material from other countries.

PURPOSE

This introductory essay provides the reader with an overview of both the nature of Indian claims in Canada and of past attempts to deal with them. The bibliography is a classified guide to a substantial part of the Research Resource Centre's holdings.

ISSUES AND FINDINGS

Major themes of the essay are the Indian view of trusteeship as a fundamental element of Indian claims, and the lack of resolution of outstanding claims.

Three major groups of Aboriginal peoples are identified: status Indians, non-status Indians and Métis, and Inuit. Also, three major categories of claims are identified: Aboriginal rights; treaty and scrip settlement grievances; and band claims (i.e., other specific claims). Recognition is given to the notion that Aboriginal rights underlie all Aboriginal claims in Canada.

The historical relationship between Indians and the federal government is identified as a primary reason for their insistence on continuing special status as the original people of Canada. Indians have insisted that the Crown act to resolve their grievances and claims in respect of land, resources and the management of their internal affairs. These claims were based on Aboriginal rights or on agreements made with the Crown.

The essay also points out that Indians consider trusteeship, involving both protection and assistance, as a fundamental element of their claims. They believe that in assuming political control over Indians (including responsibilities for reserve and band finances and imposing special limitations on status Indians) the federal government adopted a protective role in relation to Indians and their affairs.

In addition, it is noted that Indians of the day viewed treaty texts as not reflecting the thrust of verbal promises made during treaty negotiations and accepted by peoples with an oral tradition: their ancestors understood the treaties to be specifically designed to protect them, and to help them adapt by developing an agricultural base to complement their traditional livelihood of hunting and fishing. Another point of controversy is the government's open policy of "detribalization", and its goal of assimilation of Indian people into non-Indian society. Indians reject this concept and believe they must initiate and control the development effort themselves.

Many claims contest the legality or status of surrenders of reserve lands. In general, the legal system has not responded positively or adequately to Aboriginal claims issues. A foreign "legal" system and inadequate funds have hindered Indians in litigation. Many of the early but significant decisions regarding Indians rights with respect to land and resources were, in fact, more the result of federal/provincial legal battles. Also, the essay recognizes that although there had been a lack of clear direction taken by the courts in deciding land loss grievances, they were beginning to respond more favourably to Indians claims, thus providing a basis future negotiations.

RECOMMENDATIONS

The essay does not make any specific recommendations. However, it does point to the need for a mechanism to facilitate agreements in principle which would create a new negotiation-centred era of activity in claims resolution.

▲ Native Peoples and Justice: Reports on the National Conference and the Federal-Provincial Conference on Native Peoples and the Criminal Justice System

AUTHOR: Solicitor General of Canada
YEAR: 1975
ABORIGINAL GROUP: All Aboriginal Peoples
TOPIC: Administration of Justice
SUB-TOPICS: law enforcement, courts, sentencing and corrections
SOURCE: Federal Department

BACKGROUND

This three-day conference was held in Edmonton in response to concerns over the disproportionately large numbers of Native peoples being jailed in Canada. Delegates included representatives of Aboriginal people, cabinet ministers and officials. This meeting was unusual in that the third day was a formal Federal-Provincial Conference to which meeting delegates were admitted as observers.

PURPOSE

The aim of the conference was to gain a better understanding of the problems of Native peoples in the criminal justice system and to facilitate meeting the needs of the Native population within the criminal justice system.

ISSUES AND FINDINGS

The conference covered virtually every aspect of criminal law and the administration of justice as it relates to Native peoples, and identified problems that needed to be addressed in order to ensure a more equitable treatment of Native peoples within the Canadian criminal justice system.

The Report was divided into two sections. The first classifies findings according to urban and rural categories in relation to a range of subjects considered in a planning session and in workshops. Areas covered included probation, parole and aftercare administration of justice, prevention, policing, courts, institutions and Inuit concerns. The recommendations from these sessions were formulated into draft resolutions of the ministers, debated and resolved.

Over 25 resolutions were debated; the majority were adopted. Some highlights of the Report's findings are as follows:

1. that where possible, court proceedings should be held in Native communities;
2. alternatives to incarceration, developed in conjunction with Native communities, must be given important consideration in sentencing;
3. legal services available to Native people need to be improved and extended;
4. the goal of probation, parole and aftercare must be primarily to reorient Native peoples in their communities; and
5. where incarceration for Native offenders is necessary, it should be in an institution in close proximity to their normal place of residence and preferably in a community-based treatment facility.

RECOMMENDATIONS

The most influential resolution the made by the ministers (outside of the resolutions that recognized the above mentioned problem areas), was for the establishment of the Canadian Advisory Council on Native Peoples and the Criminal Justice System. Membership in the Council would consist of one representative from each of the four federal departments involved in Native matters (Justice, Secretary of State, Solicitor General and Indian and Northern Affairs), one representative from each of the six national Native organizations, and up to four representatives from each of the provinces and territories. In addition, each one of the provinces and territories would set up an advisory council with government and Native representation.

The importance of establishing the Canadian Advisory Council was that its mandate specified that it was to implement the resolutions adopted at the conference. This was seen as valuable because previous recommendations that were made to improve the relationship between the Native community and the criminal justice system were often not implemented because of a loss of momentum and direction.

1977

▲ Commissioner of Indian Claims: A Report

AUTHOR: Indian Claims Commission, Commissioner, Lloyd Barber
YEAR: 1977
ABORIGINAL GROUP: All Aboriginal Peoples
TOPICS: Treaty Land Entitlement, Claims
SUB-TOPIC: comprehensive claims
SOURCE: Federal Commission

BACKGROUND

The report was compiled at the end of Lloyd Barber's appointment as Commissioner of the Indian Claims Commission. A new body, the Canadian Indian Rights Commission, was established to resume his responsibilities, including the facilitation of co-operative resolution of claims issues.

PURPOSE

The report is a representative sample of the Commission's work. The Research Resource Centre in Ottawa brought together a compilation of numerous speeches, submissions, and discussions to assist both Indian groups and governments in coming to a better understanding of each other's views, and thereby to establish a broader base for the resolution of claims.

ISSUES AND FINDINGS

The major theme of the report is that Indian claims are not simply contractual disputes that can be solved through arbitration and adjudication. Negotiation is a method of resolution preferred by all parties.

With respect to this theme, the statements and submissions are divided into three broad categories:

1. Native aspirations and Aboriginal rights;
2. Claims (Treaty, Métis and non-status, and band); and
3. Settlements (approaches, structures and framework)

With respect to Native aspirations, the report notes that underlying claims in all parts of the country is the position that Indians have a right to continuing special status within Canada because the land was originally theirs. Further, the Indian position held the view that non-Indians and governments have never dealt in a satisfactory way with Indian claims, and have not lived up to the spirit and intent agreements already reached.

In non-treaty areas, Native people claim to have rights to the land which derive from original possession. In August 1973, the federal government formally acknowledged a willingness to address Aboriginal claims (i.e., non-treaty areas) excluding those originating in the Maritimes and southern Quebec.

As for treaty claims, the grievances of Treaty Indians relate primarily to the various provisions of the treaties. For its part the Commission notes that future programs and Indian/government relationships can be shaped very much on the basis of the spirit and intent of the treaties: the original treaties clearly embodies a concept of government assistance to Indians to enable them to make a transition to a new life.

Métis claims are based on claims that

1. the distribution of land and scrip was unjustly and inefficiently administered;
2. this form of compensation was inadequate to extinguish the Aboriginal title of the Métis; and
3. Métis are Indians under the terms of the *British North America Act* and therefore are entitled to special consideration by the federal government.

Band claims are identified under several categories including claims relating to the loss of land and other natural resources from established reserves, as well as issues pertaining to the government's stewardship of band financial assets. Underlying all these claims is the issue of trusteeship.

RECOMMENDATIONS

The report's recommendations focus on the notion of settlement. Negotiation is emphasized as a preferred method of resolution as opposed to adjudication.

It is also noted that claims-related issues have reached critical proportions, should be given high priority within government, and should directly involve members of the cabinet.

Settlements must be structured to encourage better relationships between Native people and other Canadians: differences of opinions between these two groups must be narrowed through claims negotiation. One procedure for dealing with claims would allow basic issues to be brought up through provincial and territorial Indian associations and presented to a committee of cabinet ministers. If a basis for agreement exists, general principles and parameters for settlement mechanisms could be established. Such agreements would then allow for more detailed treatment of issues either through secondary level negotiations, adjudication, court referrals, or through specially-created arbitration tribunals. Settlements would be tailored to the particular circumstances at hand, and based on agreement on principles.

▲ Northern Frontier, Northern Homeland: The Report of the Mackenzie Valley Pipeline Inquiry

AUTHOR: Mackenzie Valley Pipeline Inquiry, Commissioner, Justice
   Thomas R. Berger
YEAR: 1977
ABORIGINAL GROUP: All Aboriginal Peoples
TOPICS: Economic/Social Development, Environmental Protection,
   Claims, Resources
SUB-TOPICS: minerals, oil and gas, comprehensive claims
SOURCE: Federal Commission

BACKGROUND

The Inquiry was established in response to applications from Canadian Arctic Gas Pipelines Ltd. and from Foothills Pipe Lines Ltd. for the construction and operation of a natural gas pipeline from the Mackenzie Delta in the Northwest Territories down the Mackenzie River Valley to connect with pipelines in Alberta.

By Order in Council, Mr. Justice Thomas Berger was appointed as the Commissioner on March 21, 1974. Preliminary hearings were held in April and May 1974 at Yellowknife, Inuvik, Whitehorse and Ottawa on the scope and procedures of the Inquiry. On March 3, 1975, in Yellowknife, participants were given an opportunity to give their opening statements. From March 11, 1975 to November 19, 1976, hearings were held in all 35 communities affected, in Yellowknife, and in 10 major cities in southern Canada.

PURPOSE

The mandate of the Inquiry was "to inquire into and report upon the terms and conditions that should be imposed in respect of any right-of-way that might be granted, having regard to:

(a) "..the social, environmental and economic impact regionally; and

(b) any proposals to meet the specific environmental and social concerns set out in the Expanded Guidelines for Northern Pipelines.."

Mr. Justice Berger was authorized to hold hearings (at the time and place of his choosing), to summon and examine witness under oath, to set his own procedures, to recruit staff support and experts, and to rent space for offices and hearings.

ISSUES AND FINDINGS

The first issue to be addressed by the Berger Inquiry was how to deal with the issue of Native claims. Immediately, the Inquiry was operating beyond the scope of its mandate. In a precedent setting decision, Justice Berger decided to expand the work of the inquiry to include this area of concern.

The significance of this Inquiry is found in the which it adopted extensive input from ordinary community members and in the broad interpretation of the Inquiry's terms of reference by Justice Berger.

Beyond the technical and environmental issues involved in the report, the issues were divided into

1. cultural impact;
2. economic impact;
3. social impact; and
4. Native claims.

Cultural impact: "So the future of the North ought not to be determined only by our own southern ideas of frontier development. It should also reflect the ideas of the people who call it their homeland." Following a review of the history of contact, the introduction of government/welfare state, the creation of settlements/local governments, and the move toward a wage economy, the Inquiry makes the point that Native values continue to be different from southern values. In particular, the Inquiry found a widespread evaluation of land as being inseparable from Aboriginal identity and sense of long-term security. Further the Inquiry found there were distinct differences between Native and non-Native values of sharing and respect for elders. The Inquiry noted that Native societies were egalitarian and that models of leadership were based on respect, knowledge and ability. In part the persistence of these values and cultural differences were reflected in the persistence of the Native economy.

The Inquiry's appreciation of these cultural differences forms an important element to understanding the general approach of the Berger Inquiry recommendations.

Economic impact: "..the real danger of such developments will not be their continued failure to provide employment to the Native people but the highly intrusive effects they may have on Native society and the Native economy." Berger was convinced that the Native economy not only existed but that it had vitality and potential. Accordingly, he was much concerned that a pipeline development should not undermine what was already in place. Similarly he was interested in forms of economic development that enhanced Native values and preferences. Thus, he strongly favoured a strengthening of the Native economy.

In the evaluation of the economic benefits of the project, Berger felt that its principal beneficiaries would not be the people of the North. It was noted that although wages would rise, so too would prices. Given the supply (transportation) problems of the North, an increase in demand would be to the detriment of Native peoples and communities. In the long run, this type of economic development and expansion would result in a loss of control over the rate and extent of growth. Further he felt that the impact would be not only serious but irreparable.

Social impact: "The social impact...if we build the pipeline now, it will be devastating...and quite beyond our capacity to ameliorate in any significant way." Berger rejected the argument that an increase in economic activity would be accompanied by a decrease in welfare payments. In his analysis, he found the opposite to be true in the Alaskan, Tuktoyaktuk and Coppermine experiences. He found that the basis for increased social problems was industrial development.

Basing his view on the extensive community testimony received, he agreed that crime and violence were increasing in those communities which were more involved in wage economies and dominated by the "frontier mentality". Within the report, it was felt that the resource development in the current social climate would contribute significantly to an increase in alcoholism, crime, violence and welfare. There would be a 'tearing of the social fabric" with an increase of social pathology and a loss of a collective, cultural identity.

The potentially dramatic increase in the number of non-Native residents, would reduce Native people to a minority and lead to a subsequent loss of control over their own affairs. At the same time, employment as a result of development would only accentuate social inequalities, with Native people employed as unskilled workers in jobs that would not continue beyond the construction phase. There would be an associated loss of self-esteem and self-respect.

Native claims: Berger was convinced there was a need for a fundamental re-ordering of the relationship between Native people and Canada. He called for a new social contract "based on a clear understanding that they are distinct peoples in history". Accordingly he appreciated their claims to self-determination, self-government, and their own political institutions, as well as control over education and renewable resources.

For this Inquiry, the test of the acceptability of resource development project proposals was not just its national economic impact or its environmental impact. Rather the test was its impact on the Native people who would be living with the results of the project.

The Inquiry was successful in focusing an industrial development exercise on the people affected, and in its demands that affected people be involving in the formulating decisions which ultimately affect them. Using a democratic philosophy, the Inquiry not only welcomed the input of Native people but often evaluated their views and expertise as superior to any other source.

RECOMMENDATIONS

The recommendations are divided between the two volumes. In the first volume (tabled in May 1977) the recommendations address the question of whether there should be an approval of a pipeline application.

The Inquiry recommended that no pipeline should be built until Native claims are settled, and that the approval of a pipeline should be delayed for 10 years. The rationale was that any settlement would need to enable Native people to participate in decisions, through the new institutions and programs established by Native people under settlement agreements.

In the second volume (tabled in November 1977), the recommendations centred around conditions to be imposed upon a licence to construct and operate a pipeline. Included were the specific recommendations that Native people, their communities and organizations be involved in renewable resource projects (related to fur, fish and game), in environmental protection, in manpower delivery (recruitment), in orientation and training programs, and in forest management.

It was recommended that Native project employees should have the options of receiving country foods and culturally-based recreation, as well as instructional programs (training, safety instruction, and orientation) in their Native languages.

It was recommended that control over health programs for Native people rest with Native peoples. Similarly Native social workers and para-professionals might work with both Native workers and their families in the communities and to provide financial and social counselling.

Other recommendations included protection of Native harvesting rights, including within pipeline construction areas, promotion of an orderly and balanced development of the Native economy, and co-operation and co-ordination between Native people and unions.

▲ Report of the Alaska Highway Pipeline Inquiry

AUTHOR: Alaska Highway Pipeline Inquiry, Chair, Kenneth M. Lysyk
YEAR: 1977
ABORIGINAL GROUP: First Nations
TOPICS: Land and Resources, Economic/Social Development, Claims, Resources
SUB-TOPICS: minerals, oil and gas, comprehensive claims
SOURCE: Federal Commission

BACKGROUND

The 1970s was a time of rising petroleum prices and the discovery of massive oil and gas reserves in the North (both Canada and the United States). The predictions were that by the 1980s Canada and the United States would need access to these reserves. It was also a time of a growing awareness of Aboriginal rights and claims (particularly in relation to development) and of environmental issues. The Alyeska pipeline, with its attendant bad publicity, was seen as a model not to be replicated in northern non-renewable resource development. At the same time, the Berger Inquiry was thought by some in government as having gone well beyond its mandate and the national interest.

PURPOSE

The Lysyk Inquiry was charged with the responsibility to prepare a preliminary socio-economic impact statement concerning the construction and operation of a proposed pipeline through the Yukon. In addition to the impact implications, the Inquiry was to report on the "attitude to the proposal of the inhabitants" and to address deficiencies in the proposal.

The Inquiry board consisted of three members: one appointed by the minister of Indian and Northern Affairs, one nominated by the Yukon Territorial Council and one nominated by the Council for Yukon Indians. Board members were given the option of releasing minority reports, but the final report was given unanimous support. Beyond the hiring of staff by the Inquiry, the minister of the Environment sent a member of the Environmental Assessment and Review Panel to all hearings.

The Inquiry conducted public hearings in 17 Yukon communities to seek views and receive submissions. This Inquiry conducted its work according to a relatively tight schedule. Hearings were conducted through the summer of 1977 and, the final report was submitted by the deadline of August 1.

ISSUES AND FINDINGS

This inquiry (beyond the technical and environmental concerns) focused on three main areas with which Aboriginal people would be involved: economic impact (including employment and training), social impact, and land claims. Besides the gas pipeline to follow the highway route from Alaska to Canadian gas pipelines in Alberta and British Columbia, there was a consideration whether lateral pipelines from the Mackenzie Delta should follow the Dempster Highway or alternatively run through the Mackenzie Valley of the Northwest Territories, and thereby avoid the Yukon.

The Inquiry points out early on in the report that the circumstances of the Yukon are unique, and therefore, the Berger inquiry was seen as not entirely relevant. They see the Yukon as being much more like Alaska except the community of Old Crow which is seen as being like its neighbours to the east. They point to a history of development, of boom-and-bust, and of the massive highway construction program which sets them apart as to the type of impacts they will experience. They point to the minority status of Aboriginal people and the concentration of population (75% along the Alaska Highway) as significant. They have chosen to look to Alaska and the Alyeska experience as the most relevant for predicting possible impacts on their population.

Economic impact: The Inquiry was concerned over the lack of meaningful employment opportunities for Indian people. There was a fear that the only jobs that would exist for Indian people would be those requiring unskilled labour in, for example, the clearing the right-of-way. In addition, the Alaska experience pointed to local people being lured away from present jobs by higher wages but for short-term jobs. Similarly there was a concern that many positions would be filled through unions and would exclude Indian people as non-members.

There was a concern that employment on the pipeline would conflict with the mixed economic strategies of Indian people. Thus there was a desire that some kind of accommodation be achieved to allow for mixed economic strategies (inclusion of hunting and trapping) alongside pipeline employment.

There was an acceptance by the Inquiry that the only lasting benefit of pipeline construction for Indian people would be the acquisition of useful skills. Accordingly, there was a concern that training programs must be in place in advance of the project (provided by the proponent and others) to qualify interested individuals for high-paying jobs.

Additionally, the Inquiry was concerned that Indian people should be prepared to participate fully in the operation and maintenance phase. Here they strongly advocated a preference for Indian people in the selection, hiring and training aspects of this phase.

In general, the Inquiry was concerned with the impact of in-migration on both the labour pool and on communities. While primarily focused on Yukoners, the Inquiry did see Indian people as an important element in the equation. They were quick to promote schemes to discourage southern Canadians and Americans from moving to the Yukon and thereby displacing northerners' access to available positions. (They noted that the vague hope of employment had already attracted several people.)

One key area of review, though not specifically aimed at Indian people, was the problem of pipeline induced inflation. The Inquiry felt that efforts had to be made to reduce the impact on price that the pipeline would cause.

(They point to a 30% inflation rate in Alaska during the construction phase of the Alyeska pipeline.) Similarly, this inflation was to effect the mining, tourism, transportation, retail/small business, construction/housing and communications sectors of the Yukon economy. Besides the compensation that Yukoners would need to balance the impact, there was a need to develop compensation for Indian communities from disrupted land based economic activities (trapping, hunting and fishing) and from a perceived loss of land rights.

Social impact: While the Indian population is a minority in the Yukon, its presence is strongly felt, particularly in communities such as Carmacks, Old Crow and Pelly Crossing. The Inquiry and others were concerned that pipeline development not be seen as a racial issue. However, a pipeline would mean massive in-migration by non-Aboriginal people, thus diminishing the proportion of the population of Indian origin, and diminishing their influence.

Because of the history of the Yukon, many Indian people expressed fears of social disruptions similar to those experienced as a result of construction of the Dempster highway construction and the Canol pipeline in the 1940s, and the establishment of mines. There were concerns about increases in the incidence of alcoholism as well as the forced movement of families. Indian communities, in particular, expressed concern about the impact on wildlife and traditional lifestyles.

Additional problems that concerned the Inquiry (though not focused on Indians) included increases in child neglect, venereal disease, stress related mental illness, poor housing, alcohol and drug abuse, and crime.

The Inquiry found that Indian people in the Yukon were already disproportionately involved in criminal and quasi-criminal behaviour (51% of inmates, 85% of juveniles admitted to Wolf Creek Juvenile Training Home). A pipeline would undermine recovery from the social and economic dislocation caused by the highway construction. The Council for Yukon Indians noted "the expansion of southern-oriented social agencies and programs would emphasize the Indian's subordination and inability to participate effectively in the delivery and direction of social services".

Land claim: Through the Inquiry, representatives from "the Council for Yukon Indians and the majority of Indian witnesses at the community hearings expressed grave concern about the impact of a pipeline on their lives. They stated their view that construction of a pipeline before the completion and implementation of a land claim settlement would seriously prejudice the achievement of a just settlement." The Inquiry recognized there was a clear and valid claim that needed to be dealt with in order to promote greater equality and facilitate the development of greater self-government for all Yukoners.

The Inquiry recognized a land claims settlement would indeed be prejudiced and would set a dangerous precedent in giving priority to development over land claims settlement.

RECOMMENDATIONS

The Lysyk Inquiry report contains many recommendations. While it did not come out clearly either for or against pipeline development (though it did recognize that the national interest may require the transmission of natural gas), it did propose both specific and general guidelines for pipeline approval.

The Inquiry was, however, preliminary to the establishment of final terms and conditions. It did recommend, in view of land claims, that no construction should commence before August 1, 1981 in order to allow Indians to complete their settlement and land selection processes and to prepare for development.

The Inquiry strongly recommended against a lateral route parallel to the Dempster Highway because of the environmental sensitivity of the area, the lack of firm markets for the gas, the lack of acceptance by the people of Old Crow and the concern that their way of life would suffer without any evidence that the route was preferable to the "Maple Leaf" route down the Mackenzie Valley.

The Inquiry suggested there should be a focus on the development of the skills of Indian peoples to include skills they would be able use beyond the construction phase. They recommended people be given the opportunity to prepare themselves for participation. In this effort, it was suggested Indian organizations be involved in a Manpower Delivery Service and the recruiting, hiring and training of Indian people.

The Inquiry recommended efforts be made to reduce stresses on the economy as a result of in-migration. Compensation for those who would suffer inflated prices should be made from the increased tax revenues generated by the project. In addition, renewable resource harvesters should be compensated. Research would be needed to establish a data base to evaluate impacts. It was also recommended that a Yukon Impact Information Centre based on the Alaska model be established.

The Inquiry was unanimous in their support for the settlement of the outstanding land claim. It recommended:

1. the continued constraint on land grants (until August 1, 1980) to assist in land selection; and

2. the immediate deposit of fifty million dollars as an advance payment for ensuring adequate financial resources to proceed with the settlement.

▲ Terms of Reference for the Special Inquirer for Elder Indians' Testimony

AUTHOR: Privy Council Office
YEAR: 1977
ABORIGINAL GROUP: All Aboriginal Peoples
TOPIC: Claims
SUB-TOPIC: commission/institutions
SOURCE: Federal Department

BACKGROUND

The terms of reference note that a joint committee of cabinet ministers and representatives of the National Indian Brotherhood had been established to provide an opportunity to "discuss problems of concern to the Government of Canada and the status Indians of Canada." In addition, a joint sub-committee consisting of three members of each party had been established to reach agreement on Indian rights and claims.

The report indicates that questioning knowledgeable elderly Indians would be a good method of obtaining information concerning past events related to grievances about the rights and claims of status Indians. It is also noted that while such information may be useful in negotiating the settlement of grievances, "it is the position of the Government of Canada that such information may not be admissible in whole or in part in subsequent legal proceedings."

The terms of reference also recommend that Dr. Lloyd Barber be appointed as Commissioner and be known as the Special Inquirer for Elder Indians' Testimony.

▲ A Collection of Summaries of 13 Task Force Reports to the American Indian Policy Review Commission, 1976

AUTHOR: Department of Indian Affairs and Northern Development (Jesse Reiber)
YEAR: 1978
ABORIGINAL GROUP: First Nations
TOPIC: Federal Government/Aboriginal Relations
SUB-TOPICS: jurisdiction, federal trust responsibilities, rights
SOURCE: Federal Department

PURPOSE

The American Indian Policy Review Commission (AIPRC) commissioned 11task forces to examine the United States Government-Indian relationship. The Research Branch, Corporate Policy of Indian and Northern Affairs Canada, requested that the findings of the task forces, as well as two additional reports, be summarized.

ISSUES AND FINDINGS

The Task Forces and other reports related to the following issues:

1. trust responsibilities and the Federal-Indian relationship;
2. Tribal Government;
3. federal administration and structure of Indian Affairs;
4. Federal, State, and Tribal jurisdiction;
5. Indian education;
6. Indian health;
7. reservation and resource development and protection;
8. urban and rural non-reservation Indians;
9. Indian law revision, consolidation and codification;
10. terminated and non-federally recognized Indians;
11. alcohol and drug use; and
12. the special Joint Task Force Report on Alaskan Native Issues.

Trust responsibilities: There were five specific issues identified by Task Force I:

1. There was lack of consensus on the issue of sovereignty, including a definitional analysis of the character and status of Indian Nations.
2. It was unclear whether Indian Title referred to lands that were public, private or federal.
3. All three major branches of the federal government failed to give definitive form or statement to the specific character and force of the Trust Relationship.
4. History did not disclose any early claim of congressional authority over Indians or their property.
5. States did not give positive recognition of tribal rights in their legislation.

Tribal government: Task Force II identified three problem areas:

1. It found that the Secretary of the Interior and its sub-committee, the Bureau of Indian Affairs (BIA) were doing a poor job of protecting the Trust status. True Tribal government would not be achievable as long as the Interior had veto power over Tribal decisions.
2. There was a lack of adequate resources to support Tribal government initiatives.
3. Tribes feared termination of the Trust relationship if they demonstrated self-sufficiency.

Federal administration and structure of Indian Affairs: Task Force III reported that there were two major problems with the administration of Indian Affairs:

1. The Trust responsibility cut across all federal departments.
2. The BIA performed two divergent functions as advocate for both Indian and government interests.

Federal, state and tribal jurisdictions: Task Force IV found that throughout all levels of American society there was substantial ignorance and misinformation concerning the legal-political status of Indian Tribes and the history of their unique relationship with the government. This lack of understanding, evident at all levels of government, had a significant negative impact on Native peoples.

Indian education: Task Force V noted that the education of Indian Peoples had been a primary tool for instituting overall congressional and BIA policies, including isolation and assimilation policies. It found that materials and funding were constantly inadequate and school curriculum were devoid of Indian culture and values.

Indian health: The health of American Indian peoples remained significantly below that of the general U.S. population. Five different areas of deficiency in health care were discovered by Task Force VI:

1. There was inadequate policy to solve the problems of Indian health.

2. The mechanism for funding the Indian Health Services (IHS) was unsatisfactory.

3. There was no adequate mechanism for delivery of services.

4. State and local agencies failed to respond to the needs of Indian people, assuming they were the responsibility of IHS.

5. IHS lacked an adequate system of accountability. Goals were not set in any measurable, quantifiable manner.

Reservation and resource protection and development: A review of historical information led Task Force VII to conclude that existing law and policy failed adequately to protect Indian lands from encroachment. The slow rate of economic development on Indian reservations was attributed to the use of federal funds, where resources were directed to addressing the symptoms of poverty rather than the cause.

Urban and rural non-reservation Indians: Policies related to services for off-reservation Indians were basically attempts to diminish federal commitments. The belief that the Trust relationship does not extend to these people was not legally founded, but born out of convenience. Where legislation was in effect that addressed the needs of Non-Reservation Indians, it was found that it was circumvented by administrative neglect.

In general, it was felt that the difficulty was not one of changing existing laws, policies and practices, but rather that the problems were related to enforcement of the rights which non-reservation people already had as members of the Indian community.

Legislative consolidation, revision and codification: This report recognized that some court decisions and a greater number of congressional statutes, although sustained in their legality, violated the nature and basis of the Government-Indian relationship.

Terminated and non-federally recognized Indians: The Task Force concluded that termination had resulted in the loss of tribal lands and disintegration of tribal society. Its worst effects were evident in relation to

Indian youth, elders, and the sick who did not have adequate assistance programs.

The non-recognition of some tribes was found to be an administrative action that lacked substantive legal foundations. The results of non-recognition had been devastating.

Drug and alcohol use: Indian peoples identified alcohol and drug abuse as the most pressing problem facing them. The roots of these problem were traced back to systemic alienation. The long-range approach to prevention emphasized a return to traditional heritage and culture, and use of Indian treatment programs.

Special Joint Task Force Report on Alaska Native Issues: The Task Force noted the complexity of the issues and the lack of knowledge regarding Alaskan Native peoples. The uniqueness of tribes in Alaska created confusion regarding the *Indian Self-Determination Act.*

RECOMMENDATIONS

With regard to federal/Indian relations, Task Force I called for reform in governmental systems and relations. Specifically, it recommended that the BIA be phased out and replaced by the Department of Indian Affairs, which would be an agency of both Tribes and the federal government.

It was also viewed as essential that a tripartite federal/Aboriginal/state relationship be restored.

Task Force II recommended the reaffirmation of congressional commitment to the right of tribal self-government, superseding earlier inconsistencies in federal law.

Task Force III proposed the BIA be maintained as a separate agency for Indian issues, but that a mechanism be established to permit adjustments in the delivery system to meet changing circumstances and to address conflicts.

Task Force V recommended a comprehensive education bill ensuring quantity and quality of services to Indian people. It also recommended consolidation and enhancement in the numerous bills that had been passed at various points in the past.

Task Force VI found the entire approach to Indian health problems inadequate and recommended a complete overhaul of the system. Major recommendations were:

1. that all Indian programs be consolidated in a cabinet-level agency;

2. that Indian peoples be guaranteed a basic health care package without an arbitrary funding limit;

3. that a preventive and environmental health program be instituted;

4. that urban Indians be entitled to the same services available to all Indians regardless of where they live;

5. that Indian Health Boards be set up to promote Indian involvement and self-determination in health.

Task Force VII recommended the establishment of a constitutional amendment to protect Indian lands. As an interim measure, it proposed the establishment of an American Indian Trust Protection Commission charged with protecting Indian resources and reviewing proposed federal actions which might affect them.

With regard to reservation resource development, the Task Force proposed Congress establish the American Indian Development Authority as an independent federal agency that would provide technical assistance funding and capital to prepare and implement comprehensive development plans.

Task Force VIII concluded there was a need for total restructuring of the federal Indian Affairs administration in order to include non-reservation people.

Task Force IX proposed a Congressional Declaration of Policy vis-à-vis the government-Indian relationship. The intention was to remove the major pieces of past legislation, such as the Termination Act, which had violated the original spirit of the U.S.-Indian relationship. The intent was clearly to establish and retain the original relationship, from the basis of trusteeship and domestic nation sovereignty, and build on more recent legislation which had been supportive of Indian peoples.

Task Force X recommended Congress restore federal Indian status to those tribes who so desired. It also urged the federal government to include non-federally recognized Indians in its services.

Task Force XI made three suggestions:

1. that prevention and comprehensive treatment of drug and alcohol abuse receive the highest priority at all levels of Indian policy and programs;

2. that a joint resolution of Congress recognize a continuing commitment to provide resources needed; and

3. that a separate and distinct national Indian alcohol and drug abuse agency be established.

The Special Joint Task Force on Alaska Native Issues recommended that the eligibility requirements of the *Indian Self-Determination Act* be modified to reflect the unique tribal structures found in Alaska.

◆ *Indian Commission of Ontario: Terms of Reference* (1978), see **Volume 3, Ontario.**

1979

▲ **Constitutional Development in the Northwest Territories**

AUTHOR: Special Representative for Constitutional Development in the Northwest Territories, C.M. Drury

YEAR: 1979

ABORIGINAL GROUP: All Aboriginal Peoples

TOPICS: Constitutional Development, Self-Government, Political Development/Relationships, Land and Resources, Environmental Protection

SUB-TOPICS: constitutional development, political development, lands and resources

SOURCE: Federal Commission

BACKGROUND

In 1977 the prime minister appointed a Special Representative to report to him the results of consultations to be held with the government of the Northwest Territories (N.W.T.) and Native and non-Native northerners regarding constitutional development.

PURPOSE

This Report focuses on the need for political and constitutional change in the N.W.T. While the Report does not set out an agenda for change; rather, it describes the conditions for "better government" in the N.W.T.

The Special Representative spent two years in consultation, mediation and study preparing this Report. He met with federal government departments, territorial councils, Indian groups and individual residents of the N.W.T.

Ultimately, the purpose of the Report was to provide recommendations to the prime minister regarding constitutional development in the N.W.T.

ISSUES AND FINDINGS

This Report identifies six issues:

1. territorial division;
2. claims;
3. government in the N.W.T.;
4. federal jurisdiction;
5. public finance; and
6. the process for constitutional change.

Territorial division: The numerous arguments for division share many common objectives, including improved representation, increased direct accountability of elected officials, transfer and decentralization of federal powers, recognition of the uniqueness of the N.W.T., representation of permanent residents in government, and most important, achievement of more effective government.

The federal government had some concerns regarding territorial division particularly that any increase in the present fiscal burden of the federal government would be subject to parliamentary scrutiny. As well, the distribution of powers would need to resemble, and not exceed those held by the provinces. Finally, there was a concern that the legislative and executive functions be carried out responsibly by the new government.

It was recognized that the long-term external consequences of division had not been adequately considered by those involved. Changes that might occur would need to promote increased representation, accountability and responsiveness of the government throughout the N.W.T.

Claims: In 1975 and 1977, the federal government took the position that structures and functions of government were not negotiable as part of land claims settlements. Federally, the negotiation of claims is important to the constitutional and political future of the N.W.T. It was recognized as equally important to Native peoples in regard to the political, economic and cultural benefits that might be achieved. The substance of the claims focus on land ownership, control of resources and choice of lifestyle. Aboriginal peoples viewed claims settlements as the primary issue of government in the N.W.T.

Drury suggested that the goal of Native claims should be the protection and promotion of Native economic and cultural interests. To meet the needs of Aboriginal peoples any approach would need to include:

1. Native claims;
2. the devolution of authority to territorial/community governments; and
3. extended representation and responsibility in territorial government processes and constitutional renewal. It was suggested that any agreements reached be incorporated into any future N.W.T. legislation. Finally, it is stressed that any revised *Northwest Territories Act* should recognize the municipal order of government and the protection of Native languages.

Government in the N.W.T.: The principle problem regarding government in the N.W.T. was that authority and responsibility were in the hands of the federal government. There is a great deal of confusion about the degree of authority that had been vested in the N.W.T. government. The system of local government was seen as hierarchical. As a result there were three primary problems:

1. relating the level of decision-making authority to population size and revenue potential makes it difficult for small communities to assume local responsibility;
2. local councils have little or no authority over cultural, social, educational programs, etc.; and
3. existing legislation is complex and does not facilitate the use of local or traditional practices.

Drury felt that to achieve effective government, any political institutions that might evolve would need to embody the following essential principles:

1. accountability to the people of the N.W.T.;
2. reflection of their values and concerns; and
3. acceptance of institutional changes by the majority of northerners. The conclusion was that community government can be strengthened by increasing political authority and responsibility at the local level. Proposed changes to structures and procedures included:
   (a) elimination of the local hierarchy;
   (b) new ordinances to allow flexibility and variation;
   (c) local options for the use of preferred languages at work;
   (d) modification to intergovernmental relations;
   (e) Territorial Council and government of the N.W.T. to encourage, not hinder development of regional councils; and

(f) establishment of new roles and responsibilities for the government and council of the N.W.T.

Federal jurisdiction in the N.W.T.: Areas of federal responsibility of concern are in respect of

1. Native peoples, and

2. the ownership and regulation of land and natural resources.

Aboriginal peoples favoured transfer of certain jurisdictional areas to the government of the Northwest Territories, including:

1. jurisdictions directly affecting N.W.T. peoples;

2. ownership and regulation of land and resources; and

3. services that are a provincial responsibility in the provinces.

There were identified problems associated with these jurisdictional areas and uncertainty as to whether the rights of N.W.T. government employees would be the responsibility of the federal or territorial government. Regarding the regulation of lands and resources, there was the problem that federal jurisdiction did not reflect or significantly acknowledge territorial interests in the following areas:

1. land use planning;

2. inland waters;

3. forests;

4. non-renewable resources;

5. the environment;

6. agriculture;

7. national parks;

8. inland and marine fisheries;

9. power utilities; and

10. roads and highways.

With respect to services typically falling within the purview of provincial responsibility, the federal government was providing these services to the N.W.T., including criminal prosecutions, labour relations, some health and housing services, and community airport services. In conclusion, the general trend was seen to be toward transferring responsibilities to the government of the N.W.T., with two significant exceptions: Native matters, and ownership/regulation of land and resources.

Public finance in the N.W.T.: Present financial arrangements in the N.W.T. reflected the existing and anticipated limited territorial tax base. They illustrated fiscal dependence on the federal government. The federal government had previously and wished to continue to influence the expenditure of federal funds and to control accountability for expenditure decisions.

Responsibility accompanying any transfer of power in fiscal management to the government of the N.W.T. would include

1. responsibility for revenue raising through taxation and federal negotiations, and

2. accountability to the legislature for expenditure of resources. An identified deficiency in the system was that it failed to encourage the development of local government fiscal responsibility. Thus, because decisions were usually made by the government of the N.W.T. or by the federal government, fiscal dependency limited local decision making and accountability. Thus, greater fiscal responsibility for the N.W.T. was desirable, although two impediments stood in the way:

   (a) the final responsibility for determining budget levels and accounting for financial management lies with the federal government, through DIAND; and

   (b) at the territorial level, representatives who control the budget process are appointed, not elected. Nonetheless, Drury recommended that local responsibility and accountability be encouraged.

Processes for constitutional change: The primary issue regarding constitutional change was that no formalized constitution for the N.W.T. existed. To gain an understanding of the constitution, federal statutes, territorial ordinances, ministerial instructions to the Commissioner, federal policies, territorial regulations, territorial and federal conventions, customs and practices would need to be reviewed.

Constitutional development processes were seen as problematic, because the direction and specific details of change were being determined in Ottawa, not by the people or government of the N.W.T. Interest groups also tended to focus their attention on the federal government, not the government of the N.W.T.

RECOMMENDATIONS

The Special Representative made a number of summary recommendations. These included the overall recommendation that the people of the N.W.T. should assume more authority over the determination of their own political future. This should be accompanied by an increase in local authority and responsibility, and by extension, a reduction in federal intervention. By implementing these measures, a government-to-government relationship between the federal government and the government of the N.W.T. would develop, eventually leading to the exclusion of DIAND in northern affairs.

A major question to be addressed was whether the Northwest Territories should be divided. To arrive at a decision, a number of questions would need to be answered by both the federal government and by the people of the N.W.T.

To accommodate the people of the N.W.T., it was suggested that the Council divide the issue of constitutional development into two questions regarding:

1. short-term incremental change; and
2. the long-term question of division through the use of a forum.

Drury's final conclusion was that constitutional development and a transfer of authority and responsibility to the government of the N.W.T. must occur.

◆ *To Have What is One's Own* (1979),
see **Reports by Aboriginal Organizations.**

1980

▲ Report of the Advisory Commission on Indian and Inuit Health Consultation

AUTHOR: Advisory Commission on Indian and Inuit Health Consultation, Commissioner, Justice Thomas R. Berger
YEAR: 1980
ABORIGINAL GROUP: All Aboriginal Peoples
TOPICS: Health, Community Services and Infrastructure
SUB-TOPIC: primary and secondary health care
SOURCE: Federal Commission

BACKGROUND

The alarming state of ill-health among Canada's Aboriginal peoples and the need to improve health care services had become a priority issue for Aboriginal organizations. In late 1978, the federal government established guidelines for uninsured health services. These were objected to by Indian organizations across the country. Protests led to demands that the federal government explicitly acknowledge its responsibility for Aboriginal health care.

As a result, the federal government adopted a new Indian Health policy in 1979 that stated that the remedy to Indian ill-health required the increased participation by Indian peoples in the management of health care programs.

The Inuit Tapirisat of Canada was also calling for a greater commitment by the federal government to the improvement of Inuit health care.

At the same time the Berger Commission on Indian and Inuit health was proceeding, Justice Emmett Hall was reviewing federal public health insurance programs for non-Aboriginal Canadians.

PURPOSE

The task of this inquiry was to address two specific questions:

1. What methods of consultation are available to ensure that there is substantive participation by Indian and Inuit people in decisions relating to their health care programs? and
2. Which of these methods present the best alternative?

ISSUES AND FINDINGS

Mindful that Indians and Inuit face different health problems, the two Aboriginal groups are treated separately in the report.

Indian health: The present state of Indian health was attributed to early contact with Europeans. Europeans introduced diseases previously unknown in the Americas. Generally it was felt that the problem was fundamentally a result of centuries of oppression, and that in order to remedy the situation, Indian peoples must control the provision of their own health care at all levels and rely less on government.

To foster self-reliance in the health care field, it was agreed that structures must be set up for band representation in decision making, budgeting, conversion to community-based designs, etc. The guiding objectives would be increasing community reliance on local Indians as providers of health services and care, and a greater emphasis on preventive health care approaches.

To determine the best method of consultation available to Indians, the author assessed present methods of health care delivery, and three alternatives as suggested by the Medical Services Branch of the Department of Health and

Welfare (MSB), the National Indian Brotherhood (NIB) and the Provincial and Territorial Indian Organizations (PTOs).

In the past, consultations between the Aboriginal people and MSB, (which is responsible for Indian and Inuit health programs) consisted of irregular and informal meetings focusing on current problems, usually at the request of Indian leaders. There were no effective consultations at the national or regional level.

MSB recommended to the Advisory Commission that future consultations be funded separately from ordinary operating expenses, as was the current practice. Funds would be provided through MSB regional offices and channelled to communities.

The NIB and the Provincial/Territorial Organizations proposed that funds be administered by the National Commission Inquiry on Indian Health (NCI) – a sub-committee of the NIB's executive council. The NCI would receive a per annum sum of $150,000 and PTOs would receive core funding and additional funds based on a formula that would take into account their population size. Funding would be extended to Indian bands and organizations not presently affiliated with the NIB. PTOs would have responsibility for the management of consultation processes.

A third alternative was suggested, whereby the consultative process would become the responsibility of a new body, independent of MSB and Indian organizations. The author felt that this suggestion entailed the establishment of a cumbersome new bureaucracy.

The author concluded that the NIB/PTO proposal best suited the objectives of the federal government's new Indian health policy and that it would lead to a more co-ordinated effort than in the past. It was noted that the MSB process continued to pursue consultations on a band-by-band basis, and that this led to a fragmentation of interests, whereas the PTOs had already devised well-articulated plans for local participation in consultations on Indian health.

The commissioner stressed that it was vital to make use of existing political organizations rather than establishing new ones.

The Advisory Commission believed that bringing together the National Commission Inquiry on Indian Health and representatives of the PTOs, would be an ideal precursor to the eventual establishment of a National Indian Health Council. Such a council would be able to review all of the initiatives in Indian health taking place across the country, and provide each

Indian community with information that it could use in deciding on health care issues and priorities.

Inuit health: The commissioner noted that most of the problems associated with Indian health issues were also evident in the case of the Inuit. However, the infant mortality rate of the Inuit in the N.W.T. was double that of Indians. This was partly attributed to the young age of mothers, excessive births and geographic isolation.

The Inuit advanced essentially the same opinion as Indian representatives: the restoration of health depends on the Inuit people finding a distinct and contemporary place for themselves in Canadian life.

Differences from the Indian situation arose in relation to land claims issues. Should the territory of Nunavut be established, its government would be responsible for health care in the new territory. The agreement in principle between the federal government and the Committee for Original Peoples Entitlement (COPE) included provisions for social development. Further, it was recognized the Inuit had become very active in health care forums in the N.W.T.

RECOMMENDATIONS

Based on its findings, the Commission set out four major recommendations.

1. $800,000 per annum should be distributed to the provincial and the territorial Indian organizations affiliated with the NIB for the purposes of developing a consultation process.
2. The National Commission Inquiry on Indian Health (NCI) should be funded, on a permanent basis, $150,000 per annum out of funds appropriated for consultation.
3. Funds should be made available to the Inuit for purposes of developing Inuit awareness and expertise in the field of health care, and for consultations.
4. The federal government should hold a national conference on Native health that would be attended by representatives of all Native peoples.

1981

▲ In All Fairness: A Native Claims Policy

AUTHOR: Department of Indian Affairs and Northern Development
YEAR: 1981
ABORIGINAL GROUP: All Aboriginal Peoples

TOPIC: Claims
SUB-TOPIC: comprehensive claims
SOURCE: Federal Department

BACKGROUND

Prior to this new policy the government of Canada had attempted to resolve comprehensive land claims through negotiation processes which were only moderately successful. It was recognized that many more claims were in need of resolution through new processes.

PURPOSE

The purpose of the document was to set out federal policy for the resolution of land claims based on the concept of unextinguished "Aboriginal title". The policy statement re-affirms the government's commitment to resolve comprehensive claims but does not preclude government consideration of "band claims" (i.e., specific claims).

ISSUES AND FINDINGS

The report outlines three major objectives of the government of Canada in responding to Indian and Inuit land claims:

1. negotiation of fair and equitable settlements;
2. settlement of claims in a manner which will allow Aboriginal people to live the way they wish; and
3. finding terms of settlement which will respect the rights of all other people.

The statement builds on the 1973 policy under which the federal government was prepared to accept land claims based on the criteria of traditional use and occupancy. A key element of the policy was that entering into negotiations did not constitute an admission of legal liability by the federal government. The policy dictated that the Office of Native Claims (est. 1974) would decide which claims were to be accepted for negotiation, and which would be rejected (with reasons for rejection provided). Funding for research, the development of positions, and negotiation of claims was provided by the department of Indian and Northern Affairs in the form of grants and loans. It was also a policy requirement that those who benefited from claims settlements be Canadian citizens of Aboriginal origin and from the claimed area, with beneficiaries to be defined according to mutually agreed upon criteria.

The thrust of the policy was to exchange undefined Aboriginal land rights for concrete rights and benefits guaranteed in settlement legislation. Any land claims settlements would be considered final.

Negotiation, as opposed to arbitration, mediation, or litigation, was a preferred method of settlement as it permitted the representation of the concerns of Aboriginal peoples affected, as well as a recognition of the interests of all Canadians.

With respect to settlement benefits, negotiable components included lands, wildlife, subsurface rights, and monetary compensation. Other settlement provisions could include the establishment of corporate structures, taxation authorities, and social and economic programs. All these elements were seen to relate to the government's overall objective of achieving final and fair settlements which would allow for relative autonomy of Aboriginal peoples while respecting the rights of other Canadians.

RECOMMENDATIONS

Policy statement – no specific recommendations made.

▲ Native Women – Labour Force Development

AUTHOR: Joint Native Women's Association of Canada/Canada
   Employment and Immigration Commission Working Group
YEAR: 1981
ABORIGINAL GROUP: All Aboriginal Peoples, Aboriginal Women
TOPICS: Employment Development, Traditional/Contemporary
   Roles
SUB-TOPICS: training/skills development, discrimination
SOURCE: Bipartite Task Force (Federal/Aboriginal)

BACKGROUND

In January 1981, the Native Women's Association of Canada (NWAC), invited the minister of Employment and Immigration to meet with its board of directors to discuss concerns about the Canada Employment and Immigration Commission's (CEIC) delivery of programs and services to Native women. This request came in the aftermath of the Native Employment Policy and

Implementation Strategy of the late 1970s, and the subsequent designation of Indigenous peoples as a special target group within the CEIC's policy and program mandate. As a result of the meeting, the minister proposed, and NWAC agreed to, the establishment of a joint NWAC/CEIC Working Group to address the participation of Native women in the labour force.

PURPOSE

The purpose of the joint working group was to investigate the specific employment issues affecting Native women and to propose ways in which obstacles inhibiting the full participation of Native women in the labour force might be removed.

The mandate, jointly developed and approved, called for the development of policy recommendations concerning existing programs and strategies of the Native Employment Policy, as well as the formulation of a long-term strategy for CEIC and NWAC to meet effectively the employment needs of Native women. This, the first report of the working group, focuses on shorter-term, less comprehensive solutions for immediate implementation; a stronger focus on long-term recommendations was deferred to subsequent reports of the working group.

ISSUES AND FINDINGS

Several employment barriers and concerns specific to Native women were identified in the report. Statistics indicate that females make up the largest segment of Native residents in the city, as well as the largest segment of recent migrants, and that many of these Native women are young, single mothers with little education and limited employment experience. Employment among Native women was found to be irregular and heavily concentrated in low skill/low entry level/low wage occupations within the service and manufacturing/processing industries. Turnover rates among employed Native women were found to be relatively low.

The working group identified three distinct sets of factors which appear to inhibit Native women's labour force participation:

1. labour market segmentation based on gender and Native ancestry;
2. levels of education, skill development, and occupational training; and
3. family responsibilities and other demographic constraints.

According to the report, it is these conditions which might logically be the focus of policy and program responses.

RECOMMENDATIONS

The report's recommendations are subdivided into short- and long- term recommendations, with a specific focus in this report on the former; i.e., the emphasis was on moving forward without delay in those areas where it was agreed that short-term solutions were possible. Consequently, the working group submitted to the minister of Employment and Immigration selected short-term recommendations which it felt were feasible, easily implemented, and represented low or no cost to the Commission, as priority items for immediate action. These recommendations are as follows:

1. the continuation of the working group and the establishment of a Secretariat within CEIC to oversee the implementation of this report's recommendations;

2. the provision of funding to Native women's groups to facilitate liaison with the proposed CEIC employment needs assessment committees and between national, provincial and territorial Native women's organization;

3. the development of an adequate statistical data base for research purposes;

4. an intensive effort to increase the dissemination of labour market and employment program information to Native women;

5. the establishment of Native Women's Centres as pilot projects, particularly in urban areas having a high concentration of Native female single parents;

6. the establishment of pilot projects to explore "semestering" (i.e., programming delivered through a series of phases, the content and timing of which can be tailored to individual requirements) as a vehicle for providing the flexibility required by many Native women in order to undertake training/employment counselling; and

7. the establishment of pilot employment counselling/job orientation projects for Native female single parents.

The Working Group also identified a number of potentially longer-term solutions to the employment problems faced by Native women, including the use of community employment facilitators for rural areas, the execution of research to identify the specific training needs of Native women and the effectiveness of CEIC employment development programs, and the establishment of mechanisms to promote interdepartmental/intergovernmental consultation on employment issues of relevance to Native women.

◆ *Report of the Tripartite Local Government Committee Respecting Indian Local Government in British Columbia* (1981), see **Volume 3, British Columbia.**

▲ James Bay and Northern Quebec Agreement Implementation Review

AUTHOR: Department of Indian Affairs and Northern Development (John Tait)

YEAR: 1982

ABORIGINAL GROUP: First Nations, Inuit

TOPICS: Federal Government/Aboriginal Relations, Land Use, Development and Management, Economic Development, Administration of Justice, Education, Social Development

SUB-TOPICS: legislation, development, fiscal relations/responsibilities

SOURCE: Federal Department

BACKGROUND

After the Cree and the Inuit (the Makivik Corporation) alleged that Quebec and Canada had not fulfilled their responsibilities in the James Bay and Northern Quebec Agreement, they presented their case in front of the House of Commons Standing Committee on Indian Affairs and Northern Development on March 26, 1981. The Standing Committee endorsed the Aboriginal claims, and the Hon. John Munro initiated this review. The report focuses on the allegations raised by the Aboriginal parties. It does not examine the allegations regarding Quebec's responsibilities.

PURPOSE

The purpose of this report is to review Canada's performance in implementing its obligations pursuant to the James Bay and Northern Quebec Agreement. The terms of reference indicate that the review was to determine whether Canada had fulfilled the provisions of the Agreement and to examine Canada's overall performance regarding its implementation responsibilities.

ISSUES AND FINDINGS

The issues identified in the report are categorized as follows:

1. Factors Relating to Grievances

The first factor relating to the grievances is the wording and interpretation of the Agreement. The review found that Canada has met, or is meeting, its commitments to the extent that they are set down in the Agreement, but its performance in satisfying the "spirit" of the Agreement has been less satisfactory.

The second factor refers to the dynamic nature of the Agreement, which demands a long-term process of implementation; this allows for ongoing interaction and for the evolution of self-government. This design, however, has only led to problems, such as the obscured perception of the Agreement's benefits to the Aboriginal peoples, and the gap between the high expectations and the actual provisions of the Agreement. There is also the problem of federal budgetary restraint limiting the achievement of these goals.

2. Grievances Themselves

The first category of grievances deals with the problems relating to the provision of the federal programs, services, and benefits and the overall pattern of federal expenditures. The Aboriginal peoples allege that the federal government has not upheld its commitments and responsibilities.

The second category addresses the problems relating to the provision of "special" programs, services and benefits. The Aboriginal peoples allege that the provisions of the Agreement have been applied very narrowly, sometimes preventing or impairing the attainment of their entitled benefits. These grievances encompass the issues of housing and infrastructure, where it was found that although the programs fell short of Aboriginal expectations, Canada was attempting to act in the best interests of the Inuit. The issue of health services is also noted. The Cree allege that the federal government has failed to fulfil its obligations, and the report finds that health and sanitation problems exist and must be resolved through tripartite negotiations.

The Aboriginal peoples further allege that Canada has failed to encourage economic development. The report finds that Aboriginal economic development has been slow, and that this is attributable primarily to the failure to implement a comprehensive development strategy.

The issue of core funding is also raised. The report finds that a special funding program is required.

In terms of the administration of justice, the Aboriginal peoples contend that the provisions of the Agreement have not been fulfilled by the government. The report notes, however, that the Department of the Solicitor General has begun examining the existing programs.

In the area of education, the report finds that all parties must co-operate to ensure that the educational goals are attained.

3. Overall Implementation Costs and Co-ordination

The Aboriginal peoples allege that they were forced to use compensation funds for legal fees and other unintended costs. The report found that the expenses were not accurately forecast and that the problem should not be addressed through interpretation of the Agreement, but rather by ensuring its effective implementation.

The issue of the implementation process itself was also raised. The Aboriginal peoples claim it is an impediment to their rights and achievements. It was found that the lack of proper mechanisms, structures, and attitudes is a major obstacle to efficient implementation.

4. Other Issues of Concern to the Inuit

These issues include the extinguishment of title, Inuit political representation, and offshore islands. The report found that these issues extended beyond the mandate of the review.

RECOMMENDATIONS

The report emphasizes the need for clarification and understanding of the Agreement, largely due to the fact that many of the problems have been the result of misinterpretation. Regarding federal programs, services and benefits, the report found that the entitlements of the Cree and Inuit were respected, although the funding was not necessarily optimal. In terms of the "special" programs, services, and benefits, the report found that the federal government had not typically fulfilled its responsibilities. Reviews of existing programs, as well as the development of comprehensive strategies and negotiations, are recommended. With respect to the implementation process, the report recommends the establishment of a more effective system.

▲ Outstanding Business: A Native Claims Policy

AUTHOR: Department of Indian Affairs and Northern Development
YEAR: 1982
ABORIGINAL GROUP: All Aboriginal Peoples

TOPICS: Self-Government, Federal Government/Aboriginal
Relations, Provincial Government/Aboriginal Relations, Treaty
Land Entitlement, Claims

SUB-TOPICS: negotiation structures and processes, treaties, federal
trust responsibilities, policy, political participation/representation,
claims, commissions/structures/negotiation processes, specific claims

SOURCE: Federal Department

BACKGROUND

This booklet outlines the federal government review of its current policy on
Native land claims, particularly "specific claims". The review was stimulated
by the recognition of problems inherent in the current procedures and
processes regarding Native land claims. In response to these concerns, the
government of Canada undertook a series of consultative meetings with
Native groups across Canada to gain a better insight into Native concerns.
It is an admission of outstanding business, not liability, between the government
of Canada and Native peoples.

PURPOSE

The purpose of this booklet is to outline the policy, as of 1982, regarding Native
land claims and other assets which fall under the authority of the *Indian Act*.

ISSUES AND FINDINGS

There are various issues running throughout this policy, which reflect the
concerns of Native peoples: the lawful obligation criterion; the assessment
of claims; consultation and participation in the claims process; and the issue
of compensation.

1. Lawful Obligation Criterion

The Native groups view the lawful obligation criterion as too narrow to solve
major differences; they believe that it is not only a legal obligation that the federal
government has toward them but also a moral one. Furthermore, the Native
groups want the lawful obligation criterion to extend to the time before
Confederation and not merely to be interpreted as having relevance after
1867. It was also charged that the federal government had not fulfilled its
responsibility in keeping trust arrangements for bands and their assets and that
there have been past breaches of these arrangements by Canadian governments.

2. Assessment of Claims

The Native groups also contend that the laws regarding the assessment of claims ought to be relaxed. The procedural defences open to the Crown, such as time limitations and/or rules of evidence, should be softened. They should consider Native oral tradition admissible and statutes of limitations impractical for the fair resolution of "specific claims".

3. Consultation

It was also argued that during the claims assessment process, Native people should have access to the opinions of the Department of Justice so that adequate responses could be prepared. This position reflects the Native attitude that governmental review of a claim should not be a unilateral affair. Instead, greater effort should be made at reaching a consensus based on facts and merit. To this end, the Office of Native Claims should be given more freedom in its settlement of claims; in particular, it should be more supportive of Native efforts to establish their claims. This could be achieved by assisting in the preparation of claims and by making access to internal documents more readily available.

The Native groups also argued that independent third parties, specifically mediators, should be involved in the claims process to facilitate settlement. In the event that legal action is used, Native groups should be able to call upon the government to fund their legal actions.

4. Compensation

In terms of compensation, the general view of bands is that they should be granted the lands they had before "loss" or treaty. Lands occupied by third parties would be expropriated and if necessary, those involved would be compensated.

These issues figured prominently in the concerns of the bands. They reflected frustration and a sense of injustice at the slow and painful process of claims settlement. The Native peoples argued that any new claims policy must be developed in consultation with Native peoples and not merely on their behalf.

RECOMMENDATIONS

The revised governmental policy on "specific claims" responds to the previously cited concerns of Native peoples:

1. Lawful Obligation Criterion

In terms of the lawful obligation criterion, the federal government felt that the provision was inappropriate unless such limitations were expressly stated.

2. Assessment of Claims

According to the policy, the statute of limitations question is not grounds for the non-negotiation of claims. The federal government will not use time limitations as a defence against pursuing claims unless litigation ensues. The same procedure applies to oral evidence accepted during the negotiation process unless that process ends up in the courts. The federal government then reserves the right to call for "inadmissible evidence" as a defence in litigation proceedings.

3. Consultation

The bands were concerned with their relative lack of access to Department of Justice opinions and the internal documents of the Office of Native Claims (ONC). The policy does make it clear that there will be an exchange of documents between the ONC and Native bands. In addition, other federal or provincial departments may be called in to consult during the claims process. Immediately prior to referring the claim to the Department of Indian Affairs and Northern Development for validation, the Department of Justice will review with the claimant group any and all elements of the legal advice given to the ONC on the lawful obligation criterion of the federal government.

While the system does seem to be becoming more inclusive, the federal government has not addressed the issue of an independent third party being present during the claims process. Furthermore, should the negotiations end up in a courtroom, the federal government may or may not cover a reasonable portion of the band's court costs, depending on justification and sanction by the Department of Justice.

4. Compensation

The issue of non-Indians on "claim land" has been handled in the past and will be handled in the future as one which is generally not subject to negotiation. It is government practice not to accept settlements which will result in the dispossession of third parties, with or without compensation.

▲ Report of the Sub-Committee on Indian Women and the Indian Act

AUTHOR: Standing Committee on Indian Affairs and Northern Development, Chair, Keith Penner, M.P.

YEAR: 1982

ABORIGINAL GROUP: First Nations, Aboriginal Women

TOPICS: Membership/Citizenship/Constituency

SUB-TOPIC: membership and the *Indian Act*

SOURCE: House of Commons Committee

BACKGROUND

This is the sixth report of the Standing Committee on Indian Affairs and Northern Development to the House of Commons, and the first report of the Sub-Committee on Indian Women and the *Indian Act*. Important events at the time of the Committee hearings included a United Nations declaration that Canada was violating the international covenant on civil rights and political rights by the continued application of subsection 12.(1)(b) of the *Indian Act*, and the repatriation of Canada's Constitution including entrenchment of Aboriginal rights and a charter of rights and freedoms.

Most of the recommendations of the Committee were reflected in changes to the *Indian Act* in 1985, through Bill C-31, including reinstatement of women and their children who had lost status as a result of discrimination under the Act. Changes made to the Act also contained new provisions allowing bands to assume control over membership through the development of membership codes (subject to the minister's approval). Another significant element of Bill C-31 was that, in the case of those bands who did assume control over membership, Indian status and band membership no longer went hand in hand.

PURPOSE

The Standing Committee was charged with the task of studying provisions of the *Indian Act* dealing with band membership and Indian status, and to make recommendations on how the Act could be amended to remove those provisions that discriminated against women on the basis of sex.

The Sub-committee was also empowered to review all legal and institutional factors affecting the status, development and responsibilities of band governments on Indian reserves and to make recommendations for improvements concerning these matters.

ISSUES AND FINDINGS

The major finding of the report confirms that the *Indian Act* did contain provisions that discriminated against Indian women on the basis of sex. This fact had been recognized by the United Nations, the department of Indian Affairs, the Canadian Human Rights Commission, as well as several Native organizations.

The Sub-committee recognized that the issue of discrimination was closely linked with broader issues, including definition of band membership, difference between Indian status and band membership, the relationship of individual rights and collective rights, recognition of traditional and customary practices and the need for additional funds and additional lands for reinstated women and their descendants.

The report states that there was a clear indication from the testimony received that Indian bands would like to control band membership. Control was seen as an essential right of self-determination and exercisable through self-government. The report also noted that human rights should not be decided on a financial basis and that the reinstatement of women who had been discriminated against would have associated increased funding needs.

The Sub-committee noted that a general consensus existed that the goal of survival of Native culture is legitimate and, therefore, criteria to determine who belongs to Native groups – even though it is discriminating – must be determined. Recognition was also given to the fact that the *Canadian Charter of Rights and Freedoms* would likely be used as the basis for legal action regarding the status of women in the *Indian Act*. It was also noted that any new changes in the Act would have to give consideration to the International Covenant on Civil and Political Rights (1976) and the Convention on the Elimination of All Forms of Discrimination Against Women (1981).

RECOMMENDATIONS

The Sub-committee made several recommendations for amendments to the *Indian Act* including amendments:

1. to ensure that the status/membership of women and minor children are not dependent on the status/membership of their husband/father;

 2. to ensure all children of male and female Indians receive equal treatment and that discrimination on the basis of illegitimacy be eliminated; that children of an Indian and a non-Indian parent be granted Indian status, and that these children become members of the band of the Indian parent;

3. in the future, non-Indian persons should not gain status under the *Indian Act* by marriage, and new provisions should not be retroactive;

4. to allow bands to establish regulations concerning non-Indian spouses and their political and legal rights including such matters as residency, inheritance, retention rights on death, divorce or separation, and provision of services;

5. to ensure that descendants of children born of an Indian and a non-Indian shall not be eligible for registered Indian status, unless further provided for under band membership codes, or unless such descendants otherwise gain status;

6. to ensure subsection 12.(1)(b) has no effect on the status of Indian women who marry after the date of amendment, this recommendation should be retroactive to reinstate all affected women and children, regardless of whether the mother is still living;

7. to ensure that band membership is not lost immediately upon marriage and that either spouse has the option of applying to transfer to the band of their wife of husband, according to the band's criteria for admission; and

8. repeal sections of the Act in order that involuntary enfranchisement be eliminated from the *Indian Act*.

The Sub-committee also noted that in certain recommendations, it had suggested movement toward band control of membership. Therefore, it encouraged all bands to begin, or continue development of regulations, codes, criteria, and procedures which would be in accord with international standards.

The Sub-committee also recommended that Parliament appropriate sufficient funds to cover the costs of reinstating the affected women, and that the federal government repay the band any per capita shares for women readmitted to band membership. It was also recommended that the federal government fund an independent study in consultation with Aboriginal peoples on the number of non-status Indian women affected by the discriminatory provisions of the *Indian Act*, and the number who would be reinstated if they so wished.

▲ Turning the Tide: A New Policy for Canada's Pacific Fisheries

AUTHOR: Commission on Pacific Fisheries Policy, Commissioner, Peter H. Pearse

YEAR: 1982

ABORIGINAL GROUP: Not specific to Aboriginal peoples

TOPICS: Resources, Economic Development, Employment Development, Intergovernmental Relations

SUB-TOPICS: fishing/fisheries, regional non-Aboriginal, regional Aboriginal; tripartite (Aboriginal/federal/provincial)

SOURCE: Federal Commission

BACKGROUND

On January 12, 1981, the Governor in Council appointed the Commission on Pacific Fisheries Policy. The order charged the Commission to find ways to improve the conditions of Canada's Pacific fisheries, which were recognized at that time to be at a crisis point. Commercial fisheries were plagued by chronic instability and poor economic performance. The fishing stocks, especially salmon and roe-herring, were at low levels, or were staging recovery from previous periods of overfishing. Poor understanding of Aboriginal peoples' rights regarding fishing had led to conflicts, particularly with sport fishermen. Widespread uncertainty existed concerning government policy and regulations.

PURPOSE

The Commission's terms of reference directed it to inquire into and report upon:

1. the condition of the stocks of fish within Canada's jurisdiction off the Pacific coast;

2. the provisions for conservation, management, protection and development of the fish resources;

3. the structure and size of the commercial fishing fleet and the relationship between the capacity of the fleet to harvest fish and the optimum rates of harvesting the stocks;

4. the policies and procedure for licensing commercial fishing, and for regulating the size and structure of the fishing fleet; and

5. the nature and amount of non-commercial fishing in tidal waters and non-tidal waters for salmonid species, its impact on the stocks and on the commercial fishery, and the policies and procedures for regulating non-commercial fishing.

The Commission was further requested to make recommendations on the legislation, policies, procedures and practices affecting the management and use of the fish resources and more specifically on means to ensure that:

1. Canadians receive the maximum economic and social benefits of the fisheries resource;

2. granting of fishing privileges to commercial, recreational and Aboriginal food fishermen is conducive to proper management and conservation, to an equitable division of the catch among sectors, and to economic efficiency in the development of the commercial fishing fleet;

3. charges levied by the government for rights to fish commercially or otherwise are consistent with the value of the resources recovered;

4. the vitality of the fishing industry is maintained, while encouraging the development of its structure, ownership and control in accordance with industrial efficiency; and

5. provisions for management, enhancement and protection of the fish resources, the administration of fisheries policy, and consultation and communication between the government of Canada and private groups involved in fishing activities are systematic and efficient.

ISSUES AND FINDINGS

The Commission's findings were extensive, and most of the issues addressed were not exclusive to Aboriginal peoples. As a result, for the purposes of this summary, the Commission's general findings are divided into 10 categories below; these findings are then followed by a discussion of the Commission's Aboriginal-specific conclusions.

General Findings

1. **Resource management**: The Commission found that the condition of the fish stocks was better than many had suggested, though there was concern over the salmon stock and the effectiveness of the salmonid enhancement program. The Commission felt that the greatest threat to stock enhancement efforts was the existing fishing patterns.

2. **Fisheries and habitat management**: Current management efforts were found to be deficient, due largely to a lack of management information, a slow decision-making process, the absence of evaluation, and the lack of co-ordination with provincial agencies.

3. **Commercial fisheries**: The biggest economic problem in the fishing industry was found to be the chronic overcapacity of the fleets. To address this problem, the Commission suggested that Canadian licensing policy should ensure control of total catch and composition of the catch, efficient development of the fleet, relative security for the fishermen, appropriate public revenues, and consideration of social concerns.

4. **Sport fishing**: The greatest impediment to a more effective sport fishing management policy was found to be the limited availability and quality of sport fishing data. The Commission emphasized the need for special regulations intended for specific areas along the coast or specific rivers, and adapted to local stock conditions and sport fishing demand.

5. **Enforcement**: The Commission found a number of problems related to the enforcement program, including the relatively small enforcement capacity of the Department, the complexity of current regulations and laws governing fishing, and problems associated with detection and apprehension, prosecution, and penalties.

6. **Consultative arrangements**: Despite efforts by the Department to improve consultative mechanisms, the Commission found that advisory groups were badly structured and lacking both direction and clear terms of reference.

7. **Federal arrangements with British Columbia**: The absence of a formal working relationship between the two governments emerged as a serious deficiency in the existing policy framework for the Pacific fisheries. The Commission found disharmony in policy, duplication of effort, and considerable conflict, confusion, and suspicion.

8. **Administration**: The Commission found that the Department was subject to frequent reorganization, unresponsive to urgent needs, and characterized by slow and cumbersome procedures.

9. **Yukon fisheries**: In general, the areas of concern in the Yukon paralleled that of the overall Pacific fishery.

10. **Policy implementation and review:** The Commission examined existing policy instruments: legislation, regulations, and licences. The *Fisheries Act* was found to be narrow in scope, ambiguous, and inconsistent. The Commission found regulations to be piecemeal, static, and subject to duplication and inconsistencies.

Aboriginal-Specific Findings

The Commission reported Indian participation in the commercial fishery to be in decline, resulting in serious social and economic problems in many British Columbia and Yukon Indian communities. The Commission found that commercial fisheries offer a better chance of success for employment and economic enhancement of Indian communities than many other economic development schemes that have fewer connections to traditional activities. A major obstacle to greater Indian participation in the commercial fishery was seen to be the lack of financial assistance from traditional lending institutions.

The Commission found the existing policies governing the Indian fishery to be unsatisfactory. Some of the main problems identified by the Commission included:

1. uncertainty concerning whether the Indian fisheries have priority over the commercial and sport fisheries;
2. the requirement that government issue fishing permits for what many Indians consider to be their right to fish;
3. the control of illegal sales of fish;
4. the enforcement of fishing times, places, equipment allowances;
5. the belief that fisheries regulation and management excludes Indian participation and needs; and
6. the ambiguous and incoherent legal framework for Indian fisheries.

RECOMMENDATIONS

Based on the terms of reference, the Commission established a number of objectives as a framework for making its recommendations. The following summary of the recommendations is organized according to this framework. Once again, Aboriginal-specific recommendations follow the summary of the Commission's more general proposals.

General

1. **Resource conservation:** The Commission recommended that a major inventory of fish habitats be jointly established by the provincial and federal governments, that new procedures be developed to protect fish habitats from development projects, that new arrangements be made for data collection, planning, and evaluation, that the salmonid enhancement program be continued on a more modest scale under a modified intergovernmental

agreement, and that the management of fishing and enhancement programs be more integrated. The Commission also proposed a series of specific regulatory changes.

2. **Maximizing the benefits of resource use**: The Commission recommended a complete overhaul of the existing licensing system. According to the report, licences should authorize more specific privileges regarding timeframes, species, and defined areas. The Commission recommended that licence fees and royalties be consistent and related to the value of the fish, that new licences be issued through competitive bidding, and that a new administrative structure for issuing licences, processing appeals and retiring excess licences be established that would separate these responsibilities from those related to resource management. The Commission further recommended a reduction target of one-half the licensed fleet capacity over 10 years, assisted by a joint industry-government voluntary licence retirement program. The Commission also called for abolishing direct and indirect subsidies for new vessel construction.

3. **Economic development and growth**: In order to discourage the concentration of fishing privileges, the Commission recommended strict limits on the permitted holdings of any licensee. The Commission also made recommendations encouraging support of the mariculture industry and ocean ranching of salmon.

4. **Social and cultural development**: The Commission's recommendations for fleet rationalization contain provisions for securing the fishing privileges of long-established fishermen, and focusing any reductions on voluntary withdrawals over a 10-year period. The Commission proposed a five-year program aimed at preserving sport fishing opportunities while holding sport catches to their then-current levels, improving the information available for management and planning, and developing a long-term sport fishing policy.

5. **Returns to the public**: According to the report, recommendations for the rationalization of the fishing fleet should improve the public's return on labour and capital employed in fishing. The Commission recommended adjustments to the royalty schedules to correspond to the value of fish taken. In addition, increased sport fishing licence fees should increase the public's return.

6. **Flexibility**: The Commission's recommendations concerning licensing and other arrangements were intended to accommodate unanticipated disturbances, and to provide the government with the flexibility to adjust to changing conditions without disrupting explicit or implied commitments. Several

recommendations were made regarding collecting and developing data, which, in part, were intended to provide the information necessary to anticipate changes.

7. **Administrative simplicity**: The Commission recommended that enforcement efforts be enhanced, that responsibility for habitat management and enforcement be consolidated, that research be co-ordinated and that certain lines of reporting be streamlined. Additional recommendations called for the establishment of a policy development group within the Department, and a thorough budget and administrative review. It was further proposed that certain regulations and restrictions be streamlined, and that the *Fisheries Act* be updated. The Commission recommended greater federal-provincial co-ordination, including the establishment of an inter-governmental consultative group to plan and supervise co-operative programs and to resolve mutual problems. The Commission recommended the establishment of a Pacific Fisheries Council that would provide general policy advice to the minister and channel the advice from a more systematic consultative structure involving specialized advisory committees. Finally, the Commission suggested the establishment of a special temporary minister of state for Pacific Fisheries to expedite the implementation of the report's recommendations.

Aboriginal-Specific

The Commission recommended a variety of measures to support Indian fishing organizations, including:

1. new approaches to securing tribal bands' rights to defined quantities of fish;

2. extension of rights over the use of their catch to include consumption and sale; and

3. constructive involvement in fisheries management and enhancement programs.

1983

▲ Community-Based Research: Report of the SSHRC Task Force on Native Issues

AUTHOR: Social Science and Humanities Research Council of Canada, Task Force on Native Issues

YEAR: 1983

ABORIGINAL GROUP: All Aboriginal Peoples
TOPICS: Community Institutions, Social/Cross-Cultural Relations
SUB-TOPIC: co-operation
SOURCE: Federal Agency

BACKGROUND

SSHRC began a consultation process in 1980 to consider its potential role in supporting research in respect of Native peoples and communities.

The process involved consultation with a broad range of representatives from universities, Native organizations and communities, and government departments to determine the kinds of program that would be beneficial to both academic researchers and Native communities.

A Task Force on Native Issues was established, and a series of regional workshops was held to develop and encourage broader participation and input into the planning process.

In 1983, the Task Force, following a series of workshops, recommended that SSHRC approve in principle the introduction of a new strategic grants program to support community-based research on Native issues, for implementation in 1984-85.

SSHRC was not yet prepared to accept this recommendation as it felt further study on the operation of the new research program was required.

PURPOSE

Following the SSHRC decision that further study was needed, the Task Force on Native Issues set up a National Symposium on community-based research that brought stakeholders together to study the issue further.

ISSUES AND FINDINGS

A number of issues were addressed during the Symposium. A key issue was the participation of members of the various Native communities in the administration of the new grants program and, at the community level, in the various projects that would be undertaken once funding had been made available by SSHRC.

Also central to the participation issue was the recognition that it was important for researchers to be able to receive special training. This would be accomplished either by way of a special workshop or through apprenticeships while research projects were under way.

Training for those individuals who would be members of the Council and administering the grant program was also considered important. These individuals would need to be trained in the evaluation of various project proposals to be submitted. It was seen as particularly important that those assessing research applications have not only the experience and background needed to evaluate technical aspects of proposals but also cultural sensitivity and awareness of the particular problems of Native communities.

Another issue addressed was that of research priorities. Since this was a program of community-based research, it was felt that issues of a local nature should receive funding on a priority basis.

The language and communications policies of SSHRC were also reviewed. While publication relating to the grant program would continue in both official languages, it was felt that advertising in local Native magazines and newspapers would need to be in the local Native languages.

RECOMMENDATIONS

The Task Force on Native Issues made four recommendations to SSHRC:

1. approve, in principle, the introduction of a new strategic grants program to support community-based research on Native issues.

2. make funds available under three categories: seed money grants, grants for special research projects, and workshop grants.

3. establish a national adjudication committee with the majority of its 12 to 14 members being of Native ancestry, and with members selected from each of the following six regions of the country – Atlantic Canada, Quebec, Ontario, the Prairies, British Columbia, and the North.

4. request that the Task Force develop a guide for applicants outlining the terms and conditions of the new programs, with appropriate application forms and suggested communications plans, for consideration by the Council.

▲ Federal Expenditures and Mechanisms for their Transfer to Indians

AUTHOR: Coopers & Lybrand for the Special Committee on Indian Self-Government

YEAR: 1983

ABORIGINAL GROUP: First Nations

TOPICS: Financial Arrangements/Responsibilities/Public Finance, Self-Government, Federal/Aboriginal Relations

SUB-TOPICS: financial arrangements/mechanisms, financial management/administration, federal trust responsibilities, institutions, negotiation structures and processes

SOURCE: House of Commons Committee

BACKGROUND

This study was commissioned by the Special Committee on Indian Self-Government to assist the Committee in discharging its terms of reference as these related to the review of institutional factors limiting band development, and more particularly, the review and consideration of current and future financial transfers, control and accounting mechanisms in place between bands and the federal government and the accountability of the minister of Indian Affairs to Parliament.

Appendices contained in the report examine in detail elements of the specific terms of reference (identified below). The research report appendices themselves constitute a valuable and unique collection of data, which is complimented by a level of commentary and analysis in relation to different aspects of fiscal relations.

While the report identifies and comments on possible solutions to existing funding problems, it contains no specific recommendations.

PURPOSE

Specific terms of reference for the research report requested that it:

1. identify, for the current year, total direct and indirect federal expenditures for the benefit of Indian people;

2. identify funds specifically provided for the benefit of Indian people by provincial/territorial governments;

3. identify proportional levels of funding associated with the transfer of responsibilities (i.e., program/service delivery and administration) to bands and tribal councils;

4. identify costs incurred by federal departments and agencies in securing information required to meet the accountability requirements of Parliament;

5. identify trends in federal expenditures in respect of certain program activities (housing, education);

6. comment on the 1980 Auditor General's report and reported discrepancies between project expenditures and public accounts;

7. review current program delivery arrangements;

8. identify alternative approaches to funding arrangements and

9. review structures and funding mechanisms associated with international development as possible models for future funding of Indian governments.

ISSUES AND FINDINGS

For the purposes of summary, the main report addresses issues under three broad categories:

1. funding;

2. administration; and

3. accountability.

It also samples the views of Aboriginal organizations who appeared before the Special Committee as witnesses, in relation to each of these three broad areas.

Funding: The research report generally reflects the view that the current top-down resource allocation systems of government, which retain decision making at the level of central agencies and departments contrast with the objectives of self-government, in which the beneficiaries of the use of government funds participate more directly in funding decisions and, in particular, in decisions relating to the allocation and management of financial resources.

While the federal government has traditionally chosen to provide funding to Indian organizations through conditional grants and contributions for programs/service delivery, this has been at the expense of efficiency. The research report contains the view that unconditional grants are the only acceptable funding mechanism for self-governing organizations.

It was felt there was a need to assure delivery of certain services (health care, social services) to Indian peoples through statutory (mandatory) funding and payments to Indian governments. The report favoured the transfer of funds direct to the provinces for the provision of certain public services, provided the concurrence of Indian people is obtained.

The report suggested combining core and administrative funding for Indian governments through a per capita formula, to be reflected in negotiated

75

five-year agreements. In effect, this would establish a transfer system similar to those in place with the provinces under Established Programs Financing.

However, funding for economic development and infrastructure should be treated differently, though still apportioned on a per capita basis. These funds would be provided according to five- and ten-year plans, rather than on an annual basis.

Finally, under Indian self-government, special funding arrangements would need to be accessible to those bands who did not wish to pursue a more ambitious self-government arrangement, and in situations where bands were unable to fulfil their responsibilities under self-government.

Administration: The report found that the transfer of administrative responsibility (under devolution policies) had not resulted in any changes in decision-making responsibilities, created conflicts in the roles of DIAND, led to duplication of activities, did not enhance either band acceptance of responsibility or improved administration, and generally did not lead to any economic savings.

The view at the community level was to the effect that while bands and tribal councils had assumed many of the administrative responsibilities of the Department, this had not been accompanied by a transfer of sufficient resources, and stretched existing human and financial resources at the community level to their limit.

The research report favoured a completely new structure and system of financial adminstration in which a new funding agency would be established to assume the former funding/adminstration responsibilities of DIAND, and to distribute grants and contributions to Indian governments (who would have greater decision making powers in relation to the use of funds). The new funding agency would have a small staff and would involve Indian representation in decision making, to ensure that the agency would not be tempted to impose its own terms and conditions in the transfer of resources.

DIAND would have a residual role in the delivery of services not otherwise provided by other line departments or by provincial governments and agencies.

Under new structural arrangements, Indian governments would be able to select servicing agencies/organizations in areas where programs/services were not delivered directly by Indian governments themselves, although federal funding responsibility would remain.

Accountability: Present accountability requirements impose significant and unnecessary burdens on both government departments and on Indian recipients, and are inefficient, primarily as a result of inefficient processes for the allocation of funds to delivery agencies; program by program accountability systems; poor consultations and communications between DIAND and bands in relation to budgeting and funding decisions; audit problems associated with lack of clarify in situations where authority and responsibility is "shared" (between DIAND and bands).

New funding processes would need to incorporate the following elements: total funding to be settled by independent formula or through a separate "envelope"; bands to identify and negotiate total requirements and allocate resources as they see fit; self-government funds to be appropriated separate from appropriations in relation to the continuing roles of DIAND or other line departments; unconditional grants from Parliament delivered through a new funding agency; audited financial statements and budgets submitted to band members and to funding agency by bands; additional information provided only in cases of insolvency or in accordance with wishes of the band; renegotiation of funding arrangements every five years.

New political and legal frameworks would need to be implemented to accommodate new systems of accountability. The report identifies major elements as they are reflected in the municipal model; i.e., chief elected officers, elected councillors, independent administrators and auditors.

RECOMMENDATIONS

The report contains no specific recommendations, but clearly favoured new financial arrangements which would incorporate many elements of current government-to-government fiscal arrangements and relations, and which would facilitate decision making by Indian governments in relation to the management and allocation of resources, and appropriate systems of accountability as between Indian governments and their members, and Indian governments and funding agencies including Parliament.

▲ Indian Self-Government in Canada: Report of the Special Committee

AUTHOR: Special Committee on Indian Self-Government, Chair, Keith Penner, M.P.

YEAR: 1983

ABORIGINAL GROUP: First Nations

TOPICS: Self-Government, Constitution, Federal/Aboriginal Relations

SUB-TOPICS: rights, negotiation structures and processes, jurisdiction, structures and institutions, treaties, jurisdiction, legislation, federal trust responsibilities, policy

SOURCE: House of Commons Committee

BACKGROUND

In 1982 the Standing Committee on Indian Affairs and Northern Development requested a mandate and authority to examine financial and other relationships between Indian peoples and the government of Canada. This request followed numerous representations to the Committee by Indian peoples recounting their experiences and frustrations with current financial, legislative and institutional arrangements.

The House of Commons responded with orders for the establishment of two special committees: one to investigate these issues, and the other to review *Indian Act* membership and status provisions.

The Committee's work was conducted in the shadow of the First Ministers' Aboriginal Constitutional Conference in 1983, and at a time when national level Aboriginal organizations were focusing their efforts on seeking constitutional recognition of the Aboriginal right to self-government.

Although the Special Committee established an excellent forum for Indian representations on a broad range of matters, there was considerable mistrust and uncertainty regarding the role of the Committee vis-à-vis constitutional developments and legislative changes proposed at the time. There was also some fear that the work of the Committee might lead to another "White Paper", or some similarly unacceptable federal policy proposal.

The Committee held extensive hearings across the country and commissioned research in the following areas: federal expenditures and transfer mechanisms; Crown/Indian trust relationship; Aboriginal/government relations in other countries; and the economic foundations of self-government.

PURPOSE

Formal orders of reference for the Special Committee on Indian Self-Government called for the review of legal and institutional factors affecting the status, development and responsibilities of band governments on-reserve.

Specific issues to be addressed included legal status and accountability of band governments, powers of the minister under the *Indian Act* and accountability to Parliament, financial issues, legislative powers of bands and jurisdictional questions, and Indian women and the *Indian Act* (eight items referred from second special sub-committee). The Committee was asked to carry out its responsibilities in view of federal jurisdiction under s. 91(24), constitutional recognition of Aboriginal and treaty rights, the government's economic restraint program, and the First Ministers' Conference on Aboriginal rights.

ISSUES AND FINDINGS

The Special Committee report addressed a range of areas relating to Indian self-government, including education, child welfare and health; recognition of self-government; structures and powers of Indian governments; economic foundations of self-government; financial arrangements; lands and resources; and the trust relationship.

The Committee considered the *Indian Act*, and the paradox inherent in Indian views which recognize the constraints imposed by the Act, as well as dependence on the Act for protection of special status and rights. The Committee also pointed to difficulties inherent in pursuing devolution policies within the context of the *Indian Act*.

The Committee encountered almost unanimous rejection of the government's 1982 proposals for legislative change which were touted as facilitating greater local control and exercise of authority by band governments. Opposition to these proposals was on the basis that they involved a delegation of power to "inferior" Indian "municipal" governments, rather than a recognition of sovereignty of Indian First Nations, and would radically alter the special trust relationship, relieving the federal government of its fiduciary and special responsibilities.

With respect to education, child welfare and health care, the Committee found these to be areas where Indian government jurisdiction was essential, particularly in the design, implementation and administration of delivery systems, programs and services.

The Committee recognized the need for a new relationship based on a constitutional recognition of Indian First Nations governments as a distinct order of government in Canada. In the Committee's view, such a new relationship would need to effect dramatic change to current arrangements, respect the diversity, rights and traditions of First Nations, have as an objective the ending of dependency, and be flexible enough to accommodate the full range of government arrangement sought by Indian First Nations. The Committee considered options for the achievement of such a new relationship, including constitutional recognition of the right of Indian self-government, special enabling legislation to set out a broad framework of general principles under which Indian governments would be developed, and the continued pursuit of bilateral and treaty-making processes. The Committee made recommendations in relation to all three options.

The Committee found no international examples upon which Indian self-government might be modelled.

With respect to the structures and powers of Indian governments in Canada, the Committee found common agreement that the primary political unit of Indian government must be the band, but that self-government arrangements should accommodate situations where First Nations might choose to associate on a different basis for various purposes (i.e., administrative, economic). Further, structures of government would need to be chosen by First Nations members themselves, with systems of accountability developed under new arrangements.

The Committee considered legislative requirements to accommodate Indian government and the exercise of Indian government powers and jurisdictions, and found there was a need for:

1. legislation demonstrating federal commitment to recognizing First Nations governments,

2. legislation authorizing the federal government to enter into agreements which would identify the jurisdictional fields to be occupied by recognized First Nations, and

3. federal legislation to occupy fully the legislative field relating to Indians and lands reserved for the Indians, which would then be vacated by the federal government and occupied by Indian governments.

The scope of powers to be exercised by First Nations would be comprehensive of legislative, policy, program and service delivery, law enforcement and judicial functions. Jurisdictional fields to be occupied, however, would be identified through negotiated agreements. To ensure that at no point a jurisdictional vacuum would be created, until a First Nation chose to exercise its authority within an area the status quo would prevail (i.e., until replaced by Indian government legislation, federal or provincial laws would continue to apply). Areas of jurisdictional overlap between federal, provincial and a First Nation would need to be subject to joint control and authority.

The Committee identified the need for new mechanisms to resolve disputes in relation to all types of new arrangements and agreements including treaties, jurisdictional agreements and service delivery contracts.

In considering the economic foundations of self-government, the Committee identified the following as obstacles to development and self-sufficiency: non-recognition of the economic value of treaties and treaty rights to pursue traditional economies; erosion of Indian moneys gained from sale of assets as a result of mismanagement; *Indian Act* restrictions on band control of development and on the use of reserve land as security; limited legal capacities of band governments; economic development programs administered by multiple agencies; and limited creative use of welfare funds. The Committee recognized the need for bands to able to implement economic ventures at the community level, through, for example development boards, corporations, and the need for the development of innovative financing mechanisms and institutions.

The Committee considered in detail issues relating to current and future financing of Indian governments. The Committee found current arrangements to be generally dissatisfactory to both DIAND and bands, inefficient and inappropriately conceived. Current arrangements were seen as more appropriate for agents (i.e., government agencies) than for governments.

The research report on financial arrangements examined in detail alternative funding methods and arrangements which might be appropriate for Indian self-government. The Committee recognized that the central features of any new financial arrangements would need to:

1. incorporate clear lines of financial accountability;
2. accommodate both direct Indian government accountability to membership and ministerial accountability to Parliament;
3. establish high quality First Nations financial management and administrative systems; and
4. include innovative and flexible funding mechanisms and methods for the determination of funding levels as well as longer-term, negotiated funding arrangements, new mechanisms and institutions for the negotiation and distribution of financial resources to Indian governments.

The Committee found that non-Indian perceptions of reserve land had over time contributed to the paternalistic legal framework of the *Indian Act* and reflected an entirely different interpretation from that held by Indian people who viewed reserve lands as completely within their control and authority (i.e., lands were never "given" away, and therefore could not be "given back" by non-Indian governments). Further, the land regime established through the *Indian Act* stood in direct contrast with customary Indian land holding practices. The Committee recognized a significant continued Indian interest in traditional lands and resources, and in areas where title had not been alienated, as well as the desire by First Nations to participate in decisions affecting those lands and resources. The Committee recognized the need for additional lands to accommodate future growth in First Nations populations, including increases as a result of the reinstatement of individuals under the *Indian Act*. The primary methods for achieving such increases would be through the fulfilment of outstanding treaty obligations and the settlement of land claims.

With respect to the settlement of claims, the Committee found a high level of frustration with claims policies and processes. This was attributed to the slow pace of claims review/ acceptance/negotiation processes; perceived conflict of interest on the federal government's part; the fact that claims processes were based on policy rather than legislative enactments and therefore were wholly within the purview of executive powers; limitations on claims arising from pre-Confederation treaties, the concept that claims may be superseded by law (laws passed since the situation arose have the effect of erasing government obligations); and the doctrine of extinguishment wherein all residual Aboriginal rights and title not be specifically negotiated as part of or recognized in a final settlement terminate.

Finally, in respect of the federal/Indian trust relationship, the Committee encountered Indian support for improving, renewing and reaffirming the special relationship in the context of a new government to government relationship. The Committee recognized the need for continued federal advocacy of Indian interests and the protection of Aboriginal and treaty rights, as well as the need for a mechanism (an ombudsman) to monitor federal Indian relations and the actions of government vis-à-vis Indian peoples. Further the Committee found a need to make changes in the federal government's management of trust accounts, and in particular identified the need to clarify uncertainties surrounding the Department's role in the management of revenue and capital moneys, and to develop appropriate accountability mechanisms.

RECOMMENDATIONS

The Committee made no particular recommendations in relation to its examination of education, child welfare and health, but did conclude that Indian control and jurisdiction within these areas were essential to cultural survival.

With respect to a broad basis for Indian self-government, the Committee recommended the establishment of a new relationship based on a constitutionally entrenched recognition of Indian self-government.

More immediate 'self-government' measures reflected in Committee recommendations included the introduction of enabling legislation committing the federal government to recognition of Indian governments, if those governments met certain criteria such as accountability mechanisms (proposed *First Nations Recognition Act*). The scope of powers and jurisdictions to be exercised by Indian governments on Indian lands and in relation to Indian peoples would encompass jurisdictional fields currently occupied by federal and provincial governments. Indian governments would negotiate the jurisdictional powers they would exercise, but would retain the right to enter into arrangements for program/service delivery with federal/provincial governments.

An independent secretariat jointly appointed by federal/Indian leadership would provide a neutral forum for the conduct of Indian government negotiations, and a special tribunal would, over the longer term, resolve disputes between the parties in relation to negotiated agreements. Other institutions recommended included a Ministry of State for First Nations Relations, linked with PCO, to manage and co-ordinate federal/First Nations relations.

With respect to membership issues, the Committee supported full jurisdictional authority for First Nations determining their own membership. The First Nation membership would choose whether they wished to be constituted as an Indian First Nation government.

The Committee recommended continued federal government responsibilities for Indians (for individual Indians) regardless of their status as First Nations members, and the establishment of a "special list" (separate from First Nations membership lists), to identify all persons who are "Indian".

The Committee identified pre-requisite economic foundations as including an adequate land and resource base; the settlement of claims, and the correction of deficiencies in community infrastructure. The Committee also supported the establishment of new funding arrangements based on Indian government accountability to the community. Recommended arrangements included direct grants based on a modified per capita formula, and a five-year global funding base for operations, economic development, and correction of infrastructure deficiencies.

The Committee recommended full First Nations authority over lands and resources and establishment of a First Nations land registry (separate from federal and provincial registries). The Committee acknowledged the importance of Aboriginal and treaty rights to hunt, fish and trap, and the significant and positive economic benefits associated with enhanced control of mineral, oil and gas revenues, but made no specific recommendations in relation to these matters.

With respect to claims, the Committee recommended fulfilment of outstanding treaty land entitlements; the provision of a reserve land base for communities without such a base; and the settlement of claims through a new claims policy. A new claims policy and process would encompass pre-Confederation treaties and promote the resolution of claims consistent with constitutional protection of Aboriginal and treaty rights. Further, the Committee rejected the doctrine of Aboriginal title being superseded by law, and the requirement for extinguishment of all Aboriginal title and rights in claims settlements.

In respect of Indian moneys, the Committee recommended a centralized trust management system for capital trust funds, and the transfer of revenue moneys from DIAND to each First Nation for direct administration.

Finally in relation to trust responsibilities, the Committee recommended these be renewed and enhanced with federal responsibilities defined in the Constitution, in legislation, and legally enforceable. Related to this recommendation was a call for the appointment of an independent officer to report to Parliament on official actions vis-à-vis Indian peoples and communities, and an Indian Advocacy Office to be established under Indian auspices, with funds to represent First Nations interests in legal disputes affecting their rights.

The Committee recommended phasing out the programs of the department of Indian Affairs within five years.

With respect to political representation, the Committee was of the view that this was not the best way to promote Indian self-government, but might in the future have some benefits

1984

▲ Report of the Task Force on Northern Conservation

AUTHOR: Task Force on Northern Conservation

YEAR: 1984

ABORIGINAL GROUP: Not specific to Aboriginal peoples

TOPICS: Land Use, Development and Management, Resources,
Environmental Protection

SUB-TOPICS: land use planning, development, management,
hunting/wildlife, trapping and gathering, fishing/fisheries,
forestry/forests

SOURCE: Federal Commission

BACKGROUND

Prior to the 1970s, there were few, if any, policies, legislation or administrative frameworks for the management of the North's renewable resources. The lack of any organized system or conservation guidelines left the Department of Indian Affairs and Northern Development (DIAND) in a difficult political position in trying to manage its conflicting responsibilities for both social and resource development, as well as for co-ordinating the northern activities of other federal agencies. Though the Department finally adopted a policy for the North that emphasized the protection of the environment in 1972, the Task Force asserted that DIAND did little in practice to promote conservation through active resource management or through designation of additional protected areas.

The minister of Indian Affairs and Northern Development, responding to the recommendations of participants in a 1983 National Workshop on Northern Conservation Policy in Whitehorse, established the Task Force on Northern Conservation in the fall of 1983.

PURPOSE

The purpose of the Task Force was to advise the minister of Indian Affairs and Northern Development on the following matters:

1. a framework for a comprehensive conservation policy for northern Canada;

2. a strategy, and ongoing mechanisms, for implementing the policy; and

3. specific actions that could be taken over the next two years.

ISSUES AND FINDINGS

The Task Force identified six problem areas that needed to be addressed:

1. the current reliance on a regulatory system that tends to be restrictive, narrow and reactive;

2. institutional competition between governments and among government agencies;

3. inadequate valuation of resources and consideration of alternatives for both development and conservation initiatives prior to making decisions on land use;

4. insufficient involvement of northerners in the decision-making process;

5. legislation that is deficient with respect to conservation measures such as planning, management, protection and restoration; and

6. lack of sustained political commitment to ensure that decisions on resource use reflect conservation requirements.

The Task Force adopted a holistic, sustainable view of conservation that included protection and development of the North's resources for present and future generations. It outlined four principles for managing resources and six steps for achieving two primary conservation goals. The principles identified are as follows:

1. that genetic diversity of natural organisms and essential ecological processes should be maintained;

2. that resource management should reflect the concept of stewardship and should be aimed at achieving the integrated use of resources to the extent that they can be made mutually compatible;

3. that sustainable utilization of species and ecosystems should be assured for the benefit of the people of the North, as well as for all Canadians; and

4. that projected benefits should meet the needs and values of the people of the North, as expressed through their participation in the conservation and development processes.

The conservation goals are:

1. to manage the human use of natural resources, renewable and non-renewable, so that they may yield the greatest sustainable benefit to present generations, while maintaining their potential to meet the needs and aspirations of future generations; and

2. to establish a network of protected areas where necessary to maintain in perpetuity cultural resources and representative or unique ecosystems, their ecological processes and genetic diversity.

The report also outlines the steps required in order to achieve these goals:

1. establish management systems that maintain and/or enhance overall resource productivity;

2. establish a process for the selection and designation of protected areas that will contribute to the most effective management and use of land and water resources;

3. ensure the establishment of a land use planning process for the implementation of a northern conservation policy and a supporting advisory mechanism as appropriate;

4. increase the public's awareness of the need to apply the principles of conservation in the development and utilization of natural resources;

5. increase the level of research to improve baseline data and the understanding of natural ecosystems, particularly in the marine environment; and

6. amend or supplement existing resource legislation in order to provide the necessary legal basis for implementing northern conservation.

A significant portion of the report is devoted to the Task Force's conservation strategy and guidelines for implementation. Its strategy involves two mutually dependent components: integrated resource management; and a comprehensive network of protected land and/or water areas. An integrated resource management approach is intended to correct several of the problems outlined above; it is intended to end the institutional and jurisdictional separation that currently confounds resource planning and management in the North, and to increase understanding of the interrelationships among all of the various resources, the users, and the ecosystem.

The Task Force also emphasized the protection of limited areas, including marine areas, from development or other destructive uses. The types of areas identified by the Task Force for protection are areas of cultural or natural importance. Examples of cultural heritage sites would include prehistoric and historic archaeological sites, burial grounds, and areas used by the Native population for traditional activities (hunting and trapping, gathering soapstone for carvings, etc.). Natural areas would include outstanding, representative and unique landmarks and landscapes, critical fish and wildlife habitat, such as marine mammals or migratory bird sanctuaries, calving grounds, or habitat for rare and endangered species; this would also include sites for the preservation of genetic diversity in both plants and animals. Additionally, unique, sensitive, or representative natural areas would be set aside for education and research purposes and, where possible, for recreation and tourism.

The Task Force made special mention of marine areas within its conservation strategy. Members felt that the unbounded, transient quality of marine ecosystems and inhabitants, the special problems accompanying conservation approaches for Arctic ice cover, the importance of the sea for the subsistence of the North's Native people, and Canada's responsibilities under international environmental agreements, made marine conservation an important area for policy development, including the establishment of protected areas.

The Task Force identified several mechanisms which might be effective in implementing its conservation strategy:

1. the comprehensive land claims agreements, such as that for the Inuvialuit of the Western Arctic, which contain provisions for conservation;

2. the land use planning agreements between the two territories and the federal government which contain many of the conservation approaches called for in this report (the Task Force expressed concern, however, over the slow pace of putting the land use planning process in place and the resultant continuation of the existing make-shift resource management processes, and consequently the frustration of development plans and the continued exposure of sensitive areas to risk);

3. an interim conservation advisory board to advise the appropriate ministers on conservation strategy until more formal mechanisms, such as the land use planning process and the comprehensive land claims, are initiated;

4. changes to the institutional arrangements between and among the respective governments to begin to correct problems associated with the current regulatory approach to conservation and the weaknesses stemming from interdepartmental and inter-agency competition; and

5. a system of conservation management agreements between the government and private industry, which would outline the details of obligations for conservation, require developers to follow sound conservation practices, and perhaps involve a certain amount of support for research, communication with local people, or special restoration, enhancement, or protection efforts.

The Task Force also pointed out areas where the legislative base was inadequate for managing the North's natural resources effectively. The legislation was found to be poorly integrated into a larger management philosophy, and there was a tendency toward duplication in legislation or in many cases an absence of legislation regarding certain resource management questions. The Task Force found the existing legislation to offer little guidance or structure for administrators.

RECOMMENDATIONS

The Task Force made a number of recommendations to support the development of a new resource management and conservation process in the

North. The recommendations are divided into two sections, Conservation Strategy and Implementation.

1. Conservation Strategy

The Task Force called for the establishment of an integrated management process as described above, but recommended that priority be placed on plans for specific areas of conflict, such as the northern Yukon, the Mackenzie Delta-Beaufort Sea and Lancaster Sound. The Task Force also called for the immediate establishment, according to a predetermined set of criteria, of a comprehensive network of protected areas. Furthermore, it recommended the withdrawal from general use of endangered or potential protected areas until the status and boundaries of the areas in question can be determined through the land-use planning process.

2. Implementation

In addition to recommending the implementation of the land-use planning process between the Governments of Canada, Yukon and Northwest Territories as the basic mechanism for the conservation process, the Task Force recommended establishing a Conservation Advisory Board to perform interim and long-term roles. The interim role would be to help establish the system and make the decisions. The long-term role would be to provide the public with a forum and to provide the appropriate ministers with continuing advice on northern conservation policy and strategy.

The Task Force also recommended a number of changes in institutional arrangements, such as:

1. the establishment of a cabinet committee of those federal ministers with responsibilities for northern natural resources;

2. consolidation of all territorial government responsibilities for administering and managing land and other natural resources within one department in each of the territorial governments;

3. integration within federal and territorial government departments of the administration and management of natural resource programs;

4. acceptance and implementation by the Department of Fisheries and Oceans of its legitimate responsibility as the lead agency for Arctic marine conservation; and

5. development of federal-territorial agreements whereby the territorial governments carry out resource administration and management including freshwater fisheries either by transfer or on behalf of the federal government under federal legislation.

To assist in the implementation of the management approach the Task Force recommended a number of special efforts in the area of communication, education, and training. These efforts would be aimed at improving understanding of the new processes and the conservation ethic and its principles. It would also be designed to increase public participation and communication among governments, their agencies, industry and the public.

Finally, the Task Force recommended a number of changes to the legislative base. Included were recommendations to establish a conservation/management frame of reference and to reduce or eliminate existing or potential conflict or duplication in the law. The Task Force also called for the enactment of legislation to fill existing legislative gaps in areas like comprehensive fishery resource management, the establishment of marine and terrestrial protected areas, and protection of cultural heritage resources. It recommended supplementing existing legislation to provide for conservation management agreements between government and industry or other similar management mechanisms. The Task Force proposed that federal marine legislation be enacted to give effect to Canada's recognized off-shore jurisdiction to implement and enforce effective conservation measures respecting the marine environment. Finally, the report recommends that the laws of general application pertaining to natural resources and conservation apply to all land in the Yukon and the Northwest Territories.

1985

▲ Improved Program Delivery: Indians and Natives Study Team Report to the Task Force on Program Review

AUTHOR: Task Force on Program Review (the Nielsen task force)
YEAR: 1985
ABORIGINAL GROUP: All Aboriginal Peoples
TOPICS: Federal Government/Aboriginal Relations, Provincial Government/Aboriginal Relations, Intergovernmental Relations
SUB-TOPICS: policy, jurisdiction, program and service delivery, federal trust responsibilities
SOURCE: Federal Commission

BACKGROUND

The federal government was aware that the relative deprivation of most Native communities persisted, despite numerous government programs. It appeared that the net impact of government stewardship over the social and economic development of Native people had been marginal. In an era when the rationalization of services was a predominant philosophy, a review of the federal government's Indians and Native programs was commissioned.

PURPOSE

The Terms of Reference for this study highlighted two major objectives. First, priority was given to the identification of significant gaps, overlaps and duplication of services. The second aspect involved describing alternative programs that were simpler, more understandable and more accessible to clients.

ISSUES AND FINDINGS

The study team reviewed 106 programs, delivered by 11 federal departments. The programs were grouped into 15 subject areas. These were reserves and trusts; economic development; training and short-term job creation; regional development agreements; major resource development; natural resource agreements; Native claims; local government support; infrastructure; housing; Indian and Inuit health services; social assistance and welfare; culture and communications; and the administration of justice.

In general, the study team found that both gaps and overlaps in programs and services were more the by-products of overall policy, rather than problems inherent in programming. It found that the existing framework of federal policy in Native affairs was inconsistent, uncoordinated and rooted in the anachronism of the *Indian Act*. The report therefore focused on two policy themes. The first theme involved restructuring the relationship between Native peoples and the federal, provincial and territorial governments. The second theme was that Aboriginal peoples should be given more responsibility to manage their own affairs.

In terms of the relationship between Aboriginal peoples and the federal government, the authors stressed that the government of Canada had historically provided more for Native peoples than it was required to under section 91(24) of the *Constitution Act, 1867*. Because of this reliance on the federal government, the Department of Indian Affairs and Northern Development (DIAND) had been put in the unique position of trying to provide a full array of services, without the expertise associated with other federal departments. It was the view of the study team that specialized services to Native people should be provided by specialized line departments.

The review team felt the federal government directed too many resources to Aboriginal political organizations. They advocated that organizations should be required to demonstrate accountability to their membership, and that there be an indication of membership support for some form of self-financing.

The universal nature of DIAND's programs was criticized as inefficient. Because economic development proceeds in stages, each stage requires a different level of support. The authors advocated more focused programs dealing with specific opportunities.

With respect to provincial governments, the report noted that historically the provinces had been intransigent about discussing responsibilities for service delivery to Native people, since they had no incentive to question the federal government's jurisdiction. The authors pointed out that Aboriginal peoples have tended to reject any efforts to involve provinces in their affairs. This partitioned approach had been the main feature of federal/provincial/Native relationships and a consistent characteristic of programming efforts at the federal level.

The authors advocated a management approach to Native program reform. The underlying principle would be that legal responsibility for Aboriginal peoples involved both levels of government, regardless of status. Indeed, the sharp distinction of status was deceptive since Native people move on- and off-reserve with some frequency. It was also criticized because the needs of non-status Indians and Métis were not fully addressed.

The study team stressed that economic development was a regional issue that extended beyond reserve boundaries and that opportunities involved more than one category of Native Canadian.

The programs of the federal and provincial governments were found to be poorly co-ordinated, with duplication of effort. There were too many programs offered by two or sometimes three levels of government that had different eligibility criteria and decision-making mechanisms. The study team concluded that much Native entrepreneurship was absorbed in coping with government. To resolve this problem, there was a need for close federal/provincial program co-ordination on a decentralized basis.

RECOMMENDATIONS

The authors recommended amendments to the *Indian Act* that would provide for greater Aboriginal autonomy. In the interest of promoting financial independence, the authors proposed the transfer of Indian financial assets from the Crown to an independent national Indian trust company.

To promote less reliance on government, it was recommended that entrepreneurial expertise be encouraged, focusing on private sector activities.

The report suggested that expenditures be capped to place more responsibility on Native communities to solve their own problems. The concept of a "user-pay" system, whereby communities made some contribution to the capital and operating costs of their services was put forth as a possible way to promote responsibility.

It was suggested that a senior federal review committee be established to redefine the relationship between the federal government and the bands, and to examine DIAND's role.

To bridge the efforts of the federal and provincial/territorial Native programs, the report recommended a Ten Year Memorandum of Understanding be drafted between the federal government and each of the provinces/territories. The delivery of programs would be negotiated on the basis of which party was best equipped to deliver the particular services.

The study team proposed an ad hoc co-ordinating committee of social, economic and regional development ministers be established to oversee progress and the suggested approach to federal/provincial relations on Aboriginal issues.

The report recognized that the provinces/territories might reject a 50/50 cost-sharing scheme. It was suggested that, as a fall-back position, the federal government could pay 100% of the costs that were estimated to be attributable to status Indians.

With regard to program efficiency, the study team recommended expenditures be targeted toward those believed to benefit most (e.g., education and youth) and those who have the greatest need; and establishing exit-strategies for some programs.

▲ Living Treaties, Lasting Agreements: Report of the Task Force to Review Comprehensive Claims Policy

AUTHOR: Task Force to Review Comprehensive Claims Policy, Chair, Murray Coolican

YEAR: 1985

ABORIGINAL GROUP: All Aboriginal Peoples

TOPIC: Claims

SUB-TOPIC: comprehensive claims

SOURCE: Federal Commission

BACKGROUND

This Task Force report was the first in-depth examination of comprehensive claims policy since the 1981 policy statement, In All Fairness. Important events leading up to a reconsideration of the federal policy included entrenchment of Aboriginal and treaty rights in the *Constitution Act, 1982* and further clarification of these rights in the *Constitution Amendment Proclamation, 1983*.

PURPOSE

The Task Force was appointed in July 1985 to conduct a full review of the federal comprehensive claims policy and to make recommendations for a new policy.

ISSUES AND FINDINGS

The main issues addressed in the report concern the reformulation of comprehensive claims policy and the identification of negotiation processes.

The federal government's insistence on finality and on blanket extinguishment of all Aboriginal rights is identified as one of the most significant obstacles in reaching final settlement agreements. Other difficulties were seen to be a result of the government's refusal to include political rights, decision-making power on land and resource management boards, revenue sharing in relation to surface and subsurface resources, and rights in relation to the offshore in negotiations.

The report indicates the need to update the claims policy in place at the time *(In All Fairness)*, to reflect the entrenchment of Aboriginal rights in the Constitution. Any new policy would also need to reflect the Penner Report's call for constitutional entrenchment of the principles of self-government.

The Task Force considered two alternative processes for the negotiation of comprehensive claims:

1. a constitutional amendment on self-government; and
2. devolution of powers from the federal government to the Northwest Territories and Yukon.

RECOMMENDATIONS

The Task Force report contains a number of recommendations which relate to the fundamental objectives of a comprehensive claims policy and to essential principles which would lead to the achievement of those objectives.

The report states that the objectives of a comprehensive claims policy should be to reach agreements that

1. define the relationship between governments and Aboriginal peoples in Canada;

2. establish a framework concerning lands and resources which will provide the opportunity for economic, cultural and social development of Aboriginal societies; and

3. enable Aboriginal societies to develop self-governing institutions and to participate effectively in decisions that affect their interests.

Some basic principles for achieving these objectives were noted. Agreements reached would need to recognize and affirm Aboriginal rights. The policy would need to permit the negotiation of Aboriginal self-government while simultaneously recognizing the need to accommodate the different priorities and potential within each region. Provincial and territorial governments should be encouraged to participate in negotiations, and the scope of negotiations should include all issues that will facilitate the achievement of the objectives of the claims policy. The new policy would need to encourage Aboriginal communities to become economically self-sufficient, and to establish political and social institutions that will allow them to become self-governing.

In addition, the report suggests an independent authority be established to monitor progress and to ensure accountability in claims processes to the public. The policy would also need to provide for the effective implementation of agreements.

The Task Force also made recommendations for a workable alternative to extinguishment:

1. it would require Aboriginal consent;

2. it would enable granting of secure rights to land and resources;

3. it must be simple (to promote legal certainty); and

4. it must define rights so that they fit within the dominant property law system.

▲ Native Women and Economic Development Task Force Report

AUTHOR: Task Force on Native Women and Economic Development, Chair, Mary Richard
YEAR: 1985
ABORIGINAL GROUP: All Aboriginal Peoples, Aboriginal Women
TOPICS: Employment Development, Economic Development
SUB-TOPICS: training/skills development, discrimination
SOURCE: Federal Commission

BACKGROUND

In 1974, David Smith, then Small Business and Tourism minister, announced a strategy for the Native Economic Development Program (NEDP), which would involve a $345 million capital allocation over a four-year period. The strategy comprised four elements:

1. the development of Aboriginal economic and financial institutions to assist Aboriginal people to become economically self-sufficient;

2. the stimulation of community-based economic development;

3. support for special projects, including scholarship programs, innovation, research and marketing activities, and special studies; and

4. the co-ordination of federal government programs and policies in support of Native business and economic development. This fourth element is to be accomplished through an advisory and advocacy role for the NEDP vis-à-vis other federal departments.

In order to ensure that the special concerns and unique circumstances of Native women would be taken into account when distributing the funds, the program's Advisory Board established a Task Force on Native Women and Economic Development. This report outlines the findings and results of the Task Force, as submitted to the Advisory Board of the Native Economic Development Program for its consideration.

PURPOSE

The mandate of the Task Force was to:

1. identify a comprehensive strategy for integrating existing services for Native women, for improving their knowledge and use of services, and for identifying barriers to their participation in government programs;

2. examine the economic needs of all Native women in order to develop priorities to guide the distribution of funds; and

3. review and identify special projects for funding by the NEDP.

ISSUES AND FINDINGS

The mandate of the Task Force was realized through a series of 24 meetings held across the country where:

1. participants were briefed on the NEDP;

2. attempts were made to determine the current level of Native women participation in the economy and the potential for further development; and

3. submissions and recommendations were received for increasing the participation of Native women in economic development.

The concerns which emerged during these meetings are as follows:

1. many of the Native women presented viable business opportunities, but they were small in scope and designed primarily for their local Native communities;

2. barriers to the participation of Native women in business were found to include lack of education, lack of business skills, lack of business "connections", inadequate daycare services, racial and gender discrimination, and the inability of Native women to break free of the male dominance of their societies;

3. many of the Native women expressed a desire to remain within their communities during training programs and in the development of their businesses;

4. Native women lacked information and understanding of the NEDP and other government economic development programs;

5. funding for the National Indian Arts and Crafts Corporation was not seen to be reaching the local communities or the producers; and

6. the use of arbitrary criteria, such as class sizes and age limits, was found to limit Native women's participation in existing government training programs.

RECOMMENDATIONS

The Task Force report makes a number of general recommendations, a summary of which follows:

1. that a national conference, and perhaps regional conferences, on Native women and business be held to facilitate networking, information exchange, and the co-ordination of projects;

2. that the NEDP hire Native women economic development officers in the various regions to disseminate business information, assist in the development of proposals, and provide business advice to Native women;

3. that all NEDP information be developed in a manner that facilitates understanding and be translated into the appropriate language by community members for appropriate remuneration;

4. that existing Native-oriented business training institutions be used as much as possible to give Native people necessary business skills;

5. that a national Native Women's Business Newsletter be developed;

6. that a directory of Native professionals and businesses of relevance to NEDP programs be established as a resource for Native women and Native communities;

7. that the NEDP work with other government departments in an attempt to resolve the issue of daycare services for Native women;

8. that an additional funding criteria be added whereby the applicant indicates the manner in which the proposed project will involve and/or benefit Native women, or alternatively, provides adequate justification why it will not;

9. that the NEDP emphasize small business funding, given that small businesses are particularly suitable for and desirable to Native women;

10. that the NEDP ensure the protection of Native partners in joint venture business funding; and

11. that the NEDP ensure that the Indian arts and crafts industry is not adversely affected by Canada's failure to recognize international border treaties between the Indian people, Canada and the United States concerning the sale, importation and exportation of Indian arts and crafts.

◆ *Reflecting Indian Concerns and Values in the Justice System* (1985), see **Volume 3, Saskatchewan.**

▲ Comprehensive Land Claims Policy

AUTHOR: Department of Indian Affairs and Northern Development
YEAR: 1986
ABORIGINAL GROUP: All Aboriginal Peoples
TOPICS: Self-Government, Federal Government/Aboriginal
  Relations, Provincial Government/Aboriginal Relations, Treaty
  Land Entitlement, Claims, Land Use, Development and
  Management, Resources
SUB-TOPICS: negotiation structures and processes, treaties, federal
  trust responsibilities, policy, claims, commissions/structures/
  negotiation processes, comprehensive claims
SOURCE: Federal Department

BACKGROUND

This booklet outlines a revised policy approach that the government of
Canada proposed in an attempt to resolve comprehensive land claims
settlements. It addresses the growing concern of Aboriginal groups that the
current process is far too slow and that the ultimate settlement still abrogates
certain inherent rights.

PURPOSE

The purpose of the booklet is to provide guidelines for the resolution of
comprehensive land claims disputes. One of the primary concerns of the revised
federal policy is that any settlement reached be final in terms of claims to the
land; however, so that land claim settlements are not viewed merely as "real
estate" transactions, the ongoing interests of claimants in these areas will need
to be recognized and addressed. Furthermore, it is recognized that consistency
between the federal land claims policy and other legislation needs to be
assured.

ISSUES AND FINDINGS

The rights which stem from "Aboriginal title" encompass the traditional
Aboriginal view that their cultural distinctiveness is tied to the land that
they continue to use and occupy. In law, these rights stem from treaties,

which are the centrepiece of the deadlocks in the resolution of land claims settlements. It is not so much a question of whether a right exists, for by law a treaty must be honoured, but rather, it is a question of expeditious and equitable treatment, and of balancing federal, provincial and Aboriginal interests.

The spectrum of issues dealt with in this publication may be listed as follows: land selection; the involvement of provincial and territorial governments; self-government; environmental management; resource/revenue-sharing; hunting; the continuation of certain Aboriginal rights despite claims settlement; and the rights of third parties. These topics are, however, not dealt with in an in-depth fashion. Their substance is deemed to be self-evident and the Department of Indian Affairs and Northern Development (DIAND) has chosen therefore to address the resolution, rather than the expression of these issues. Therefore, the essence of the document is found in its recommendations.

RECOMMENDATIONS

1. Land Selection

The policy recommends that only those lands which are currently used by the beneficiaries shall be selected. This is due in part to the fact that not all treaties have as of yet been honoured nor has the federal government met all its obligations in these respects. In the event that more than one claimant group is involved, boundaries must be agreed upon or some other agreements such as land/resource sharing must be developed. Multilateral agreements must be established before any one group is granted entitlement to such land.

2. Involvement of Provincial and Territorial Governments

Multilateral agreements also extend to provinces, whose interests must be addressed if land claims fall within their jurisdiction. Federal jurisdiction involves "Indians, and Lands reserved for the Indians"; presumably, this means that jurisdiction flows from treaties and other arrangements into which the government of Canada has entered. Other lands and resources, with the exception of those of the Yukon and Northwest Territories, fall under provincial jurisdiction.

3. Self-Government

The idea of self-government for Aboriginal peoples is a key aspect in the harmonization process between Aboriginal and federal/provincial interests.

In terms of comprehensive land claims policy, the federal government feels that appropriate areas for Aboriginal self-government include community-based regimes on designated lands. In other areas, Aboriginal representatives would be participants on management boards concerned with possible resource initiatives; this participation would be subject to federal and/or provincial jurisdiction in those areas. The precise nature of local self-government matters, however, will need to be set out in specific framework agreements which reflect differing circumstances.

4. Environmental Management

The environmental management objective is one in which Aboriginal people would serve a participatory function on advisory committees, boards or other governmental decision-making bodies. Any actions in this respect, however, are subject to the overriding obligations of the federal and provincial governments in matters of resource conservation and renewable resources.

5. Resource Revenue Sharing

Resource revenue sharing will also involve participation by Aboriginal peoples. Such arrangements employ neither resource ownership nor joint management boards to manage sub-surface or sub-sea resources. Instead, this is more or less a royalty-sharing scheme which is derived from the extraction of minerals in the settlement areas and offshore areas. Revenue sharing is also subject to some limitations, such as an absolute dollar cap, a time cap of not less than 50years from the first payment of the royalty share, and a reduction in the percentage of the royalties.

6. Hunting

Hunting, fishing and trapping are recognized by the federal government as having economic, social and cultural importance to Aboriginal peoples; therefore, settlements may include preferential wildlife harvesting rights on unoccupied Crown lands and exclusive harvesting rights on selected lands. Terms of settlements which do not provide for these rights are subject to the normal laws and procedures with respect to hunting, fishing, trapping, public safety and conservation measures.

7. Continuation of Certain Aboriginal Rights

Perhaps the most controversial topic with regard to the final settlement of comprehensive land claims is the extinguishment of all Aboriginal rights and title following claims settlement. The federal government has decided that there may be exceptions to this policy provided that certainty with respect to lands and resources has been established. Some defined rights may be granted in specified or reserve areas or in the entire settlement area. Only those rights related to the use of and title to the land and resources are to be relinquished. Where provincial jurisdiction is concerned, the province must play a major role in the exact course to be followed toward a resolution of the concerns.

8. Interests of Third Parties

All of the above policy changes will take into consideration third party interests. Any party directly affected by settlements will be dealt with equitably. The rights of the public to the continued use of Crown lands with respect to recreation, hunting and fishing will also be taken into consideration.

▲ The Fur Issue: Cultural Continuity and Economic Opportunity

AUTHOR: Standing Committee on Aboriginal Affairs and Northern Development

YEAR: 1986

ABORIGINAL GROUP: All Aboriginal Peoples

TOPICS: Land Use, Development and Management, Resources, Environmental Protection

SUB-TOPICS: management, hunting/wildlife, trapping and gathering

SOURCE: House of Commons Committee

BACKGROUND

This is the first report of the Standing Committee on Aboriginal Affairs and Northern Development.

PURPOSE

The Committee's mandate is to make certain that the needs and aspirations of Canada's Aboriginal and northern peoples are met and to propose measures to enhance their viability. This report looks at the anti-fur campaign and the effect on Aboriginal trappers.

ISSUES AND FINDINGS

The Committee found that although the anti-fur campaign is not directed at Aboriginal people, they will be adversely affected if their economy, based on hunting, trapping and fishing, collapses. They have already been influenced by the anti-sealing campaign. Many Aboriginal and northern people still pursue a traditional lifestyle of hunting and trapping; however, they manage their wildlife resources with great care.

The Committee found that the campaign against trapping may be detrimental to the wildlife it is claiming to protect. Loss of habitat and the effects of overpopulation destroy more animals than does the fur industry. An effective way of protecting the habitat and the animals is to ensure their continued social, cultural and economic importance to society. The Aboriginal people who live in harmony with nature offer the best hope of wildlife protection.

The Committee established that Canadian trappers use the most humane methods of trapping available today and are on the forefront of continued research. Humane trapper education courses specifically designed for Aboriginal people are not offered due to lack of funds, but the Committee found that the Department of Indian Affairs and Northern Development (DIAND) recognizes this need.

The Committee found that there is a lack of precise data available which might be used to counteract the data presented by the anti-fur campaign.

According to the report, trapping has become an essential part of wildlife management. In Aboriginal societies the trapper is also a wildlife manager. If he does not manage properly, he and his family will suffer. Constant contact with land and animals provides trappers with an understanding of the habitats, patterns and cycles of animal populations which would be difficult for any trained biologist to acquire.

Indigenous people themselves are taking the leadership in protecting their harvesting rights. In 1985, an organization called Indigenous Survival International was created to protect and promote Indigenous harvesting rights and to maintain a market for Aboriginal fur products. The Aboriginal Trappers Federation of Canada was also established to provide an umbrella organization for hunters and trappers associations across Canada. The industry has agreed to take the lead in publicizing its position but sees a supporting role for government. The Committee found that the government needs to take an official position on trapping as a way of life and to organize to meet the anti-fur challenge more effectively.

RECOMMENDATIONS

The report contains 36 recommendations. These may be broken down into eight areas: the federal role; financial assistance; traps; information; harvesting; an interdepartmental committee; conservation; and the role of the Department of External Affairs.

1. Federal Role

The Committee recommends that the federal government issue a statement on the importance of trapping and that it make a commitment to the preservation of the traditional way of life for Aboriginal peoples.

2. Financial Assistance

The Committee recommends that social assistance regulations be more flexible in providing start-up funds for those wishing to begin or return to living off the land, and that the federal government fund secondary industries and Aboriginal cottage industries related to the fur trade.

3. Traps

The Committee recommends that the federal government assign high priority to the development of alternate trapping methods and consult Aboriginal groups to ensure regional differences are recognized. When new traps are developed, the federal government should consider providing incentives for trap replacement programs. A specific definition of humane death must be developed as must a federal-provincial-territorial commission to develop standard legislation on trap methods, education and trap checks. Aboriginal education programs should include a business and tax management component.

4. Information

The Committee recommends that government departments and agencies, in conjunction with the fur industry, consider compiling data which may be useful in responding to the anti-fur campaign. This information could then be disseminated to the public.

5. Harvesting

The Committee recommends that the federal government play a substantial role in the management of wildlife and conservation and that it recognize and fund Indigenous Survival International as well as the Aboriginal Trappers

Federation of Canada and continue to fund the Fur Institute of Canada. The Fur Institute of Canada should work with Aboriginal peoples to encourage their involvement in other aspects of the fur trade.

6. Interdepartmental Committee

The Committee recommends that an interdepartmental committee of the federal government be created, chaired by DIAND, to develop strategy, allocate funding, and to disseminate accurate information to the public on matters relating to the fur industry. The government of Canada should provide this committee with a budget as well as the required personnel.

7. Conservation

The Committee recommends that the Department of the Environment play an active role in the World Conservation Strategy and include Aboriginal groups in this role.

8. Role of External Affairs

The Committee recommends that the Department of External Affairs undergo an attitudinal change in order to recognize the legitimacy of trapping as an economic activity and disseminate the facts about trapping to the international public. The Committee further recommends that External Affairs play an active role in countering the threat of the anti-fur campaign that is occurring overseas.

▲ Report of the Cree-Naskapi Commission

AUTHOR: Cree-Naskapi Commission, Chair, Justice Réjean Paul
YEAR: 1986
ABORIGINAL GROUP: First Nations
TOPICS: Self-Government, Federal/Aboriginal Relations
SUB-TOPICS: self-government implementation, structures/institutions
SOURCE: Federal Commission

BACKGROUND

This was the first biennial report of the Cree-Naskapi Commission. The Commission was established as an independent agency to monitor the implementation of the *Cree-Naskapi (of Quebec) Act*. The Act was an outcome of the James Bay and Northern Quebec Agreement and the Northeastern Quebec Agreement and is considered to be a statute of great significance because it is the first Indian self-government legislation in Canada.

PURPOSE

The duties of the Cree-Naskapi Commission, as stipulated in section 165 of the Act, are to prepare a report every two years on the implementation of the Act; to receive and investigate representations of interested persons regarding implementation of the Act; and to prepare reports and recommendations on matters investigated.

In the course of performing these duties in the first two years of operation, the Commission became involved in a number of areas of disagreement involving the Cree and Naskapi bands and the federal government. This first report, therefore identifies and examines the more contentious issues and provides suggested solutions.

ISSUES AND FINDINGS

There are three major issues identified in this report. They are

1. the development of Cree and Naskapi governments under the Act;

2. fiscal relations with the federal government; and

3. the nature and basis of bilateral relations between the two parties.

All three issues are interrelated with a fundamental difference of opinion regarding the legality of the Statement of Understanding, which is the negotiated funding package that accompanies the *Cree-Naskapi (of Quebec) Act*. The nature of this disagreement is more fully explained in the section dealing with the issue of fiscal relations.

In the implementation of Cree and Naskapi governments under the Act, difficulties were encountered, most notably as a result of the lack of qualified personnel and training associated with implementation of the new self government arrangement. This problem also appeared in respect of land registration, and was exacerbated by the Department of Indian Affairs and Northern Development's (DIAND) adoption of new land registration regulations, which had no provisions for training.

It was the Commission's view that the lack of adequate training was a significant obstacle to the implementation and establishment of Cree and Naskapi governments and government administrative structures and systems.

Law enforcement and the administration of justice were identified by the Commission as another area where implementation had been less than successful. The Act gives the Cree and Naskapi bands the power to make by-laws of a local nature. However, bands were reluctant to adopt by-laws relating to areas other than administration and financial administration/management, primarily as a consequence of the lack of funding to support by-law enforcement measures. In addition, although the minister of justice for Quebec is responsible for administration of justice within the territory, provincial Crown prosecutors were found to be often unavailable, thus placing additional financial burdens on the bands.

Fiscal relations between the Cree and Naskapi bands and the federal government were identified by the Commission as the major area of dispute. The central disagreement revolved around the issue of whether the Statement of Understanding (relating to financial arrangements) was binding on the government of Canada. The Cree and Naskapi believed this to be the case, with the federal government in disagreement. This dispute precipitated difficulties in respect of the transfer of annual subsidies to the bands and annual adjustments to the federal subsidy, with the bands experiencing revenue shortfalls.

After examining the sequence of events that led to this impasse between the Cree and Naskapi and the federal government, the Cree-Naskapi Commission came to the firm conclusion that the Statement of Understanding was legally valid and binding on the federal government. The Commission emphasized that an assured level of federal funding was fundamental to the Cree and Naskapi when they agreed to the Act and suggested that a failure to provide this funding threatened the existence of the *Cree-Naskapi (of Quebec) Act*.

A final issue addressed by the Commission in its report concerned bilateral relations. Specifically, the roles and responsibilities of the Department (DIAND) in the implementation of the Act were called into questioned. It was the view of the Cree and Naskapi bands that the Department was not structurally geared toward the implementation of self-government. The bands were also of the view that the *Cree Naskapi Act* established a government-to-government relationship and placed obligations upon the government of Canada, not just the Department. The federal government's attempt to address these concerns through the use of a mediation/negotiation process, and its subsequent failure were outlined in the report.

RECOMMENDATIONS

The only formal recommendation contained in this report concerns the issue of bilateral relations. The Commission recommended the establishment of an implementation mechanism with a government-wide mandate to deal with the concerns of the Cree and Naskapi bands. Specifically it proposed the appointment of a special representative of the prime minister who would have direct access to the prime minister and cabinet.

The importance of the other issues, the development of Cree and Naskapi governments under the Act and fiscal relations with the federal government, were validated, but no specific recommendations were made. The main finding of the report was that the federal government should treat the Statement of Understanding as legally binding.

▲ Seals and Sealing in Canada: Report of the Royal Commission

AUTHOR: Royal Commission on Seals and Sealing in Canada, Chair, Hon. Albert Malouf

YEAR: 1986

ABORIGINAL GROUP: Inuit

TOPICS: Resources, Economic Development, Employment Development

SUB-TOPICS: hunting/wildlife, regional Aboriginal economic development, types of employment

SOURCE: Federal Royal Commission

BACKGROUND

The Royal Commission was established in 1984 following the dramatic collapse in world seal markets as a result of the European Community Directive of 1983 which banned the importation of products made from harp and hooded seal pups. The seal industry in Canada has not recovered since that directive was issued.

The Royal Commission was established in view of the reality that sealing was not simply a technical issue of concern only to fishermen, scientists and administrators. Rather, it was an issue which had garnered much public interest and concern, with a wide variety of views encompassed in the public debate about sealing and the sealing industry in Canada.

Aboriginal peoples of the Arctic regions of Canada have depended for thousands of years upon seals and seal by-products to provide many of the basic necessities of life: food, clothing and heat. In more recent times, the Inuit have been active participants in the international sale of seal products. In fact, the EC Directive of 1983 specifically exempted the sale of Inuit seal products from the ban. Nonetheless, the reality has been that with the overall decline in domestic and international markets, the commercial sealing activities of northern Aboriginal peoples and communities have suffered along with sealing industries in other parts of the country.

PURPOSE

The Commission was established by federal order in council in August 1984. Its report was delivered two years later, in August 1986. The mandate of the Commission was to review all matters pertaining to seals and the sealing industry in Canada, to assemble relevant information and make recommendations based on findings for the purposes of policy development.

Although the terms of reference contained no specific provisions respecting Aboriginal peoples and communities, those elements which were particularly relevant included the requirement to examine the social, cultural and economic aspects of sealing, management of seal stocks, domestic and international commercial sales/markets, and alternatives for individuals and communities dependent on the seal harvest.

ISSUES AND FINDINGS

The Commission addressed issues in the following categories:

1. ethical issues and public concerns about sealing;
2. economic, social and cultural issues;
3. biological issues; and
4. management issues.

Particular attention was given to Aboriginal issues in relation to the following:

Economic, social and cultural issues: The main income from sealing for all those engaged in the industry comes from the sale of seal skins. However, in the case of Aboriginal participants, many families and communities are close to depending entirely upon seal products to meet their subsistence needs at certain times of the year. Furthermore, cash from the sale of seal skins had contributed to the overall cash income of Inuit families. This cash was needed to operate and maintain mechanised equipment used in all hunting activities. The Commission estimated that the collapse in world seal markets reduced the cash income of seal hunters by as much as two-thirds their 1983 levels. This further contributed to a decrease in hunting activities (because of limited cash supply to operate machinery) and subsequently to poor nutritional habits of Aboriginal families.

The Commission concluded that sealing is one of the most economical ways of maintaining nutritional levels in northern communities. The sale of seal products is the most feasible and environmentally appropriate means of meeting the cash requirements of a contemporary Inuit society which used motorized vehicles in their hunting pursuits. The Commission felt that further decline in the sealing activities of northern Aboriginal people would increase dependence upon imported food and result in poorer health conditions, and higher health costs.

The Commission also found that up to $4 million would be required annually to support subsistence hunting at levels prior to the EC Directive and ban.

It was also suggested that Aboriginal peoples and communities in other parts of Canada, and especially in Labrador, Quebec, and B.C., likely suffer greater hardships as a result of federal sealing regulations which are intended to manage the commercial hunting activities of primarily non-Aboriginal communities, and which therefore failed to take into account the special and unique needs and uses of Aboriginal subsistence sealing activities.

With respect to biological issues and methods of killing seals, it was suggested that changes in the seal hunting patterns of Inuit were in all likelihood more humane than traditional methods of killing.

The Commission considered alternative economic activities which might be pursued by northern Aboriginal peoples and sealing communities, but concluded that fur harvesting, tourism and commercial fishing would have limited potential in the Arctic and likely would benefit only a few Inuit. Resource development as an economic alternative was seen as potentially reducing the availability of marine mammals, and would in and of itself not lead to the development of a long-term economic base in the North.

A further finding of the Commission was that the United States — unfairly, and in contravention of historical treaties with the U.K. (which allowed the free passage of Aboriginal peoples and trade across the border) — restricted importations of Canadian Aboriginal products derived from marine mammals, while protecting the sale of U.S. Inuit and Indian crafts.

RECOMMENDATIONS

The Commission's recommendations, as they related to Aboriginal sealing activities were as follows:

1. The federal government should encourage Inuit self-regulation of marine mammal harvesting, and provide scientific advice to assist these activities.

2. Temporary relief, in the form of total annual payments of up to $4 million for five years, should be provided to Inuit hunters under agreements to be negotiated with Inuit organizations including local hunters and trappers associations.

3. Discussions should proceed with the U.S. government aimed at ending discrimination against Canadian Aboriginal peoples in trade.

4. Federal government should conduct a more detailed examination of regulations as they apply to non-Arctic Aboriginal communities engaged in subsistence hunting of seals, and modify those regulations to allow certain Aboriginal communities to hunt seals in the same manner as Aboriginal people of the arctic regions.

▲ Task Force on Indian Economic Development – Summary of the Report to the Deputy Minister of Indian and Northern Affairs Canada

AUTHOR: Department of Indian Affairs and Northern Development, Task Force on Indian Economic Development

YEAR: 1986

ABORIGINAL GROUP: First Nations

TOPICS: Economic Development, Employment Development

SUB-TOPICS: business development, entrepreneurship, statistics

SOURCE: Federal Department

BACKGROUND

The deputy minister of Indian and Northern Affairs Canada established a Task Force to study and report on the state of Indian economic development in Canada and to make recommendations for future action.

PURPOSE

The Task Force was asked to

1. assess the state of Indian economic development;

2. define and measure the resource base available for future development;

3. examine programs affecting Indians;

4. examine the tax system as it affects Indian-owned business; and

5. examine the structure and responsibilities of Indian and Northern Affairs Canada (INAC) and advise on the reorganization of economic development functions within INAC.

ISSUES AND FINDINGS

The report reviewed the state of Indian economic development in accordance with traditional economic classifications of land, labour, capital and government involvement and made the following observations:

Land

Resource development is a vital and integral part of Indian economic development. Natural resources play an important role in the Canadian economy and their exploitation holds much promise for the Indian communities. However, most Indian bands do not benefit from this resource because of a lack of up-to-date technology and limited resource management skills. An additional restriction is imposed by the environmental trade-offs that must be made.

Labour

The labour component of Indian economic development is underdeveloped. Employment and education levels of Indians are below national averages. Education, particularly limited in the area of business management has led to the failure of many Indian business initiatives. This has had a large impact on employment opportunities for Indians, both on- and off-reserve. Inadequate training programs which focus on upgrading job skills for short-term vocational work compound the problem and have reduced opportunities for Indian employment.

Capital

The basic problems for Indian businesses are limited access to private sector financial capital, complex and restrictive taxation policies, limited access to non-Native joint ventures and projects, and limited contact with the non-Native, private sector.

Private sector financing of businesses located on-reserve is limited because of restriction on land and other assets as collateral. This restriction also affects a firm's ability to be bonded. The direct consequence of this limitation is high Indian unemployment, as most Indian private sector employment is located on-reserve.

The ability of an Indian business to enlist non-Indian, private sector support is limited because Indian business may face restrictions from the onset because of the firm's inability to meet the demands of joint business ventures. The concern over trade-offs (potential loss of control of resources) also restricts joint venture initiatives.

Access to the non-Indian private sector is problematic for Indian businesses primarily because of limited knowledge of the procurement requirements of many Canadian businesses. This problem is also experienced in the federal and provincial public sectors, where procurement policies are not well documented.

Government

INAC has contributed to many of the economic inequities experienced by Indian communities. Federal government programs, by and large, have been ineffective primarily as a result of the lack of co-ordination between an increasing number of programs directed toward Native communities. Lack of co-ordination and information about programs is further compounded by programs available at the provincial level.

RECOMMENDATIONS

In relation to its broad mandate, the Task Force identified three general areas seen as critical to Indian economic development. They were:

1. the need for Indians to have control of their economic development, principally through community planning and improved access to financing;

2. INAC must encourage support for Native efforts at all levels (private/public sector, increased tripartite co-operation); and

3. INAC must generate the momentum to deal with current problems and opportunities. INAC must develop policies that are long term in their approach to resolving the problems, particularly in addressing Indian unemployment. The INAC mandate must evolve to reflect the changing realities of economic development.

The report also recommended specific actions to be taken to improve Indian economic and business development through improved access to financial capital, bonding, taxation and through the establishment of linkages with the non-Native business community.

▲ Bill C-31: Equality or Disparity? The Effects of the New Indian Act on Native Women

AUTHOR: Canadian Advisory Council on the Status of Women (Joan Holmes)

YEAR: 1987

ABORIGINAL GROUP: All Aboriginal Peoples, Aboriginal Women

TOPICS: Membership, Political Participation, Federal Government/Aboriginal Relations

SUB-TOPICS: legislation, policy

SOURCE: Federal Agency

BACKGROUND

For over a century, the membership provisions of the *Indian Act* have specified who shall be recognized as an Indian by the federal government, and consequently, who could benefit from use of reserve lands, belong to Indian bands, and receive special services and benefits.

Bill C-31, *An Act to Amend the Indian Act*, was passed in June 1985 and back-dated to April 17, 1985 so that the *Indian Act* would be in compliance with the equality provisions of the *Canadian Charter of Rights and Freedoms*. These amendments made significant changes to the membership rules, and have had a profound effect on the right of Native people to be recognized as Indians, and the right of Indian bands to determine their own membership.

PURPOSE

The Canadian Advisory Council on the Status of Women commissioned this background paper on the impact of Bill C-31 to assist women's groups, both Native and non-Native, to understand better the impact of the changes to the *Indian Act* on Indian women.

ISSUES AND FINDINGS

The first sections of the report describe the history of the achievement and retention of status from the perspective of the government of Canada, and from the social experience of Native women. The remainder of the paper addresses the main issues emanating from the passage of Bill C-31, and more specifically, what its impact will be on Native women and their families. Secondary issues addressed in the paper include the impact of Bill C-31 on band control of membership, and its effect on the overall development of the Indian community.

In general terms, the amended *Indian Act* separates Indian status from band membership and creates new divisions among Indians. Although blatant discrimination against Indian women has been removed from the Act, the author asserts that the effects of that discrimination persist, and new areas of inequality have arisen. Many women interviewed for the report expressed concerns about the provisions of the Act that perpetuate past discrimination against women, and do little to repair the rifts between alienated women and their families and communities.

The changes to the Act divide status into two types, one of which is difficult for a parent to transmit to her/his child. This restricted status belongs mostly to the children of women who lost their status. In the future, however, these restrictions will affect all Indians by limiting the number of Indians eligible for status, and for its accompanying rights and benefits.

Other divisions are also created by the changes. The majority of non-status Indians and Métis people are not eligible for registration under the amended *Indian Act*, and moreover, some people accepted as band members do not qualify for Indian status. The author argues that these divisions will continue to promote disunity and inequality among Indian people.

Under the new legislation, bands have the option of either leaving control of their membership with Indian and Northern Affairs Canada, or assuming control themselves by following the process outlined in Bill C-31. According to the report, the principle that First Nations should control their own citizenship or membership is a key issue in the struggle for self-government and is therefore generally viewed as a positive change to the Act.

Many who registered under Bill C-31 indicated that they would not be interested in returning to their reserves for a variety of reasons, or at least not immediately. Some women have had difficulties getting services and benefits from their bands or exercising their rights as reinstated band members. They fear that their rights and the rights of their children are being ignored by bands, and that they have no protection. This is especially true for single mothers, whose situation is not addressed in the legislation. It is feared that this unequal and unfair treatment may cause other women to hesitate to return to their reserves.

RECOMMENDATIONS

No specific recommendations were offered in the report. There were, however, several comments included which represent the aspirations of the Indian women interviewed. Some of these are presented below.

1. Many women interviewed felt that the *Canadian Charter of Rights and Freedoms*, or a similar Indian rights charter, needs to be applied to all band membership codes, review processes, and protest provisions to assure that no one is unfairly treated.

2. They also felt that bands would be in a better position to accept new members if they received a guarantee of ongoing increased funding to match their populations and actual needs.

3. The women interviewed also emphasized the need for information and assistance programs to help eligible people to follow up their applications and access benefits, and to assist bands to understand the amendments and to develop membership codes.

▲ Gaming on Reserves: Discussion Paper Prepared by a Departmental Task Force

AUTHOR: Department of Indian Affairs and Northern Development, Task Force on Gaming on Reserves, Chair, Neil Overend

YEAR: 1987

ABORIGINAL GROUP: First Nations

TOPICS: Self-Government, Intergovernmental Relations, Financial Arrangements/Responsibilities/Public Finance, Taxation and Customs, Economic Development

SUB-TOPICS: jurisdiction, tripartite (Aboriginal/Federal/Provincial) relations, federal/provincial fiscal responsibilities, revenue generation, on-reserve economic development

SOURCE: Federal Department

BACKGROUND

This discussion paper was prepared in response to the development of friction between some Indian communities and provincial authorities over the control of gaming on-reserve.

PURPOSE

The purpose of the report is to examine the issue of gaming on-reserve. The paper examines the question of jurisdiction over gaming, provides an overview of gaming regulations by province, and reviews recent gaming trends and methods of provincial control.

ISSUES AND FINDINGS

The principal issue addressed in this report is that of jurisdiction. Other issues include the implications of gaming for self-government and the use of gaming revenues for economic development.

The issue of jurisdiction arose in 1985 when the federal government ceded responsibility for gaming to the provinces. This transfer was accomplished through a political accord signed in June, 1985, and subsequent amendments to the *Criminal Code* in December 1985.

A parallel development in the mid-1980s was the growth of interest in the revenue potential of gaming. The most visible source of this growing interest was the revenue-raising capacity of provincial lotteries.

Also during this time, Indian reserves were experimenting with gaming as a means of economic development. The interest in gaming on-reserve was fuelled by the success of several multi-million-dollar gaming operations on American Indian reserves. The efforts of bands, however, to raise revenue through gaming was being undermined by legislation which limited gaming to charitable or religious purposes. This served as a source of frustration for bands because it precluded the band from stimulating economic development through gaming, while simultaneously increasing the provincial control over gaming as a new source of revenue.

The discussion paper presents three lines of reasoning which argue against provincial authority over gaming on-reserve:

1. Provincial authority over gaming on reserves curtails the federal government's constitutional responsibility under section 91(24) of the *Constitution Act*, 1867, for "Indians, and Lands reserved for the Indians". This line of argument suggests that Indian interests should not be subordinated to competing provincial priorities with regard to licensing and the revenue-generating potential of gaming.

2. By-law powers under the *Indian Act* provide band governments with authority over "the control and prohibition of public games," (paragraph 81(m)), money by-laws (section 83), and "the raising of money from

117

band members to support band projects" (paragraph 83(f)). Through these provisions, by-laws made under the *Indian Act* should be able to undermine provincial control.

3. Provincial control in this area is inconsistent with principles of self-government. According to this line of argument, the evolving notion of self-government, which recognizes the rights of Indians to manage their own affairs, includes the inherent right to control gaming on reserves.

RECOMMENDATIONS

While the paper does not recommend a particular course of action, it does propose three strategies that might resolve the conflict between Indian bands and provincial governments over gaming on-reserve:

1 statutory changes to recognize special Indian gaming interests;

2. recognition of Indian jurisdiction over gaming as consistent with the principles of self-government; and

3. the establishment of a national Indian lottery to relieve the pressure for gaming on reserves.

▲ Indian Child and Family Services in Canada

AUTHOR: Indian and Northern Affairs Canada Child and Family Services Task Force

YEAR: 1987

ABORIGINAL GROUP: First Nations, Aboriginal Youth

TOPICS: Child Welfare, Family/Family Relations, Community Services and Infrastructure

SUB-TOPICS: adoption/foster homes, family violence

SOURCE: Federal Department

BACKGROUND

The report describes Indian child and family services provided by bands, provincial agencies and the Department of Indian Affairs and Northern Development (DIAND) in the period from 1981-82 to 1985-86. The data were gathered from national and regional offices of DIAND across the country.

PURPOSE

The purpose of the report is to describe Indian child and family services and costs nationally and regionally and to show trends in services and costs over the five-year study period.

ISSUES AND FINDINGS

The report identifies three major groups of services: prevention; protection; and adoption. Two kinds of intervention are possible under provincial law: voluntary and statutory.

In 1985-86, Indian children were placed into care about 2.7 times as often as non-Indian children. The range of placement ratios was 11.5 times as often in Prince Edward Island to 1.5 times as often in Alberta.

All bands are covered under some type of arrangement for provision of child welfare services. The earliest arrangements were federal-provincial (bipartite) in nature. More recent arrangements involve the bands directly. Thirty-six per cent of the bands in the country delivered some or all of the services of provincial child welfare programs to their own members.

The report identified various stages of transfer of responsibility and control to bands. Bands usually assume responsibility for voluntary prevention services, then voluntary protection services, then statutory protective care, and finally, the full range of child welfare services. By the end of 1985-86, it is expected that 119 bands will have assumed full responsibility.

Ontario, Manitoba and New Brunswick were found to have the highest participation rates of all regions in terms of bands delivering their own service. Virtually no bands in British Columbia were found to deliver their own services.

Statistics outlined in the report reveal that bands delivering their own services received 7.4% of DIAND expenditures in the area of child and family services under service agreements in 1981-82 and 37% in 1985-86. This varied from region to region.

According to the report, bands place greater emphasis on prevention measures, providing support services to families in distress and remedial support to families when children are temporarily placed in substitute care.

The Task Force found that provincial agencies used more intrusive and more expensive placements in group homes and institutions, and they did so more frequently than bands. Bands tended to stress placements in family homes within the community. The structure of cost sharing and funding arrangements was also found to affect costs.

RECOMMENDATIONS

There were no recommendations in the report.

▲ Suicide in Canada: Report of the National Task Force on Suicide in Canada

AUTHOR: National Task Force on Suicide in Canada,
Chair, Diane Syer-Solush
YEAR: 1987
ABORIGINAL GROUP: First Nations
TOPIC: Health
SUB-TOPICS: suicide, mental health
SOURCE: Federal Commission

BACKGROUND

In 1979, Ottawa hosted the 10th International Association for Suicide Prevention Congress, focusing national attention on suicide for the first time. Five years earlier, the federal minister of health, Marc Lalonde, had identified suicide as a major public health problem in Canada. Despite interest in the topic, it was found that little was known on the subject of suicide in Canada.

PURPOSE

Health and Welfare Canada established the National Task Force on Suicide in Canada to investigate and define the dimensions of suicide, and to consider effective strategies in responding to the problem. The Task Force was also asked to identify Canadian groups that were at greatest risk, including Aboriginal peoples.

ISSUES AND FINDINGS

The Task Force's investigation of Aboriginal peoples was limited to Status Indians, the only group for which national statistics were available. The

Task Force specifically noted that comments and conclusions might therefore not be applicable to other Aboriginal groups.

The Task Force recognized that Aboriginal peoples are two to three times more likely to commit suicide than other Canadians, and identified eight contributing factors:

1. the loss of control over collective identity;
2. social isolation;
3. education;
4. depression;
5. alcoholism;
6. physical illness;
7. internalization of feelings; and
8. vulnerability to the loss of significant others.

Loss of control over collective identity: Some researchers believed that the Canadian government's attempts to assimilate Aboriginal peoples into the dominant culture had significantly lowered their self-esteem.

Social isolation: There appeared to be an astonishing lack of personal relationship between suicidal Aboriginal people and with members of their peer group outside the immediate family. A comparison of the marital status of Aboriginal suicide victims with the general population showed a greater proportion of single individuals among the Aboriginal population.

Education: It was believed that inadequate education among Aboriginal peoples had limited their employment opportunities, thereby contributing to a sense of hopelessness.

Depression: This had been found to be the most prevalent mental disorder of Aboriginal people who commit suicide.

Alcoholism: Studies have reported that a significant number of Aboriginal suicide completers had a history of alcohol abuse and had been drinking immediately prior to their death.

Physical illness: One study found that 25% of the group of Aboriginal suicide completers suffered from significant physical illness.

Internalization of feelings: Studies have shown that among Aboriginal peoples, the most common and socially acceptable method of dealing with stress is to internalize feelings.

Vulnerability to loss of significant others: Aboriginal people inclined toward suicide were particularly vulnerable to the loss of significant others as a result of family disruption; a frequency of inappropriate parental substitutes; death in the family; death from violence and frequent moves to boarding schools.

The Task Force pointed out that it was generally agreed that the number of suicides among Aboriginal peoples was significantly underestimated because of difficulties associated with certifying that a death was indeed suicide. Reasons for confusion were the high incidence of alcohol-related violent deaths among Aboriginal people and the Aboriginal peoples' tendency to make distinctions between officially certified homicide and victim-induced homicide, which they interpreted as suicide.

RECOMMENDATIONS

The Task Force recommended that the development and implementation of suicide prevention strategies for Canadian Aboriginal Peoples should be based on a comprehensive and culturally oriented approach.

It was also proposed that a liaison and back-up network of mental health consultants be accessible to all community health workers delivering health, education and social services to Aboriginal peoples.

1988

▲ Report of the Commission of Inquiry Concerning Certain Matters Associated with the Westbank Indian Band

AUTHOR: Commission of Inquiry Concerning Matters Associated with the Westbank Indian Band, Commissioner, John E. Hall, Q.C.

YEAR: 1988

ABORIGINAL GROUP: First Nations

TOPICS: Federal/Aboriginal Relations, Self-Government, Land Use, Management and Development, Economic Development

SUB-TOPICS: federal trust responsibilities, legislation, policy, institutions, self-government jurisdiction and structures, land tenure systems, land use planning, land zoning, land development, land management, economic development on reserves

SOURCE: Federal Commission

BACKGROUND

The Westbank Indian Band is located outside the city of Kelowna, British Columbia. In the 1970s Westbank shared in the general economic growth and expansion of the area. Its economy was enhanced as a result of residential developments and associated increases in the economic value of Westbank reserve lands. The financial status of the Band was further improved as a result of a large reserve lands cut-off settlement and upgrades in the provincial highway system running through reserve lands.

The Band became a major depositor and held a substantial share position in the Northland Bank which failed in 1985.

Westbank was, and remains a sophisticated band in terms of administration and economic progress, and continues to be active in leasing not only for residential, but also commercial, industrial and recreational purposes.

In the mid-1970s a number of major land development projects, mainly mobile home/trailer parks, were under way, encouraged in part by the absence of by-laws regulating land use. In 1976, a new Chief (Derrickson) was elected to office, with a commitment to increase land regulation to ensure quality development and income generation for the Westbank Band.

At the same time DIAND was in the process of closing its district offices, as part of "downsizing", with functions centralized in regional offices. This policy effort reflected the Department's transition from the old order of Indian agent style management toward greater autonomy for bands.

By the mid-1980s band members and non-Indian residents/tenants were growing increasingly concerned about the circumstances surrounding the leasing of band lands, and the state of band financial affairs in general.

The collapse of the Northland Bank, a physical attack on the Chief, and the perceived indifference of the department of Indian Affairs in relation to unfolding events at Westbank all contributed to the eruption of a high level of controversy, dissatisfaction and confusion both within the community, and without.

A new Chief and Council were elected in 1986, following the establishment of an Action Committee by disgruntled band members. The committee opposed the land and financial activities that had been pursued by the Chief of the previous 11 years and his Council.

The Commission of Inquiry was appointed by federal order in council in August 1986 to investigate and report on the specific controversies surrounding economic development, financial and land management, and relations between the Band and DIAND at Westbank.

PURPOSE

By its Terms of Reference the Commission of Inquiry was assigned tasks in two particular areas. First, it was to investigate and report on matters of controversy surrounding the management of the Westbank Indian Band and the relationship with the department of Indian Affairs between 1975 and 1986, and to look into the activities and enterprises of lessees of Westbank lands during this time.

Second, the Commission was asked to review and recommend changes to the *Indian Act* in respect of the management of Indian lands and moneys, and the policies and procedures of the department of Indian Affairs.

The Commission involved those persons affiliated with the Westbank Indian Band, and in the specific controversies in the first of its tasks, but invited Indian groups throughout B.C. to prepare submissions and appear as witnesses in relation to the second.

ISSUES AND FINDINGS

In relation to the Westbank Indian Band controversies, the Commission addressed the following issues:

1. economic development projects at Westbank supported by federal funding agencies;
2. land allotments (tenure) and conflict of interest;
3. band finances, accounting practices and investments;
4. band government structures and exercise of powers; and
5. conduct of the Department throughout the period of controversy.

With respect to possible changes to the *Indian Act*, the Commission examined interim and long-term changes for:

1. land management;
2. financial accounting and control/management of Indian moneys; and
3. self-government.

On issues strictly involving the Westbank Indian Band and DIAND, the Commission of Inquiry revealed the following:

- A need to achieve balance in government involvement in Indian enterprise, and to recognize that federal economic development funding agencies (including DIAND), are often called upon to support what may, under certain criteria, be considered non-viable projects on-reserve, often at the expense of the operation of the principles of a market economy.

• Limited enforcement of conflict of interest standards (set out by DIAND) in local decision making and, in the case of Westbank, particularly in the allocation of local interests in land (i.e., allotments); recognition of the delicacy of these issues in Indian communities where familial relations permeate local Indian government activities.

• Historical lack of consultation with the band membership on a major investment decision (i.e., the purchase of a share position in the Northland Bank), limited financial analysis to support the investment decision, and a subsequent failures by Council to inform the Band of details relating to the investment.

• Limited economic planning with respect to other band investments.

• Westbank financial accounting system had not contributed to a clarity of understanding of financial transactions. Band members were not informed of activities of incorporated and unincorporated band enterprises, nor were they informed of significant transactions between band members and the Band itself. Further, in light of new financial arrangements between DIAND and bands, the Commission recognized the need for greater vigilance by communities in the management of their own financial affairs.

• In relation to government structures and the exercise of powers, the Commission encountered lack of clarity between the Band and the federal government (DIAND) regarding who was able to exercise what authorities, particularly in relation to land management and the administration of leases on conditionally surrendered lands.

• No findings of corruption on the part of DIAND officials, but a noted inability to deal effectively with the types of problems and controversies which surfaced at Westbank, and to clearly perceive and address the respective authorities and responsibilities of the Band and the Department. The Commission suggested that the "fumbling" of the Department through the period was attributable in part to its "blind" commitment to the policies of devolution and enhanced band autonomy.

With respect to the second part of its mandate, to consider changes to the *Indian Act*, the Commission concluded that the history of the Act was a history of tension between wardship, and assimilation and independence.

The Commission reviewed and commented on current policy initiatives including: the Kamloops Amendment, which proposed broader band taxation by-law making powers, and the extension of those taxation powers to conditionally surrendered lands (formerly subject to provincial laws). The Kamloops amendment was supported in principle, though the Commission felt that many difficulties would be encountered in implementation.

The Lands, Revenues and Trusts Review (LRT), (uncompleted at the time of the tabling of this Report), which involved a comprehensive management review of federal administration, policy and statutory concerns in relation to DIAND's LRT activities and responsibilities was strongly supported by the Commission, as were the proposed *Indian Lands Act* and an upgraded Indian lands registry (i.e., administered by the federal government). It was the Commission's view that these initiatives would facilitate a clarity of roles, responsibilities and land management regimes, and thereby contribute positively to Indian economic development.

With respect to management of Indian moneys, the Commission heard calls from most Indian groups for greater flexibility in the management of capital moneys.

The Department's devolution and downsizing policies of the late 1970s and 1980s were, in the view of the Commission, modestly successful and efficient. The costs of devolution arising from the transfer of responsibilities, education/training and demands for higher standards, coupled with the loss of economies of scale in program delivery, would, in the Commission's view, exceed the costs of administration under present arrangements.

The Commission also examined the federal government's policy of supporting Indian "self-government", and concluded that self-government was subject to widely varying interpretations. In the end the Commission supported a delegated form of self-government within the Canadian constitutional context, with the federal government playing an administrative role, and facilitating the evolution of Indian self-government according to the particular needs of individual communities. The Commission also supported a statutory base for the delegation of self-government powers to bands and tribal councils.

The *Indian Act* was recognized as an obstacle to the achievement of self-government as a result of its paternalistic and intrusive nature and its failure to provide the requisite legal underpinnings to support the exercise of greater powers by Indian governments. It was also the conclusion of the Commission that the *Indian Act* and departmental policies diverged to such an extent that policies lacked any kind of underlying statutory foundation.

RECOMMENDATIONS

The Commission clearly recommended legislative change to address change in the relationship between Indians and the Crown, and the transforming economic circumstances of Indian bands. Such change was proposed regardless of the outcome of constitutional level developments. It was recommended that the scope of legislative change would need to incorporate amendments to the *Indian Act* to provide a statutory base for current practices and policies, coupled with a new *Indian Lands Act* and, over the longer term, development of alternative and optional legislative schemes, such as Bill C-52.

The Commission made a number of specific recommendations for amendments to the *Indian Act*, particularly in relation to existing land, financial management and Indian monies provisions, as well as for new Indian lands legislation and alternative legislative regimes which would permit the development of band constitutions, and enhance band by-law making powers similar to those of municipalities.

The Commission made recommendations for both long- and short-term changes to the *Indian Act* based on its investigations of the not so unique problems encountered by the Westbank Indian Band, and as identified through its broader consultations with other Indian groups and leaders.

In terms of specific amendments to the *Indian Act*, the Commission recommended such amendments should allow for management of surrendered lands by band councils; allow for the delegation of authority by the band to the band council for the management and control of reserve lands, with clear identification of band decision making authority retained; permit delegation of band authority to the band council for management and expenditure of revenue monies; facilitate band control and management of capital moneys; repeal provisions permitting per capita distribution of capital moneys.

In terms of land administration, the Commission recommended annual reporting by band councils in relation to all land allotments, public hearing procedures for granting allotments to band executive members and their families, additional funding for the Indian land registry and new regulations to improve its operation.

The Commission also recommended the enactment of comprehensive Indian lands legislation to provide a coherent legal structure for the control and management of Indian lands.

The Commission also identified a number of recommendations to improve band financial accounting and disclosure practices, including the preparation of an annual report by band councils to brief the band membership of all government activities.

With respect to Indian self government, the Commission made a number of recommendations to be implemented in the short term including:

- legislation allowing bands to enact constitutions;

- support for the Kamloops Amendments which would extend band taxation powers to conditionally surrendered lands; and

- by-law powers and legal immunities of bands similar to those governing municipalities in relation to land management and zoning

Recommendations for long-term change were primarily focused on self-government and supported a statutory basis for new arrangements, with enabling legislation favoured over individual ("private") acts such as the *Sechelt Act*.

The Commission also recommended funding to support the development of community-based "expertise" which would be required for the assumption of self-government powers and supported the pursuit of self-government through tribal councils and broader administrative structures. Under self-government the band membership would continue to participate in major land decisions and in significant financial decisions, including the approval of budgets and large capital expenditures.

With respect to land management regimes under self-government, the Commission did not support the development of unique land regimes by individual self-governing bands, and called instead for the extension of the proposed *Indian Lands Act* over all self-governing band lands.

Although no specific recommendations were provided in relation to the continued role of government, the Commission clearly favoured a continued active federal role (and responsibility) in Indian affairs, and observed that the federal government could play a useful role in the negotiation of claims settlements, in monitoring expenditures of public funds, maintaining the federal Indian land register, and administering trust accounts not transferred to local control.

1989

▲ From Here to There: Steps Along the Way, The Report of the Scott-McKay-Bain Health Panel on Health Services in Sioux Lookout District

AUTHOR: Scott-McKay-Bain Health Panel on Health Services in Sioux Lookout District, Members, Archbishop Edward Scott, Mr. Wally McKay and Dr. Harry Bain

YEAR: 1989

ABORIGINAL GROUP: First Nations

TOPIC: Health

SUB-TOPICS: primary and secondary health care, mental health, preventive health/education

SOURCE: Federal Commission

BACKGROUND

In 1988, five members of the Sandy Lake Band held a two-day fast at the Sioux Lookout Zone Hospital. These men wished to draw attention to what they felt were years of meaningless consultation, worsening health conditions and deteriorating relations between Aboriginal communities and the Medical Services Branch (MSB) of Health and Welfare Canada, which provided health services in the Zone.

The protest led to an agreement between Native leaders and the federal government, whereby the Nishnawbe-Aski Nation, representing the Native communities, and the federal government would review health services in the Sioux Lookout Zone, within a framework that supported the right of Indian people to determine their own health needs and to control the health delivery system by which their needs were met.

PURPOSE

The three-member review panel's mandate was:

1. to review, evaluate and determine the deficiencies of existing health services and programs provided in the Zone;

2. to hold community hearings to document the problems and suggested solutions from individuals, band councils and elders in the Zone; and

3. to establish a process and a plan of action which identify solutions and rectify noted deficiencies in the health care system.

ISSUES AND FINDINGS

The review panel identified five basic problems with respects to the health care system. These were:

1. the lack of Aboriginal empowerment to develop policies and services;

2. the lack of community infrastructure and economic development required to support and promote health;

3. the weakening of the traditional, extended family due to exposure to Western culture and the loss of spiritual values;

4. the failure of communication between the two cultures involved in providing and receiving health care; and

5. the focus of health care services on curative measures, rather than prevention.

Aboriginal empowerment: The panel concurred with new principles of health and health promotion. These principles stressed empowerment and individual and community collaboration. The planning and administration of health services was designed by the MSB, with little Aboriginal input except for the mental health program (NODIN), which was run by Aboriginal peoples. Aboriginal community responsibility for health services was seen as essential for efficiency and effectiveness.

The federal government's current health transfer process which transferred administrative control of the health care system to local authorities was criticized because control was not extended to policy development or fiscal responsibility. In addition, transfers were negotiated on a community-by-community basis, creating a situation where Native communities within the Zone were competing for limited resources rather than co-ordinating health care efforts.

Lack of community infrastructure and economic development: The panel stressed that long term improvements in health status would not be possible without dramatic improvements in these two areas. With regard to infrastructure, it was noted that the Sioux Lookout Zone was characterized by poor sewage disposal systems, crowded housing, inadequate supplies of drinking water and non-existent bathing facilities. Geographical isolation was also a problem, since supplies had to be flown in and were therefore expensive.

With regard to economic development, the panel noted that many of the traditional Indigenous livelihoods had disappeared and that the Aboriginal people had benefited little from development that had occurred within the region. The panel emphasized the ample evidence that lack of employment opportunities had a negative effect on both physical and mental health.

Weakening of traditional culture and spiritual values: The panel noted that often when an Aboriginal person complained about ill health he or she was really alluding to mental/spiritual health. It was felt that the greatest threat to Aboriginal health was the breakdown in the traditional family unit, loss of cultural and spiritual values and the resulting decline in mental health. This social and cultural breakdown was exacerbated by high levels of unemployment in the Zone. Several communities expressed concern over the alarming increase in suicide among Aboriginal youth and young adults.

Failure of communications between the two cultures: Language barriers between providers and recipients of health services were identified as one of the greatest weaknesses of the current system.

It was also noted that Aboriginal peoples tended to have an inflated view of western medicine capabilities, equating expensive equipment with good health. In addition, it was found that misconceptions about perceived second-class care were often based on ignorance of the system. For instance, many Aboriginal people complained that Sioux Lookout Hospital was staffed by students. These were in fact licensed doctors doing post-graduate work, a practice found in all teaching hospitals in urban settings.

Preventive vs. curative health: The panel stressed that the World Health Organization not only defined health as the absence of disease, but also as a state of physical, mental, spiritual and social well-being. This view reflected the Aboriginal peoples' traditional holistic view of health.

RECOMMENDATIONS

The panel was convinced that problems with health and health care in the region were not primarily financial, but recognized that its recommendations would require additional funding from the federal government. The panel stressed that the recommendations would lead to a long-term reduction in health care costs.

The panel believed that to ensure greater Aboriginal involvement in and control over health care, the federal government and the Nishnawbe-Aski Nation could enter into a formal agreement to transfer authority for the formation and implementation of health policies to an Aboriginal Health Authority. The agreement would include reassurances that such an organization in no way negated the federal government's trust responsibility.

The panel recommended that the Nishnawbe-Aski Nation, Health and Welfare Canada and the Department of Indian Affairs and Northern Development enter into a comprehensive agreement on a major capital program that provided a new infrastructure, comparable to neighbouring non-Aboriginal communities and culturally appropriate.

The report proposed that the federal and provincial governments work with the Nishnawbe-Aski Nation to develop culturally appropriate long-term economic goals. The communities themselves were also urged to form economic development committees to develop self-help initiatives.

Due to a perceived mental health crisis in the region, the review proposed that this aspect or health be given priority attention, and that traditional and Western spiritual leaders be encouraged to become involved in mental health services, providing support and role models for teenagers and young adults.

The panel proposed a blending of traditional Aboriginal healing practices and western medicine to provide a more holistic, culturally sensitive approach to health care.

The review panel was of the view that many health services, particularly preventive services, could be best delivered by individuals rather than physicians.

▲ Final Report: Task Force on Aboriginal Peoples in Federal Corrections

AUTHOR: Solicitor General of Canada, Task Force on Aboriginal Peoples in Federal Corrections

YEAR: 1989

ABORIGINAL GROUP: All Aboriginal Peoples

TOPIC: Administration of Justice

SUB-TOPIC: corrections

SOURCE: Federal Department

BACKGROUND

Aboriginal peoples have been an identified concern of the Department of the Solicitor General of Canada since the early 1970s. They are over-represented as inmates and under-represented as employees in the federal correctional system. Fewer Aboriginal offenders are granted full parole by the National Parole Board, and when granted some form of release, this is often later in the sentence. Aboriginal offenders are more likely to have their parole revoked. These concerns, complicated by the heterogeneity of Aboriginal offenders and the need for accurate data collection on Aboriginal offenders, led to the establishment of the Task Force on Aboriginal Peoples in Federal Corrections.

PURPOSE

Prompted by the Solicitor General of Canada, the Task Force was established in March 1987 to:

Examine the process which Aboriginal offenders (status and non-status Indians, Métis and Inuit) go through, from the time of admission to a federal penitentiary until warrant expiry, in order to identify the needs of Aboriginal offenders and to identify ways of improving their opportunities for social reintegration as law-abiding citizens, through improved penitentiary placement, through improved institutional programs, through improved preparation for temporary absences, day parole and full parole, as well as through improved and innovative supervision.

The Task Force established the following set of principles to guide the development of recommendations and strategies:

1. that the Task Force be restricted to matters within the Solicitor General's responsibilities;
2. that Aboriginal inmates must have access to all services and programs offered to the general population;
3. that Aboriginal offenders must be given the opportunity to derive maximum benefit from the correctional process even where this means making specific provisions for Aboriginal offenders;
4. that where Aboriginal-specific services are to be provided under contract, their development and delivery should normally be by recognized Aboriginal organizations, agencies and communities;
5. that where existing policies and programs already advocate a distinct approach to meet the special needs of Aboriginal offenders, the intent is to clarify and reinforce those existing policies and procedures, in addition to establishing mechanisms for implementing the recommendations contained in the report and monitoring the progress of their implementation;
6. that awareness and sensitivity with respect to Aboriginal cultures and peoples is required in order to respond to the aforementioned principles; and
7. that the report of the Task Force must offer practical recommendations and viable options which will have an impact and increase chances of the Aboriginal offender's successful reintegration into society.

ISSUES AND FINDINGS

The issues addressed by the Task Force may be classified under the following headings:

1. **Data collection:** Statistics relating to the proportion, case management, and release of Aboriginal federal offenders was found to be inadequate.

2. **Case decision-making:** The Task Force noted the following issues relating to case management: correctional assessment procedures and tools may not apply as effectively to Aboriginal as to non-Aboriginal offenders and elders may be able to provide a more accurate assessment of Aboriginal inmates; there are communications problems between Aboriginal inmates and non-Aboriginal staff; the role of the police in providing community assessment and parole supervision has caused tension between police and offenders and/or Aboriginal communities; there is a lack of cultural awareness and sensitivity among corrections decision-makers; and Aboriginal inmates waive their right to a parole hearing and/or to a parole review more frequently than other offenders.

3. **Programs and services:** The following issues relating to programs and services for Aboriginal offenders were identified by the Task Force: Aboriginal inmates in protective custody, female Aboriginal offenders, Inuit offenders, and Aboriginal offenders transferred by Exchange of Services agreements present difficult programming situations; procedural problems exist relating to the handling of medicine and sacred bundles by security personnel, the inaccessibility of elders to segregation or dissociation areas, and the frequency of sweat lodges and other ceremonies; community release programs display a need for expanded Aboriginal liaison services, and improved co-ordination of services and programs for Aboriginal inmates upon release; Aboriginal offenders often fail to understand the intricacies of the correctional and parole process and will not seek clarification because of lack of trust or difficulty in communicating; Aboriginal inmates and organizations are dissatisfied with substance abuse programs and frequently refuse to participate; and Aboriginal inmates are not receptive to the delivery of Aboriginal-specific programming by non-Aboriginal organizations.

4. **The Aboriginal community:** The Task Force identified a lack of communication and information exchange with Aboriginal communities with regard to the needs of inmates being released into the community.

RECOMMENDATIONS

The Task Force made 61 recommendations with regard to data collection, case decision-making, programs and services, and interaction with the Aboriginal community.

1. **Data collection:** The Task Force made several recommendations to improve the data collection on Aboriginal inmates at various points in their sentence.

2. **Case decision-making:** The Task Force made the following recommendations: that assessment procedures be evaluated as to their validity for Aboriginal offenders and that elders be permitted to submit an assessment to the National Parole Board; that Aboriginal employment be increased within the federal corrections system; that agents of community assessment and parole supervision other than the police be established to reduce conflict between the police and Aboriginal offenders and/or communities; that training be implemented within the Department of the Solicitor General to increase awareness and sensitivity of Aboriginal cultures; and that steps be taken to ensure that the policy on waivers is fully understood by both staff and inmates.

3. **Programs and services:** The Task Force made the following recommendations with regard to programs and services: that accessibility to Aboriginal programs by Aboriginal women, Inuit, inmates in protective custody and in provincial institutions be enhanced and increased; that elders be given the same status as Chaplains and that guidelines be developed regarding the minimum number of sweat lodges and other ceremonies; that the availability of Native liaison services be increased and that offender release preparation include greater co-ordination of community resources; that Aboriginal people be proportionately represented on Citizens Advisory Committees; that information about the correctional and parole processes be presented to Aboriginal offenders in a manner more conducive to their approach to learning; that post-release services for Aboriginal offenders be improved; that Aboriginal-specific substance abuse programs be developed; and that Aboriginal-specific contracted programs be delivered primarily by Aboriginal-controlled services.

4. **The Aboriginal community:** The Task Force recommends that the Department of the Solicitor General develop and implement an appropriate strategy for dissemination of information on corrections, especially release, to Aboriginal communities and organizations, and that other appropriate mechanisms be introduced to ensure that the needs of Aboriginal offenders are understood by Aboriginal organizations with mandates to service their needs. The Task Force also recommended greater consultation with the Aboriginal community prior to an inmate's release.

▲ Policing for Aboriginal Canadians: The RCMP Role

AUTHOR: Royal Canadian Mounted Police, Acting Commissioner, R.H.D. Head
YEAR: 1989
ABORIGINAL GROUP: All Aboriginal Peoples
TOPICS: Administration of Justice, Social/Cross-Cultural Relations, Federal Government/Aboriginal Relations
SUB-TOPICS: system (integrated vs. separate), law enforcement, racism, jurisdiction
SOURCE: Federal Agency

BACKGROUND

In 1988, an evaluation of current programs, from both RCMP and client perspectives, was requested. It was to be carried out by the Chief Superintendent of the RCMP, who was mandated to consult with Native people and leaders, officials overseeing justice, and members of the RCMP and other police forces.

PURPOSE

The purpose of this report was to recommend means, methods, and approaches to enhance Native policing services, the organizational structure for the delivery of services, and the effectiveness of the Native policing section at RCMP Headquarters.

Five separate questionnaires were distributed to Native leaders at both the provincial/territorial and band/settlement levels, government officials, Native constables, RCMP managers, and program managers. Personal interviews were also conducted.

ISSUES AND FINDINGS

The report discusses the history of the RCMP and its policing of Aboriginal people. The report found that prior to the 1950s, the RCMP provided policing services to reserves as well as to most Inuit and Métis communities. During the 1960s, band councils started effectively to manage their own affairs, and began to want greater control over their policing services. The late 1960s was characterized by co-operation between reserve governments and provincial authorities with regard to policing. In the 1970s, policing began to be considered the responsibility of the provincial government; this limited the role of the RCMP to policing only Indian and Inuit communities under contract. Indian police programs were established in the 1970s and 1980s, including the creation of "Special Constables" in 1973 to stimulate the recruitment of Indians. The RCMP justified its continued policing activities by referring to the federal responsibilities outlined in the provisions of the *Indian Act*.

The issues dealt with in the report include Native policing program management; service delivery systems; communication links to Native communities; policing by partnership and ownership; an examination of attitudes; present Native programs; and recruitment and training.

1. Program Management

As policing demands increased, more Native people were recruited as Special Constables. As the needs expanded, a Native Policing Branch was established in the Ottawa Headquarters of the RCMP to assist in program management and to develop, implement and co-ordinate programs between the field divisions. The report found that the original intent of the Native Policing Program has been lost in the maze of bureaucracy. They are not consulted on issues of importance to Native policing and are not given the opportunity to participate in national objectives or to give or solicit feedback; as a result, a working relationship with Native policing programs or political organizations has not been established. Native people do not want to be consolidated with Canada's visible minorities.

2. Delivery Systems

The report found that to be efficient, Native participation and co-ownership of Native policing programs is essential. The delivery systems have become varied and decentralized. They now include store-front operations, a patrol cabin concept, and a satellite concept. It was established that the RCMP must continue to offer police services to Native people in most jurisdictions, at least in the short run.

3. Communication

The report found that it is essential that communication between the Force and the Native communities flow in both directions. The structure of Native organizations, however, does not correspond to the structure of the Force, making communication difficult, but not impossible. The report found clear and definitive communication policy to be the key to sound operational practices.

4. Community Policing by Partnership and Ownership

The report found that Native leaders should have input into policing services and goal-setting initiatives if they are expected to co-operate.

5. Attitudes

Prejudice in the Force was found to be most often a latent yet subtle characteristic that surfaces on occasion during casual encounters. There was also found to be a comparable prejudice on the part of Native people, who at times refuse to co-operate with the Force. The importance of cross-cultural training at various stages of the careers of RCMP members is realized.

6. Native-Specific Supplemental Programs

These initiatives include special constables (who are mainly Indian-Métis or Inuit recruits), band constables, and reserve constables (i.e., RCMP reserve, not Indian reserve). Other programs in effect are the supernumerary constable summer student program, targeted at Native students, and the RCMP-Scouts Canada Venturing Program.

In Ontario, the Ontario Provincial Police (OPP) have a high profile "Indian-specific" policing program, but Native policing in Ontario has been given a low profile. It was found that policing committees were critical for success. The band has input into hiring in Ontario, but there is also the problem of special constables reporting to two bosses, the band and the OPP. Quebec utilizes detachment policing, community-based policing, peacekeepers (not approved by government), and optional policing. In addition, although many Indian bands spoke positively of the American Navajo justice and policing system, it was found that it offered little that could be applied to the Canadian context.

7. Recruitment and Training

There was found to be a shortage of Native police personnel. Additional education is usually necessary for Native recruits. Visual acuity has been questioned and found to be unequal for Native and non-Native personnel. As well the level of fitness has been considered too low. Training has been found to be a traumatic experience for many Native recruits.

RECOMMENDATIONS

The report makes over 100 recommendations. The major ones are as follows:

1. Program Management

It is recommended that the Force be restructured and that a person of Native origin be the Officer in Charge in Native communities and that he be allowed a travel budget and the authority to develop strict policy requirements.

2. Service Delivery Systems

It is recommended that the Force develop a definition for its field delivery systems, that delivery systems be expanded to Native communities, and that the Force liaise with Native leaders during planning. It is further recommended that RCMP enforcement of Federal Statutes on Indian lands be re-examined and a formal stance be determined.

3. Communication Links to Native Communities

It is recommended that the importance of clear communication be re-emphasized in policy. To encourage communication, meetings between Native communities and leaders and the Force should be held.

It is recommended that the Force undertake federal police-community relations programs with Native communities, and participate in community-based programs.

4. Policing by Partnership and Ownership

It is recommended that a "partnership and ownership" concept be developed between the Force and the Native community, and that non-political police advisory committees be established.

5. Examination of Attitudes

Also recommended is pre-hiring psychological testing and subsequent attention to detecting prejudicial attitudes. Cross-cultural training is also proposed for all members of the RCMP.

6. Native-Specific Supplemental Programs

Funding for the Native policing program should be transferred from Department of Indian Affairs and Northern Development to the Department of the Solicitor General.

In Ontario and Quebec, it is recommended that a Native policing program establish federal liaison, crime prevention and enforcement programs on reserves.

It is also recommended that the creation of supernumerary special constables be encouraged and that a Field Police Handbook be written to outline the different Native cultures, as well as the goals and objectives of the Native organizations.

7. Recruitment and Training

The report recommends that commanding officers standardize job descriptions, that the Force initiate programs to encourage Native and youth participation, that the application process be free of cultural biases, and that the special constable designation be abolished in favour of other recruitment initiatives. It is also recommended that Native people be given the same transfer considerations as non-Native members.

▲ A Review of the Post-Secondary Student Assistance Program of the Department of Indian Affairs and Northern Development

AUTHOR: Standing Committee on Aboriginal Affairs, Chair, John Reimer, M.P.

YEAR: 1989

ABORIGINAL GROUP: First Nations

TOPIC: Education

SUB-TOPIC: post-secondary education

SOURCE: House of Commons Committee

BACKGROUND

A set of guidelines for funding post-secondary assistance was approved by Treasury Board in 1975. The objectives of this policy were to increase the number of Aboriginal people with university and professional qualifications and to create a greater degree of economic self-sufficiency among Aboriginal people. These guidelines formed the basis for the E-12 guidelines approved in 1977. Between 1977 and 1982, discussions took place between the

Department of Indian Affairs and Northern Development (DIAND) and the Indian communities on revisions to the E-12 Guidelines. A full review took place between 1987 and 1989 which resulted in several changes being made.

The changes included stricter residency requirements, an obligation on the part of students to seek financial assistance elsewhere to offset funding from the program, and the discontinuation of some categories of assistance, including counselling services and some tutorial assistance. Furthermore, incentive grants for graduate and advanced studies were discontinued; there was a restriction in time limitations to complete degrees; restrictions were placed on the programs of study chosen; and assistance was limited to the main estimates as opposed to the previous practice of requesting supplementary estimates to cover all eligible applicants.

This is the first report of the Standing Committee on Aboriginal Affairs. Within 24 hours of being formed, the Standing Committee on Aboriginal Affairs moved to examine the Post-secondary Assistance Program of DIAND and to respond to widespread concern which the changes to this program had created.

PURPOSE

The purpose of the review is to recommend means and mechanisms to improve the efficiency and effectiveness of the program in providing post-secondary assistance to Aboriginal students.

ISSUES AND FINDINGS

The critical importance of education, particularly post-secondary education, to Aboriginal people was emphasized by practically all witnesses and submissions. Aboriginal groups perceived the goals of self-government, economic self-sufficiency and higher educational achievements among Aboriginal peoples as interdependent. Without exception, submissions made to the Committee indicated great dissatisfaction with many of the key program changes. Aboriginal people also emphasized that they viewed post-secondary education as an Aboriginal or treaty right.

The Committee found that there is a high level of mistrust of the federal government in the Aboriginal community and that divergent views are held by the federal government and Aboriginal groups on what constitutes proper or adequate consultation. A key demand of the students and of many of the Aboriginal groups was a moratorium on any policy change pending the completion of a bilateral consultation process.

RECOMMENDATIONS

The Committee submitted nine recommendations in four general areas:

1. Consultation

The major recommendations concerned the establishment of a full and meaningful consultation process set up between the government of Canada and Aboriginal peoples. The primary goal would be to reach a consensus on post-secondary education policies and guidelines and also to establish a shared national data base on Aboriginal post-secondary education.

2. Treaty Rights

The Committee did not feel that it could decide the legal issue of whether post-secondary education was a treaty right. It did, however, recommend that a forum be created to resolve this disagreement.

3. Program Issues

The Committee recommended that the government of Canada thoroughly and seriously consider the submissions made to this Committee on program issues and that in particular special consideration be given to the situation in the Northwest Territories and to the provisions of the James Bay and Northern Quebec Agreement.

4. Funding

The Committee further recommended that the program provide adequate funding to each eligible applicant in each year and, as a long-term goal, that management of the program be transferred to Aboriginal peoples.

1990

◆ *Discussion Paper Regarding First Nation Land Claims* (1990), see **Volume 3, Ontario.**

▲ Impact of the 1985 Amendments to the Indian Act

AUTHOR: Department of Indian Affairs and Northern Development
YEAR: 1990

ABORIGINAL GROUP: All Aboriginal Peoples

TOPICS: Membership, Federal Government/Aboriginal Relations

SUB-TOPICS: federal trust responsibilities, legislation, policy, institutions, political participation/representation

SOURCE: Federal Department

BACKGROUND

In 1985, Parliament passed a series of amendments to the *Indian Act* to make it more compatible with the *Canadian Charter of Rights and Freedoms*. The specific objectives of Bill C-31 were threefold. First, it was to remove discrimination on the basis of gender from the Act; this objective was intended to address the issue of women who had lost their status through marriage to non-Indians. Second, the Bill sought to restore Indian status and band membership rights to eligible persons, particularly Aboriginal women who made up 58% of all those who gained status between 1985 and 1990. Of this majority, 77% of the women had not just gained status but had had it restored. Finally, the provisions of Bill C-31 were to transfer the authority to control band membership from the minister of Indian Affairs and Northern Development to the band.

The increase in the number of individuals who applied for status began to put pressure on resources available to fund Native communities and governmental support programs. There were also signs that Bill C-31 registrants were viewed as an underclass by the current status Indians, which further aggravated the process.

Two years following the passage of Bill C-31, the minister of Indian Affairs and Northern Development, Bill McKnight, promised to deliver an assessment to Parliament by 1990, which addressed the new concerns that the Bill had prompted. The modules studied in this report are the result of that promise.

PURPOSE

The objective of these modules is to present the findings of a comprehensive assessment of the impact of Bill C-31 on Native Indians. Specifically, the analyses study the impacts of this Bill on registrants, on bands and reserve communities, on off-reserve Aboriginal communities, and on government programs. This study was developed in consultation with the Assembly of First Nations, the Native Women's Association of Canada and the Native Council of Canada.

ISSUES AND FINDINGS

1. Registrants

In terms of the impact of Bill C-31 on registrants, the findings are not unexpected or unusual. Since Bill C-31 sought to re-establish reserve status and band membership, it is not surprising that those who registered did so because of personal identity and cultural heritage. Health and education benefits were also important to those who registered; however, many of those surveyed who lived off the reserve at the time, expressed some concern about what life on the reserve would be like for them. Lack of employment, unavailability of housing, adjustment problems and the stigma of being a Bill C-31 registrant, deepened their concerns about moving back to the reserve or moving to a reserve for the first time.

2. Band and Reserve Communities

In the study of band and community attitudes toward Bill C-31, the general opinion was one of disdain. Many Aboriginal people saw the amendments as part of an assimilation process. They were concerned that individuals who they regarded as non-Indians (non-Native children adopted by Native people) would dilute the overall Native culture with non-Native ethnocentric attitudes if they were allowed residency. There were also problems arising from a perceived inequality of treatment because of the second generation cut-off clause. Some Aboriginal people viewed this clause as an attempt by government to limit the size of the status Indian population. A more general criticism, or rather an indictment of the process by which Bill C-31 came into being, addressed the lack of Aboriginal participation in its formulation.

The infusion of new applicants also increased band operating costs and exacerbated the already existing housing shortage. While more houses could be built, some bands did not want to see available land used for housing. The increased number of individuals also had negative and positive impacts on the educational system. Negative effects included financial strain on funding availability; positive effects included the motivation of regular band members by registrants to take advantage of educational benefits.

Overall, the study found that there were both positive and negative consequences for bands because of Bill C-31. The impact has been more pronounced in some areas and less in others. This is due to the fact that some bands "accepted" more registrants than others, and this had an impact on the availability of resources to accommodate them.

3. Off-Reserve Aboriginal Communities

The introduction of the Bill also caused problems in terms of control over band membership. Given that the bands had control over membership, difficulties arose when a particular band did not recognize the registrant as a member, despite the fact that the Department of Indian Affairs and Northern Development (DIAND) did. It is important to realize that while an individual may be a status Indian, if he or she is not living on the reserve, certain benefits may be denied. If the band does not recognize the individual, that person may not become part of the band community and is systematically denied any benefits accruing from reserve residency.

Bands also felt that Bill C-31 recipients were "different". The extent to which this sentiment was expressed in negative terms depended on a number of factors. Acceptance was based on whether the registrants had ever resided on the reserve, whether they had maintained contact with the band, or whether they had relatives living on the reserve. Confusion and lack of understanding regarding benefits and responsibility for program delivery to new registrants further aggravated band members.

4. Government Programs

Aboriginal service organizations expressed frustration with the federal government's disregard (in terms of financial and support assistance) for the increased workload (approximately 30%) that the organizations faced in assisting registrants pursuing reserve status. It is alleged that the government severely underestimated the number of individuals who would seek status and, once having recognized the problem, did little to relieve the situation. Some service organizations, however, felt that the Department had done a satisfactory job in helping them with their concerns.

These studies show that, while the government's intentions were good, the amendments to the *Indian Act* created additional problems while removing others.

RECOMMENDATIONS

This study does not contain any official recommendations. This is consistent with DIAND's desire to create an information base concerning the effects of Bill C-31, rather than a government policy. In Module 1 (Aboriginal Inquiry), however, the study does agree with Aboriginal groups who advocate greater Indian participation in government decision making with respect to such policies as Bill C-31. This approach is viewed as the only way equitable solutions can be reached.

▲ Indian Policing Policy Review: Task Force Report

AUTHOR: Department of Indian Affairs and Northern Development
YEAR: 1990
ABORIGINAL GROUP: First Nations
TOPIC: Administration of Justice
SUB-TOPIC: law enforcement
SOURCE: Federal Department

BACKGROUND

Indian communities, like others, have in recent years experienced a rapid increase in crime. Indian leaders were becoming increasingly concerned about the adequacy of policing services and the ability of existing services to deal with the unique needs of Indian communities. At the same time, the federal, provincial and territorial governments were concerned with the increasing costs associated with policing on reserves. The lack of a co-ordinated policy framework in the area of on-reserve policing prompted Treasury Board to identify the need for a comprehensive review.

PURPOSE

The purpose of the Task Force was to outline current issues, problems and findings in relation to the provision of policing services to Indian communities. The Task Force was asked to develop and propose a set of principles which would then guide more detailed discussions prior to the articulation of a new federal policy for on-reserve policing.

ISSUES AND FINDINGS

Three areas were addressed in the findings:

1. needs and programs;
2. Indian participation; and
3. government roles and responsibilities.

In the area of policing needs and programs, it was determined that there were two primary objectives:

1. provision of comparable levels of service; and

2. culturally sensitive service delivery and service delivery which meets the special requirements of Indian communities. Some of the identifiable strengths of successful programs, such as the RCMP and Ontario Special Constables programs, were identified as access to experience and established training, and operational and support infrastructure. The need for flexibility within programs to meet the varying needs of distinct communities was emphasized.

In the area of Indian participation, the Task Force examined what the government position should be and how to provide for greater participation. It was suggested that any governing structures to be established should be consistent with the objectives of Indian self-government, and a police force should reflect the composition of the community it serves. Further, policing services should be independent of band government authority, but accountable to the community.

The last issue area examined was that of government roles and responsibilities. The roles of different parties in the provision of policing services to Indian reserves was examined, as was the question of what specifically the future federal role in this area should be. It was determined that federal, Indian, provincial and territorial governments all had a legitimate and valuable role to play. Provincial and territorial governments had responsibility for establishing suitable policing legislation and for the provision of policing services on-reserve. The federal government's role was seen to be in supporting Indian-specific policing initiatives and programs, with Indian governments increasingly becoming involved in the management and administration of policing services.

RECOMMENDATIONS

Although no formal recommendations were made, the Task Force reached several conclusions. In the area of programs and needs, the Task Force concluded that the parties should consult and negotiate the issues of access to policing services, access to culturally sensitive policing services, provision of services meeting regional standards (which include extension to remote communities) and, the jurisdiction of constables.

In the area of Indian participation, the Task Force concluded that the federal government should ensure greater participation and that policing should be included in the negotiation of self-government arrangements.

In respect of government roles and responsibilities it was determined that the federal government should continue to contribute financial resources to on-reserve policing services that meet mutually agreed criteria. In applying new policy, the federal government should seek to be consistent in its level of financial participation.

▲ New Commitment: Statement of the Canadian Human Rights Commission on Federal Aboriginal Policy

AUTHOR: Canadian Human Rights Commission
YEAR: 1990
ABORIGINAL GROUP: All Aboriginal Peoples, Urban Aboriginal People
TOPICS: Self-Government, Federal Government/Aboriginal Relations, Provincial Government/Aboriginal Relations, Treaty Land Entitlement, Claims, Land Use, Development and Management, Economic Development, Health, Education, Programs and Services
SOURCE: Federal Agency

BACKGROUND

Further to the confrontations at Kanesatake and Kahnawake, Oka, and the Mercier Bridge, the Canadian Human Rights Commission, through this statement, brings further attention to the many issues and concerns facing Canada's Aboriginal peoples.

PURPOSE

The purpose of this statement by the Human Rights Commission is to call upon the federal government to re-establish as a priority the settlement of the major issues and concerns facing Aboriginal peoples.

ISSUES AND FINDINGS

At issue throughout the statement is the fact that Aboriginal affairs have not been treated with the priority they deserve by the federal and provincial governments.

A comprehensive analysis of the main issues facing Aboriginal peoples was considered beyond the scope of the report. The Human Rights Commission did, however, identify three key areas of interest:

1. Aboriginal Claims

The Commission believes the current process is flawed. Its criticism is directed toward the fact that the present system is heavily weighted in favour of the government. A claim can be rejected solely on the legal advice of the Department of Justice, without any opportunity for Aboriginal peoples to test the validity of that advice. The Commission was further troubled by the requirement that claimants relinquish their Aboriginal rights and title in return for the benefits provided in an agreement.

2. Self-Government

The Commission is critical of both the federal and provincial governments for failing to move more quickly in granting an increased measure of control for Aboriginal peoples over their own affairs, despite the number of public and parliamentary reports that have been written over the past decade that recognize that self-government is urgently required.

The Commission also takes issue with the operation of the Department of Indian Affairs and Northern Development (DIAND). It feels that the time has come to dismantle the old bureaucratic structures of the past and replace them with a more modern organization that reflects the fact that many Aboriginal communities now manage the great majority of programs themselves.

3. Economic Self-Sufficiency

The Canadian Human Rights Commission also recognizes the governments' failure to provide policy options to Aboriginal peoples that will allow them to share in the economic prosperity of this country. The Commission is critical of the policies that have allowed for the shrinking of the land bases of Aboriginal peoples through expropriation. Furthermore, the Commission recognizes the government's lack of policy direction in the battles against poverty, ill health and illiteracy problems that Aboriginal peoples face not only on reserves but in many urban centres.

RECOMMENDATIONS

One of the major recommendations made by the Commission is the creation of a new forum to discuss the many diverse issues and problems facing our

Aboriginal peoples. The statement calls upon the government to form a Royal Commission to address these concerns. Other recommendations may be categorized as follows:

1. Aboriginal Claims

The Commission calls for the creation of a third body, for example, an Independent Claims Commission, to deal with land claims in the future. It also recommends that land claims policy recognize the need to confirm and clarify Aboriginal rights, rather than to extinguish them.

2. Self-Government

The Commission recommends that the Canadian government commit itself to the replacement of the outdated *Indian Act* regime through appropriate constitutional and legislative action that recognizes the unique status of Aboriginal peoples. The Commission further recommends that serious consideration be given to replacing DIAND with a new agency for Aboriginal-federal relations.

3. Economic Self-Sufficiency

The recommendations call for the government vigorously to pursue the goal of ensuring that the fundamental needs of all reserve communities are met in this decade and that a policy is enunciated that clearly incorporates the special needs of urban Aboriginal people.

▲ Report of the Joint National Committee on Aboriginal AIDS Education and Prevention (Volume 1: Findings Document; Volume 2: Recommendations for a National Strategy on Aboriginal AIDS Education and Prevention)

AUTHOR: Joint National Committee on Aboriginal AIDS Education and Prevention

YEAR: 1990

ABORIGINAL GROUP: All Aboriginal Peoples

TOPIC: Health

SUB-TOPIC: preventive health education

SOURCE: Bipartite Committee (Federal/Aboriginal)

BACKGROUND

The Joint National Committee on Aboriginal AIDS Education and Prevention was created in 1989 as a partnership which included representatives from 11national Aboriginal organizations, Health and Welfare Canada and the Department of Indian Affairs and Northern Development.

PURPOSE

The mandate of the Joint National Committee (JNC) was to develop a culturally appropriate National Aboriginal AIDS Education and Prevention Strategy. The object of the strategy was to guide Aboriginal governments, the Federal Centre for AIDS and others in determining the most effective measures in the battle against AIDS in Aboriginal communities.

ISSUES AND FINDINGS

1. The research clearly indicated that a unique strategy was required to meet the needs of Aboriginal people in AIDS education and prevention because of their cultural, social, political, geographic and linguistic differences.

   It was found that unlike mainstream Canada, the Aboriginal population shared common characteristics with those countries defined by the World Health Organization as having a high rate of HIV infection (which leads to AIDS), and where the predominant means of transmission was through heterosexual contact. The most notable common characteristic was the high incidence of sexually transmitted diseases (STDs).

   Aboriginal youth were perceived to be at high risk of acquiring HIV infection because they were sexually active and often unprotected as evidenced by the high number of teenage pregnancies; they were under the strain of peer pressure to abuse alcohol; some had been sexually abused; and many were homeless, transient and street dwellers.

2. It was felt that a priority should be given to community-based programs, given that the circumstances of Aboriginal communities were heterogeneous and varied widely from each other.

3. Aboriginal organizations cited a lack of financial resources as the major obstacle to developing and delivering effective AIDS prevention programs. It was also found that many groups were unaware of funding available to them.

4. Although many Aboriginal communities expressed interest in developing and delivering AIDS education and prevention programs, they lacked the required skills.

5. There was a need to train Aboriginal resource people because the AIDS prevention message would be more effectively delivered by Aboriginal people to Aboriginal people.

6. An urgent need for Aboriginal-specific information was identified due to the lack of basic information on AIDS and its potential impact on the Aboriginal community. These messages would stimulate awareness and discussion by presenting ideas on how individuals and communities can prevent the spread of HIV. Effective messages to individuals who may be at greater risk were also considered important.

7. The research indicated that without the support of the entire community, sustained behavioural change was not a realistic goal. It was viewed as critical that the whole community understand that the threat of HIV transmission was not limited to homosexual/bisexual or injection drug use activities.

8. It was found that HIV data and demographic information, which were essential to monitoring the spread of the disease, program planning and evaluation and resource allocation, were incomplete and lacking in Aboriginal communities. It was also seen as important that individuals have knowledge of whether they are HIV positive so as not to spread the disease.

9. Discrimination and mistrust of the medical system were cited by Aboriginal people as major obstacles to seeking timely health care services. Some Aboriginal people expressed fear that medical staff would be judgemental.

10. The report emphasized that the preventive message would go unheeded if condoms and needle exchange programs were not available.

11. Knowledge, attitude and behaviour (KAB) studies were important tools for evaluating effectiveness and providing specific information to facilitate planning.

12. There were few historical or anthropological accounts of how Aboriginal people viewed sexuality and how the arrival and imposition of foreign values might have altered those views. It was believed that a thorough understanding of the traditional sexuality of Aboriginal people may result in culturally motivated behaviour change.

13. Although little is known of the subject, there was reason to believe that the holistic nature of traditional medicine may be beneficial for an HIV-infected person. There had been claims that traditional medicine had successfully delayed the progress of HIV diseases and AIDS.

14. The economic impact of AIDS on a small community had the potential to be disastrous because AIDS had its greatest impact on the 25-39 year-old age group.

15. The implications of the federal government's policy to transfer responsibility for medical services to First Nations governments needed to be critically examined in terms of future needs. Current transfer funding formulae did not cover the costs of medical services associated with AIDS.

16. Aboriginal people in Canada shared common concerns and problems vis-à-vis HIV infection and AIDS with Indigenous people in other countries. It was viewed as important that information be shared among these groups.

17. It was recognized that the strategy should be monitored continually because new initiatives would likely emerge, since knowledge about HIV infection and AIDS was always growing.

RECOMMENDATIONS

The JNC recommended that a specific strategy for Aboriginal AIDS education and prevention be developed and implemented by all levels of government, given the unique needs of Aboriginal populations. It was proposed that activities related to the strategy be community-based both in design and delivery.

The report proposed that available financial resources be allocated to the community-based groups and that information on funding availability be widely publicized and accessible.

The authors recommended that Aboriginal human resources be developed through training and information sharing with other communities and agencies involved in AIDS education and prevention. Linkages established between non-Aboriginal and Aboriginal community groups were promoted.

Due to the lack of awareness in Aboriginal communities about AIDS issues, it was proposed that general awareness messages be developed for use by Aboriginal groups in Canada. It was also recommended that AIDS education and prevention efforts be targeted at specific groups that may be at greater risk; i.e., Aboriginal youth (street youth).

AIDS education and prevention activities should be designed for the whole community, including elders, parents, children, policy makers and service providers.

The JNC recommended that HIV seroprevalence studies be undertaken within Aboriginal communities to monitor disease occurrence, within the ethical guidelines established by Somerville and Gilmore in 1988. It was also stated that free HIV testing should be made available to all Aboriginal people across the country.

It was proposed that the obstacles posed by the health care system, as identified by Aboriginal groups, be specifically documented and steps taken to remove them.

The report recommended a number of research areas, including KAB studies, Aboriginal sexuality, the role of traditional medicine and healing in AIDS, economic impact of AIDS analysis and the implications of AIDS on the Health Transfer from the federal government to the First Nations governments.

The JNC proposed that the federal government financially support the involvement of Canada's Aboriginal peoples in an international conference on Indigenous people and AIDS.

Finally, the authors recommended that a mechanism be implemented to facilitate the ongoing involvement of Aboriginal people in monitoring the effectiveness of the National AIDS Strategy.

▲ Unfinished Business: An Agenda for All Canadians in the 1990s

AUTHOR: Standing Committee on Aboriginal Affairs, Chair, Ken Hughes, M.P.

YEAR: 1990

ABORIGINAL GROUP: All Aboriginal Peoples

TOPICS: Self-Government, Constitution, Federal/Aboriginal Relations

SUB-TOPICS: negotiation structures and processes, implementation, treaties, policy, institutions

SOURCE: House of Commons Committee

BACKGROUND

The Standing Committee on Aboriginal Affairs completed a series of hearings intended to gauge the priorities and key policy concerns of Aboriginal people at the national level. It was apparent that the quality of life for most Aboriginal peoples in Canada was still far from satisfactory and that some very important political, legal and constitutional issues remained unsolved. In particular, Meech

Lake was still alive, with no provisions for the entrenchment of Aboriginal rights.

PURPOSE

The main purpose of the report was to share some of the understanding that the Committee had accumulated and provide an introductory overview of Aboriginal affairs. It is emphasized that the report was not intended to provide recommendations.

ISSUES AND FINDINGS

The document identified self-government as an overriding area of concern and broke it down into sub-topics, recognizing their interrelatedness. These topics were:

1. land issues;
2. constitutional issues;
3. treaty rights;
4. federal/Aboriginal relations;
5. justice; and
6. international treaties.

The report identified further issues that were not directly related to self-government. They were

7. Aboriginal women;
8. off-reserve Aboriginal people;
9. the environment;
10. social services;
11. northern issues;
12. traditional economy; and
13. human rights issues.

The process of resolving land issues was thought to be too slow, with problems identified in the definition of Aboriginal legal interests in land.

There were two aspects to the constitutional issue:

1. Aboriginal peoples wanted to emphasize to the Canadian public the need to re-start constitutional discussions regarding the Meech Lake Accord, and the distinct society clause for Quebec in particular; and

2. with respect to the provision of self-government, it was felt that the federal government should expand its activity under s.91(24) of the *Constitution Act, 1867.*

With regard to treaty rights and relations with treaty nations, there were three topics that were identified as important:

1. the spirit and intent of the treaties were not being honoured by the federal government;

2. specific claims policy was inadequate to the task of dealing with the types of political and legal rights being claimed by treaty people; and

3. there was no dispute mechanism in relation to treaties.

The concerns expressed regarding federal/Aboriginal relations had two aspects:

1. relations with the federal government in general; and

2. relations with the Department of Indian Affairs and Northern Development (DIAND) in particular.

The issue of renewing the trust relationship with the federal government in a manner consistent with Aboriginal self-government aspirations was given prominence.

There were a number of problems identified specifically in relation to DIAND:

1. It was felt that the parameters of authority set out for self-government negotiation policy were not at a sufficiently high level.

2. Many Aboriginal organizations expressed uncertainty about the Department's Lands, Revenues and Trusts (LRT) review.

3. There was continuing controversy concerning Bill C-31.

4. Fiscal arrangements were too complex and had been developed in an ad hoc manner.

5. DIAND had a poor consultation record and a history of disputes with the Aboriginal community.

The report noted that several provinces had just completed or were in the process of conducting inquiries concerning justice and Aboriginal peoples, and that they had revealed problems in all aspects of the justice system.

The Committee referred to Canadian court decisions that noted that international treaties have often had a negative impact on the rights of Aboriginal people; i.e., the *Migratory Birds Convention Act*, and that the legitimacy of such agreements was now in question.

The Committee expressed awareness of the concerns of Aboriginal women, but noted that the Native Women's Association had been unable to appear during these set of hearings.

The fact that off-reserve and non-status Indians have less access to government services was identified as an issue requiring urgent attention. The quality of life of many urban Aboriginal people was described as shockingly poor.

With regard to the environment, it was noted that Aboriginal peoples continue to experience devastating effects in relation to the development of mega-projects. The need for a resolution to the fundamental question of how competing and often incompatible values might be mediated and the need for consultation with Aboriginal communities were identified.

Issues such as housing, education, and health and welfare were raised. The existence of a housing crisis was noted as requiring urgent attention. Aboriginal peoples' desire for control over education and child care was highlighted.

The complexity of northern issues was noted, with particular reference to Inuit concerns about circumpolar matters and the division of powers among federal, provincial and territorial governments.

The critical importance of the traditional economy to Aboriginal cultures was emphasized, as was the threat to traditional pursuits from animal rights activists.

The Committee outlined four human rights issues involving Aboriginal people:

1. discrimination and employment equity;
2. Aboriginal people in the justice system;
3. international human rights initiatives; and
4. women's equality rights under the *Indian Act*.

RECOMMENDATIONS

The following are not formal recommendations, but suggestions that the Committee heard from its witnesses. Not all the issues identified have corresponding suggestions.

A recurring suggestion with regard to land claims was that claims processes, including the funding support arrangements, should be managed or monitored by a body independent of the department of Indian Affairs and the Department of Justice.

The expansion of federal activity under section 91(24) of the *Constitution Act, 1867* was also a recommendation of the Special Parliamentary Committee on Indian self-government. Federal legislative activity would encompass new subject matters affecting Aboriginal people that would otherwise fall under provincial jurisdiction.

Several sources recommended that some form of independent claims tribunal be established to deal with matters concerning treaty rights.

With regard to fiscal arrangements, it was suggested that a review of the current system of financing Aboriginal governments was needed.

The Committee recommended that there be a study conducted on consultation processes. Specifically, it suggested that views in the Aboriginal community and in government be canvassed on:

1. consultation as part of the process of policy development;

2. dispute resolution mechanisms for discretionary programs;

3. alternative mechanisms, rather than litigation, to resolve disputes over rights; and

4. how to deal with disputes that are a combination of (2) and (3).

The report stated that the federal government had an important role in reviewing provincial justice inquiries from a national perspective.

▲ You Took My Talk: Aboriginal Literacy and Empowerment. Fourth Report of the Standing Committee on Aboriginal Affairs

AUTHOR: Standing Committee on Aboriginal Affairs, Chair, Ken Hughes, M.P.

YEAR: 1990

ABORIGINAL GROUP: All Aboriginal Peoples

TOPICS: Education, Language, Cultural Affairs

SUB-TOPICS: primary and secondary education, adult education, curriculum, fiscal relations/responsibilities

SOURCE: House of Commons Committee

BACKGROUND

This is the fourth report to the House of Commons of the Standing Committee on Aboriginal Affairs. After a series of general consultation meetings with national organizations representing Aboriginal peoples, the Committee decided to study literacy as a short-term project. Public hearings were held from April 26, 1990, to June 20, 1990, in Ottawa, Vancouver, the Siksika Reserve (Alberta), Regina, Winnipeg and Halifax. A total of 68 submissions were received.

PURPOSE

The fact that 1990 was International Literacy Year brought the issue to the attention of the Committee. The Committee sought to discover how literacy affected issues such as economic development, self-government, and quality of life in general. It also investigated concerns about quality of elementary and secondary education, and access to education.

ISSUES AND FINDINGS

According to the Committee, the major issue appears to be the lack of community-based schools. The Committee found that the experiences of parents in residential schools may have caused parents to pass on negative attitudes about non-community education to their children. Furthermore, the non-community schools usually lack relevant curriculum and do not offer instruction in Aboriginal languages.

The Committee also investigated the number of Aboriginal languages that have been lost or are in danger of being lost. They discovered that little was being done to preserve these languages and the cultural traditions that they encompass.

The Committee addressed the issue of literacy in terms of empowerment and potential gains in self-esteem. It found that there is an unresolved intergovernmental jurisdictional issue concerning who is responsible for Aboriginal education.

Finally the Committee sought to determine the features of an effective literacy program. It found that the main requirements are that the programs be community-based and community-controlled, that they reaffirm the learners' language, and that the final goal be to enable students to function in their Aboriginal community and in the non-Aboriginal community.

RECOMMENDATIONS

There are 17 recommendations in this report, the most significant of which are as follows:

1. that the federal, as well as territorial and provincial governments, support mother tongue literacy among all Aboriginal peoples and that an institute or foundation be established to promote the survival of Aboriginal languages;

2. that all self-government legislation be translated into the relevant Aboriginal language as well as French and English;

3. that a National Task Force on Aboriginal Education be established to look at issues such as curriculum, Aboriginal language instruction, literacy and barriers to employment;

4. that Aboriginal peoples be included in the negotiation of Master Tuition Agreements and there be co-operation between federal and provincial governments in the resolution of jurisdictional questions pertaining to education;

5. that long-term funding to preserve Aboriginal languages be initiated within two years;

6. that communities be empowered to achieve their own literacy goals where possible and to develop their own curriculum; and

7. that the Correctional Service of Canada strengthen its literacy programs for the Aboriginal inmate population and that Friendship Centres be considered a key element in the delivery of literacy programs.

1991

▲ Building a New Relationship with First Nations in British Columbia: Canada's Response to the Report of the British Columbia Claims Task Force

AUTHOR: Department of Indian Affairs and Northern Development

YEAR: 1991

ABORIGINAL GROUP: First Nations

TOPICS: Federal Government/Aboriginal Relations, Self-Government, Claims, Treaty Land Entitlement

SUB-TOPICS: treaties, negotiation structures and processes, claims, commissions/structures/negotiation processes, comprehensive claims, specific claims, commission/institutions

SOURCE: Federal Department

BACKGROUND

On September 25, 1990, Prime Minister Brian Mulroney announced the federal government's Native Agenda. One of the four pillars of this agenda was the "fair and timely resolution of Native land claims in Canada". British Columbia faces special challenges in this area given that over 75% of outstanding comprehensive claims in Canada involve British Columbia First Nations. In order to address these difficulties, the federal and provincial governments, and British Columbia First Nations, created a joint task force to review and make recommendations on the scope, organization and process for the effective negotiation of comprehensive claims in British Columbia. The British Columbia Claims Task Force, was created in December 1990, and released a unanimous report, with 19 recommendations, on July 3, 1991.

PURPOSE

This document is the federal government's response to the 19 recommendations of the British Columbia Claims Task Force.

ISSUES AND FINDINGS

The document delineates the federal government's response to two major sets of recommendations made by the Task Force: one set of recommendations concerns the proposed negotiating process; the other concerns the proposed scope of the negotiations.

1. Proposed Negotiating Process

(a) The Federal Contribution

The federal government accepts the recommendations which relate to its role in the negotiating process. This acceptance entails the provision of resources to support an accelerated tripartite process, including the establishment of a major federal office in British Columbia, the appointment of negotiators, and the assurance of co-operation from other federal departments in the resolution of claims.

(b) The Provincial Contribution

The document proposes that the overall costs be shared, with the federal government contributing 70% of the financial costs of settlement and the provincial government providing 30% of the financial costs, plus land and resources.

(c) The British Columbia Treaty Commission

The federal government supports the creation of an independent treaty commission in British Columbia, to be established by agreement with the province and First Nations, as soon as a mandate and cost-sharing has been arranged. The Commission is to facilitate rather than negotiate settlement. The federal government also outlines its support for a system of funding whereby the Commission would use established criteria to allocate funds to support First Nations participation in the claims negotiations.

2. Proposed Scope of Negotiations

The report outlines the areas which the federal government considers to be within the scope of negotiations: land and resource arrangements, self-government arrangements, and the participation of First Nations. With regard to the participation of First Nations, the federal government commits itself to negotiation with the 20 British Columbia First Nations whose comprehensive claims have been accepted for negotiation, and agrees to deal with all other British Columbia First Nations through the Treaty Commission. The federal government further agrees to honour existing treaty rights, and to no longer require British Columbia First Nations to demonstrate continuing use of resources in order to begin negotiations.

The report contends that specific claims (concerning both fulfilment of treaties or mismanagement of Indian land or resources) will continue to be dealt with using a separate, previously established process. Other issues which call for solutions, but are not part of the formal treaties, will be pursued by the federal government and First Nations through separate discussions.

RECOMMENDATIONS

The document makes no formal recommendations. It does, however, emphasize the priority which the federal government places on a well-informed public as a key factor in the success and fairness of the process. To this end, the report outlines the federal government's commitment to support a comprehensive public education and information program directed at all residents of the province, to be developed and implemented in co-operation with the province and with British Columbia First Nations.

▲ Creating Choices: The Report of the Task Force on Federally Sentenced Women

AUTHOR: Task Force on Federally Sentenced Women
YEAR: 1991
ABORIGINAL GROUP: All Aboriginal Peoples, Aboriginal Women
TOPIC: Administration of Justice
SUB-TOPIC: corrections
SOURCE: Bipartite Commission (Federal/Non-Governmental Organization)

BACKGROUND

The Task Force on Federally Sentenced Women was established in March 1989 by the Commissioner of Correctional Service Canada, in collaboration with the Canadian Association of Elizabeth Fry Societies.

The Report cites several factors which contributed to the need for the Task Force: feminist analyses of the problems of federally sentenced women had gained credibility; Aboriginal people were demanding more control over justice for their people; a series of Charter challenges, primarily related to the inequality of services for male and female inmates; recommendations from the Daubney Report to close Prison for Women; the adoption of the Mission of the Correctional Service of Canada which embodies a commitment to ensure that the needs of federally sentenced women are met; the Task Force on Community and Institutional Programs which called for improved programming for federally sentenced women; and recent tragedies within the Prison for Women, including suicides and the manifestation of general unrest.

The Task Force also responded to a series of government commissions and task forces since 1934 which looked at the problems of federally sentenced women. These reports emphasized the following problems: the inadequacy of Prison for Women; the excessive security requirements characteristic of prisons for women; the lack of programming, particulary in the areas of substance abuse, vocational training, and pre- and post-release planning; the isolation of federally sentenced women from their families; the unmet needs of francophone women; the unmet needs of Aboriginal women; the need for shared responsibility with the provinces and the community; and the ineffectiveness of incarceration as a means of promoting rehabilitation.

PURPOSE

The mandate of the Task Force on Federally Sentenced Women required members to examine the correctional management of federally sentenced women from the commencement of sentence to the date of warrant expiry, and to develop a policy and a plan which would guide and direct this process in a manner that is responsive to the unique and special needs of this group.

The Task Force Report is recognized by the Aboriginal members of the Task Force as the first report on corrections to acknowledge the Aboriginal voice and experience, and it involved significant input from Aboriginal women, both as members of Aboriginal organizations and as representatives of federally sentenced Aboriginal women.

ISSUES AND FINDINGS

The Task Force identified several problems integral to the situation of federally sentenced women:

1. **Accommodation:** The Task Force found the Prison for Women to be inadequate as housing for federally sentenced women; it identified excessive security, noise, poor ventilation, and inadequate space for community interaction and program delivery as problems inherent in the existing physical structures. The needs of Aboriginal women were also seen as unmet within the Prison for Women because of its lack of space for ceremonies and contact with elders, and its lack of outdoor access.

2. **Geographic dislocation:** Many federally sentenced women serve their sentences at Prison for Women because they are either ineligible to remain in their home province under an Exchange of Service Agreement or because they chose the Prison for Women because of its broader program profile. These women suffer the additional disadvantage of being separated from the home and families.

3. **Programming:** Programming for federally sentenced women is seen as inadequate: there are gross disparities between the programs offered at provincial institutions, Prison for Women and institutions housing male offenders; and there are limited programs, particularly for long-term offenders and Aboriginal women.

4. **Aboriginal women:** The unique realities of Aboriginal women are not recognized: elders and shamans are not given the same status as chaplains, doctors or psychologists and programs are delivered largely by white males.

5. **Community involvement:** There are few community-based alternatives for federally sentenced women.

RECOMMENDATIONS

The recommendations are intended to provide meaningful choices for women in the more immediate term, but they are set within a context that looks forward to long-term fundamental change in the criminal justice system's response to women in conflict with the law. The changes proposed are intended as a significant step toward the long-term goals of creating and using community-based, restorative justice options and an alternative Aboriginal justice system.

The Task Force proposes a holistic approach which embodies principles of empowerment, meaningful and responsible choices, respect and dignity, a supportive environment and shared responsibility. Consistent with these principles, the Task Force outlines its Guiding Statement of Principle:

> The Correctional Service of Canada, with the support of communities, has the responsibility to create the environment that empowers federally sentenced women to make meaningful and responsible choices in order that they may live with dignity and respect.

The Task Force's recommendations have three primary components which are to be considered as a single recommendation in keeping with the focus on a holistic approach: the establishment of Regional Women's Facilities, the creation of an Aboriginal Healing Lodge, and a Community Release Strategy.

1. **Regional women's facilities:** The recommended plan includes the establishment of five Regional Women's Facilities across Canada, to be located in or near Halifax, Montreal, central/southwestern Ontario, Edmonton and the lower mainland of British Columbia; these facilities are to be completed by the fiscal year 1993-94. The facilities will provide a variety of programs, including programs for Aboriginal peoples. Aboriginal programs would include unrestricted access by elders, indoor and outdoor space for ceremonies and gatherings and dedicated space for a sweat lodge. Native Studies courses would be facilitated by contracts with Aboriginal communities and organizations. Some staff would be of Aboriginal descent and all staff must be sensitive to the spirituality and cultural priorities of Aboriginal prisoners.

2. **Aboriginal healing lodge:** A Healing Lodge where Aboriginal federally sentenced women may serve all or part of their sentences, will be established in a prairie location acceptable to both Aboriginal communities and the Correctional Service of Canada. The design, programming and operation of the Healing Lodge will be based on a holistic approach to the needs of federally sentenced Aboriginal women; it will include the involvement of elders and healers, an outreach program to facilitate community release, non-hierarchical administration, and the recruitment of Aboriginal staff who will act as positive role models for the women serving sentences.

3. **Community release strategy:** The plan recommends the establishment of additional community release centres for women in more communities across Canada. These centres will include traditional halfway houses, Aboriginal centres, satellite units, home placements, addiction treatment centres, and multi-use women's centres. The community release centres will offer a wide variety of programs and services to women who no longer need, or are legally required to be held in closed custody.

▲ Pathways to Success: Aboriginal Employment and Training Strategy

AUTHOR: Employment and Immigration Canada, Aboriginal Employment and Training Working Group

YEAR: 1991

ABORIGINAL GROUP: All Aboriginal Peoples

TOPICS: Employment Development, Education, Federal Government/Aboriginal Relations, Community Institutions

SUB-TOPICS: training/skills development, discrimination, adult, vocational/training, facilities/institutions, policy

SOURCE: Federal Department

BACKGROUND

Aboriginal organizations had expressed concern about the role of Employment and Immigration Canada (EIC) in Aboriginal human resource development and the effectiveness of its employment and training programs in meeting their needs. To address these concerns, EIC established the Aboriginal Employment and Training Working Group (AETWG). The AETWG consisted of representatives from six national Aboriginal organizations, Aboriginal training professionals from all regions of Canada, and representatives from EIC national headquarters and regional offices. This paper represents the efforts of the Working Group.

PURPOSE

The purpose of the Working Group was to review EIC programs and services for Aboriginal people, participate in the design of new programming, and make recommendations to improve and rationalize the entire Aboriginal training and employment process.

ISSUES AND FINDINGS

The document consists of two separate papers. The Background Paper provides information on EIC programs and services for Aboriginal people, and examines the extent to which these programs and services have met the needs of Aboriginal peoples. The Policy and Implementation Paper contains five partnership principles aimed primarily at improving the relationship between EIC and Aboriginal peoples. The principles are viewed as the foundation for a co-operative means of improving EIC programs and are put forth as the recommendations of the Working Group.

The Background Paper is divided into 11 chapters, each focusing on a different program or aspect of the Aboriginal employment and training system.

1. Problems and Strategies

The report describes the overall poor employment and earnings situation of Aboriginal people, with particular emphasis on the difficulties faced by Aboriginal women. EIC reported that its training and employment efforts have been only half as successful with Aboriginal participants as with the non-Aboriginal participants in its programs. In order to be successful, the Working Group concluded, delivery and control of training and re-employment activities should be in the hands of Aboriginal communities and organizations.

2. Review of the Canadian Jobs Strategy (CJS)

Aboriginal groups expressed a number of concerns about the CJS program:

(a) CJS programs did not encourage the development of the human resource planning capacity of Aboriginal organizations and communities;

(b) Aboriginal groups were often forced to make their training needs correspond to CJS requirements;

(c) CJS programs were frequently not designed to meet the particular needs or situations of Aboriginal clients and communities;

(d) the duration of most EIC programs did not allow participants enough time to improve their literacy and vocational skills;

(e) CJS programs did not incorporate literacy work into their training programs;

(f) there was poor participation of Aboriginal groups in the early stages of setting CJS budget and program priorities; and

(g) the existing year-to-year budget and resource planning cycle prevented people from taking a long-term view.

3. Services

The Working Group found that there are often negative perceptions held by Aboriginal people concerning the consistency of service delivery by EIC's Canada Employment Centres (CECs). It found that basic cultural differences account for many of the difficulties, but the size, formality and procedures of most CECs were also seen to be contributing factors. The relative freedom of individual CECs to apply rules and regulations selectively depending on client needs, had led many Aboriginal people to believe that services were arbitrary and inconsistent. The Working Group concluded that it may be impossible to overcome these perceptions given the size and nature of EIC's organizational network and the number of delivery points to Aboriginal groups. EIC Outreach programs might help, but overall, the Working Group felt the best solution would be to place the responsibility for delivery of services with Aboriginal community-based organizations and groups.

4. Employment Equity

According to the Background Paper, the success of employment equity for Aboriginal people has been poor, despite the finding that there has been a significant pool of appropriately qualified Aboriginal people available for positions. To address this problem, the Working Group felt that a number of EIC programs, such as the Native Internship Program and the Designated Group Retention Program, might be used more extensively. The need for greater consultation and co-ordination of local human resource objectives with employment equity policies was also recognized.

5. Training Allowance

Training allowances to participants of training programs were found to be inadequate for urban Aboriginal people who often must cope with a high cost of living. For single mothers, whose children require daycare, the allowance was considered insufficient to cover this cost alone. The Working Group concluded that training allowances must be large enough so as not to provide a disincentive to engage in training programs.

6. Unemployment Insurance Developmental Uses

The report indicates that any redirection of Aboriginal people from unemployment insurance (UI) income support to training programs would have minimal effects on the labour force development needs of on-reserve Indians, as only a small percentage of Aboriginal UI recipients live on-reserve. The Working Group found that UI developmental mechanisms inhibit Aboriginal people from accessing training programs because of limitations on the use of UI benefits for educational up-grading and inappropriate participation requirements in job creation programs.

7. Social Assistance Recipient Training

Efforts by all levels of government to move people off passive social assistance programs to active programs, such as job training, began in 1985 with the "Four Cornered Strategy". This strategy allowed EIC and the Canada Assistance Plan to reallocate social assistance funds to employment/training programs. The Working Group, however, found it difficult to assess the effects of this program, as the provinces did not specifically track Aboriginal clients.

8. Canadian Aboriginal Economic Development Strategy (CAEDS)

In April 1989, the government of Canada announced the Canadian Aboriginal Economic Development Strategy (CAEDS). CAEDS was to establish a new co-ordination mechanism between EIC, Indian and Northern Affairs Canada (INAC), and Industry, Science and Technology Canada (ISTC), and to appropriate $873 million over five years to INAC and ISTC for community and business enterprise development programs. The government's initiation of this program did not change EIC's budget, but it did increase its responsibilities. EIC committed itself to CAEDS objectives: involving Aboriginal people in EIC's local planning strategy; setting participation rates of Aboriginal people in EIC programs and services; providing flexibility in programming; distributing resources commensurate with the levels of Aboriginal unemployment; using

Aboriginal institutions to deliver EIC programs and services; and complementing local and provincial programs and services. CAEDS called on EIC to focus on Aboriginal skills development and urban employment through the Canadian Jobs Strategy (CJS). Given that CAEDS is primarily an economic development program as opposed to a human resource development program, EIC's influence has been marginalized among the principal government participants. Furthermore, the addition of urban Aboriginal programs has threatened reallocation of EIC funds from reserve areas to urban areas, thereby creating tension.

9. Native Internship Program (NIP)

NIP provides summer employment opportunities to Aboriginal secondary and post-secondary students. The Working Group found the program to be successful and popular among students and EIC staff.

10. Federal/Provincial Agreements on Training

The Working Group found these agreements to be too rigid, making it difficult for EIC to contract with Aboriginal training institutions for training courses. The agreements failed to provide sufficient authority at the provincial level to ensure that local Aboriginal needs were met. Direct purchases of training programs were subject to CJS program criteria, which continued to have a top-down approach rather than allowing the needs of the trainee to dictate training course purchases. The agreements also failed to provide equity provisions governing Aboriginal apprenticeship training within public institutions.

11. Consultation Mechanisms

The Working Group found a number of regional consultative mechanisms in place, most notably in British Columbia. It also reported that some consultation was occurring through client groups and Local Advisory Councils, and additional avenues for consultation existed through Community Futures Committees and Co-ordinating Groups. Nevertheless, EIC did not have an overall consultation process for Aboriginal participation in policy development and program design. The Working Group suggested that a consistent, community-based consultative process at the national, regional and local EIC levels would improve EIC officials' knowledge of labour market conditions for Aboriginal people and promote Aboriginal issues during planning and programming stages of EIC programs.

RECOMMENDATIONS

The Policy and Implementation Paper contains the Working Group's suggestions for affecting change in EIC's policies and operational procedures to improve the working relationship between EIC and the Aboriginal community. The Working Group attempted to address factors such as regional and local flexibility, joint management processes, effective program and service delivery machinery, appropriate allocation mechanisms, and the specific needs of Aboriginal women.

The Working Group's specific recommendations were based on five partnership principles:

1. **Consultation process and local control of decision making:** The needs and priorities of the Aboriginal community should be addressed and should be apparent in the design, development and implementation of EIC policies that affect them. To ensure this the Working Group proposed the establishment of national, regional and local consultation/management boards.

2. **Delivery mechanisms:** Employment and training programs and services should be managed, operated, conducted and arranged through Aboriginal infrastructures.

3. **Funding mechanisms and institutional development capacity:** Funding mechanisms should be developed which recognize the planning and operational needs of Aboriginal delivery machinery. Successful models exist on which to base these mechanisms.

4. **Employment equity:** The Working Group recommended that EIC aggressively undertake active measures to improve recruitment, training and employment of Aboriginal people both within and outside EIC.

5. **Eligibility for programs and services:** Eligibility decisions should rely more on individual counselling than on strict eligibility criteria.

▲ Reforming Electoral Democracy

AUTHOR: Royal Commission on Electoral Reform and Party Financing, Chair, Pierre Lortie

YEAR: 1991

ABORIGINAL GROUP: All Aboriginal Peoples

171

TOPICS: Federal Government/Aboriginal Relations, Political
Development, Communications/Transportation
SUB-TOPICS: electoral reform, political participation/representation,
television and radio broadcasting
SOURCE: Federal Royal Commission

BACKGROUND

The Royal Commission represents another major attempt to bring
comprehensive reform of the Canadian electoral system. Little, if any, reform
had resulted from past studies on this topic, the most recent being the White
Paper on Election Law reform. Legislation that was proposed based on the
White Paper recommendations (Bill C-79) died on the order paper with the
call of the 1988 federal election.

PURPOSE

The purpose of this Royal Commission was to inquire into and report on the
appropriate principles and processes that should govern the election of
members of the House of Commons and the financing of political parties and
of candidates' campaigns.

Areas examined included current electoral practices, procedures and legislation
in Canada, means by which political parties should be funded, limits to
funding, and how funds may be used; the qualifications of electors and the
compiling of voters lists.

Aboriginal peoples were not specifically mentioned in the mandate of the Royal
Commission. It was not until public hearings were under way that Aboriginal
peoples' concerns came to the attention of the Commissioners.

ISSUES AND FINDINGS

A series of consultations, led by Senator Len Marchand, was set up under the
Royal Commission to study issues concerning Aboriginal peoples and the
electoral process.

Key issues addressed were:

1. representation of Aboriginal peoples in the House of Commons;

2. participation of Aboriginal peoples in the electoral process; and

3. electoral reform in Canada's North.

Throughout the report, the theme of lack of participation by Aboriginal peoples in the electoral system is very evident. There was a sense that the system as it exists in no way facilitates or encourages Aboriginal participation. A number of areas were highlighted: the geographical dispersal of Aboriginal people throughout Canada does not allow for a sense that their votes affect election results, and therefore their interests and concerns are not taken seriously; lower education levels of Aboriginal peoples, who number disproportionately among the poor, the homeless, and the transient, make it difficult, if not impossible, to enumerate or register within the current framework; language problems and the lack of communication with Aboriginal people on issues of the day.

One of the key issues addressed is that of representation in the House of Commons by members of Aboriginal communities. Although they make up 3.5% of the population, only 12 self-identified Aboriginal people have been elected to the more than 10,500 House of Commons seats available since Confederation – 9 of them since 1960.

The third issue addressed in the report was the need for electoral reform in Canada's North. At issue were several key problems: lack of access to free and paid broadcasting; lack of coverage of issues in the various Aboriginal languages; the vast areas to travel and the overall expense of campaigning in the North. Again, it was felt that the system as it exists disadvantaged those who chose to live in large northern constituencies.

RECOMMENDATIONS

One of the key recommendations of the report is the establishment of Aboriginal constituencies. This recommendation addresses both the issues of participation and representation by Aboriginal peoples within the electoral process. The Commission recommendation offers a system to address the problem of under-representation in the House of Commons and accommodates the desire of many Aboriginal peoples for a greater role in Canada's institutions of government.

Aboriginal constituencies would be created in response to the number of Aboriginal voters in a province who choose to register for that purpose. A certain threshold, if attained, would allow for the creation of a constituency. Aboriginal people could choose to vote either in a general or an Aboriginal constituency.

Aboriginal constituencies would be the same as general constituencies in most respects including provisions respecting candidate's qualifications and spending limits; the appointment of returning officers and election officials (including representatives of the Aboriginal communities who can speak the languages and who have been educated in the rules governing the process); principles and procedures for registering voters, advance polling and election day, regular mobile polling stations, special ballots, counting of ballots and reporting results.

Aboriginal people would be consulted and would participate in all these constituency-related functions and activities including the determination of electoral boundaries where there may be more than one constituency per province (boundaries would be considered on the basis of treaty areas, and in recognition of the composition of the Aboriginal population, and local Aboriginal history and relationship to the land).

With respect to the North, the Royal Commission issued a series of recommendations concerning the issue of campaigning in northern communities. They included the use of mobile polls to help reach voters in remote locations and in those communities too small to warrant a regular polling station. As well, voters could vote by a new special ballot that would allow the voter to cast the vote at his or her place of residence.

To resolve the problems associated with campaigning in the north (long distances, uncertain weather, small, scattered communities, culturally and linguistically diverse population) the Commission recommended that candidates have access to 60 minutes of free time and 20 minutes of paid time on the CBC Northern Service (in addition to the time allocated nationally to the political parties). This recommendation was made in recognition that traditional forms of campaigning, which include door-to-door and telephone canvassing, are ineffective in the North, and therefore the increased use of media was to be encouraged.

Candidates in sparsely populated constituencies in the North (an average of fewer than 10 voters per square kilometre) would be allowed to incur additional election expenses of 30 cents per square kilometre in the constituency, up to a limit of 50% of the total election expenses limit. As well, reimbursement of candidates' election expenses would be increased correspondingly.

Collectively, the recommendations of the Royal Commission with respect to Aboriginal and northern peoples were designed to encourage greater access and participation in the electoral system and the institutions of governance in Canada.

The Commission did not address the issue of self-government but recognized that its recommendations were in no part offered in exchange for the demands of Aboriginal people for self-government.

◆ *Report of the British Columbia Claims Task Force* (1991),
see **Volume 3, British Columbia**.

▲ Report of the Cree-Naskapi Commission

AUTHOR: Cree-Naskapi Commission, Chair, Justice Réjean Paul
YEAR: 1991
ABORIGINAL GROUP: First Nations
TOPICS: Federal Government/Aboriginal Relations, Provincial Government/Aboriginal Relations, Financial Arrangements/Responsibilities/Public Finance, Treaty Land Entitlement, Education
SUB-TOPICS: treaties, jurisdiction, legislation, federal trust responsibilities, claims, fiscal relations/responsibilities
SOURCE: Federal Commission

BACKGROUND

This report is the third biennial report to Parliament on the implementation of the *Cree-Naskapi Act*. It was prepared on the basis of consultation with those directly affected by the Act and with government officials.

PURPOSE

The purpose of this report is to help the Cree and Naskapi and other Aboriginal people to realize their goal of self-government, and to help the government in working with the Cree and Naskapi to remedy the problems facing them and facing all Aboriginal peoples.

ISSUES AND FINDINGS

The issues identified in this report include methods for solving the issues facing Canada and the Aboriginal peoples; a review of past issues; policing and the administration of justice; housing and infrastructure; the Ouje-Bougoumou Cree; the Naskapi Band; implementation of the James Bay and Northern Quebec Agreement; and revisions to the Agreement.

1. Methods for Solving the Issues Facing Canada and Aboriginal Peoples

A new approach to remedying the existing problems is required. Increasingly popular is a call to civil disobedience, which suggests that the traditional methods – government policies, commissions, and Native litigation – have been inadequate. Many Aboriginal people see new or revised policies as an attempt to diffuse discord rather than to solve problems. The government has established Royal Commissions to deal with Aboriginal problems, but the Aboriginal peoples tended to view their mandates as too limited. Although Aboriginal groups are relying more on courts to solve their problems, the courts are only able to provide a legal framework for change and cannot change social values or attitudes.

The approach that the Cree-Naskapi Commission suggests is direct dialogue and negotiation between Aboriginal peoples and governments, coupled with dispute resolution mechanisms to resolve matters when conflicts arise. Its proposed success rests on three rationales: first, it allows Aboriginal people to express their wishes; second, it allows government to find ways to accommodate Aboriginal aspirations; and third, it incorporates a dispute resolution mechanism to overcome the obstacles that have led to previous defeats.

2. Past Issues

The past is seen as important in understanding the present and the future. The problems of training Cree as government personnel and of the lack of funding for operations and maintenance of local governments are ongoing. Land registry based on zoning and regulations are foreign concepts to this people who view land as a collective interest; they do not see it as something to be bought or sold.

3. Policing and the Administration of Justice

Recent inquiries have supported the charges that there is inequitable treatment of Aboriginal people by the criminal justice system. A Cree-developed justice system has been suggested to provide fairer hearings. According to the James Bay and Northern Quebec Agreement and the *Cree-Naskapi (of Quebec) Act*, the Cree communities have responsibility for and entitlement to policing and justice that is responsive to the community being served. At present, the provincial court is the only justice system available to the Cree. Despite the plan to establish a Cree police force, one has not yet been recognized.

4. Housing and Infrastructure

The Cree communities have a housing shortage, resulting in overcrowding, social problems and deterioration of existing housing. Funding is also a problem, in that decisions are made too late in the year to facilitate the transport of equipment and materials.

5. The Ouje-Bougoumou Cree

The Ouje-Bougoumou Cree have been displaced without compensation seven times since 1940 due to mining and forestry developments, and are living in "third-world conditions". The problem is rooted in a disagreement over the cost of construction between government offers and Cree demands. An agreement was reached in December 1990 which included negotiations for a socio-economic fund.

6. The Naskapi Band

The Naskapi Band has established self-government according to the *Cree-Naskapi Act*. An unresolved issue, however, remains, concerning who is responsible for prosecuting Naskapi by-laws – the federal government, the Quebec government, or the Naskapi. The problem is attributable to the conflicting assignment of responsibility, as is outlined in different Acts. Changes to the *Cree-Naskapi Act* have been proposed.

7. Implementation of the James Bay and Northern Quebec Agreement

The Cree report that many parts of the James Bay Agreement remain unfulfilled. The Cree claim that further developments related to the proposed James Bay II hydro-electric development breach the Agreement's provisions. The Cree are attempting to use the courts to implement the Agreement fully. Capital funding is to be based on a framework established by the Cree and the federal government; this framework is to provide for the appointment of a mediator to oversee negotiations and for the recognition of certain principles to govern the process. The Cree also assert that the federal government has an obligation to fund education as a component of the Agreement; the funding is to be comprehensive. The Commission has found that the federal and provincial governments are minimizing their financial obligations.

8. Revisions to the Agreement

The Grand Council of the Crees proposes that the Commission pursue a comprehensive examination of each provision of the Act. Some of the problem areas are quorums, taxation, seizure exemptions, audited financial statements, and trade and commerce.

RECOMMENDATIONS

The Cree-Naskapi Commission has developed some recommendations in their third report. With regard to training, they suggest the use of a community-based inventory of human resources, the incorporation of local cultural and traditional beliefs, and an educational program to enhance knowledge of the various Acts. Funds, such as the Ouje-Bougoumou Socio-Economic Development Fund, are seen as essential by the Commission and should be further developed. Also, in accordance with the Cree, the Commission recommends a comprehensive review of the James Bay Agreement, leading to revisions of the Act, which would best be undertaken by means of a questionnaire distributed to the Cree communities.

▲ Report on Aboriginal Peoples and Criminal Justice: Equality, Respect and the Search for Justice

AUTHOR: Law Reform Commission of Canada
YEAR: 1991
ABORIGINAL GROUP: All Aboriginal Peoples
TOPIC: Administration of Justice
SUB-TOPICS: law enforcement, legal representation, courts, sentencing and remedies, corrections
SOURCE: Federal Agency

BACKGROUND

The Law Reform Commission of Canada historically has advocated a uniform, consistent and comprehensive approach to law reform. This report deviates from that course by proposing reforms specific to Aboriginal peoples. The members of the Commission justify distinct treatment for Aboriginal peoples on the basis of their history of disadvantage and suffering within the criminal justice system and on the basis of their unique constitutional position.

PURPOSE

In June 1990, the minister of justice asked the Commission to study, as a matter of special priority, the *Criminal Code* and related statutes and to examine the extent to which those laws ensure that Aboriginal persons and persons who are members of cultural or religious minorities have equal access to justice and are treated equitably and with respect. In carrying out its general mandate, the Commission was requested by the minister to focus on "the development of new approaches to and new concepts of the law in keeping with and responsive to the changing needs of modern Canadian society and of individual members of that society."

The work was divided into two components: an Aboriginal justice review; and a cultural or religious minorities justice review. This report is therefore the first of two which the Commission submitted in response to the minister's request.

ISSUES AND FINDINGS

The Report, at the outset, makes an important distinction between equal access to justice and equitable treatment and respect, emphasizing that for Aboriginal persons to be treated equitably and respectfully, equal access to justice must encompass greater recognition of the distinctiveness of Aboriginal peoples.

The Report finds that the present system fails Aboriginal peoples and contributes to their difficulties; the system is seen as remote, both in terms of physical separation and in terms of conceptual and cultural distance. This remoteness pervades the following areas:

1. **Recruitment and training:** there is a pervasive lack of knowledge about Aboriginal peoples on the part of justice system personnel that makes the justice system less capable of operating equitably and with respect.

2. **Language difficulties and cultural barriers:** there are language-related problems in the use of interpreters, including the denial of requests for an interpreter if the accused can speak English, the partiality and inadequate training of interpreters, and the fact that many legal concepts have no equivalent words in Aboriginal languages.

3. **Community involvement:** there is a lack of accountability of justice system personnel to the community they serve and a lack of recognition that the actions of the criminal justice system affect not only the offender but the victims and communities as well.

4. **Customary laws and practices:** there is a lack of recognition that customary law can establish a mechanism which is just as effective as statutory law in social control.

5. **Treaty rights in criminal courts:** the primary circumstance in which treaty rights are given meaning is when they are raised in court as a defence to a criminal charge; this procedure is considered demeaning by Aboriginal peoples.

6. **Police:** the police are regarded negatively in Aboriginal communities, as a result of the overpolicing of Aboriginal communities and the large gap that exists between the values and culture of non-Aboriginal police officers and of Aboriginal people.

7. **Prosecutors:** there is a need for a more open process and the exercise of important discretionary powers by Crown prosecutors to reduce distrust and misunderstanding.

8. **Defence counsel:** problems relating to the legal representation of Aboriginal peoples include a lack of awareness or understanding of legal aid services, inequities in legal aid eligibility guidelines, and unfamiliarity of defence counsel with Aboriginal issues or culture.

9. **Courts:** the courts are almost invariably located outside Aboriginal communities; the judges, prosecutors, defence lawyers and courts staff are almost all non-Aboriginal; and when court officials are flown in to remote communities on the same plane, there is the sense that they are on the same side and have already decided the outcome of upcoming cases.

10. **Bail:** empirical evidence suggests that Aboriginal persons are twice as likely to be detained without bail than are other arrested persons.

11. **Sentencing:** there is a disproportionately high rate of incarceration of Aboriginal offenders; this situation has been associated with the effects of colonization, discrimination of the part of justice system personnel, imprisonment for fine default, and the criminalization of alcohol consumption.

12. **Corrections:** Aboriginal offenders are generally incarcerated in prisons that are geographically and culturally far removed from their communities, without programs and services sensitive to Aboriginal cultural and spiritual needs. There is a lack of culturally appropriate assessment tools and inadequate after-care facilities for Aboriginal offenders.

13. **Ensuring progress:** the Commission finds that the major difficulty in solving Aboriginal criminal justice problems lies not in finding solutions, but in instituting them. One issue is cost and the need for additional resources to implement reform.

RECOMMENDATIONS

The Law Reform Commission proposes two tracks of reform. The first track is short term and may not address the more fundamental issues. The second track, however, is long term and envisions Aboriginal communities opting for the creation of a variety of justice systems, all of which may be described as Aboriginal justice systems.

The Commission makes recommendations in 15 areas:

1. **The meaning of equal access to justice, equitable treatment and respect:** The criminal justice system must provide the same minimum level of service to all people and must treat Aboriginal persons equitably and with respect. These objectives require that cultural distinctiveness be recognized, respected and, where appropriate, incorporated into the criminal justice system.

2. **The desirability of Aboriginal justice systems:** Aboriginal communities identified by the legitimate representatives of Aboriginal peoples as being willing and able to establish Aboriginal justice systems should have the authority to do so.

3. **Criminal justice system recruitment and training:** Aboriginal persons should occupy posts throughout the criminal justice system and cross-cultural training for all participants in the criminal justice system should be improved.

4. **Overcoming language difficulties and cultural barriers:** Linguistic and cultural barriers between the criminal justice system and Aboriginal societies must be removed; the right of Aboriginal peoples to express themselves in their own languages in all court proceedings should be statutorily recognized; and qualified interpreters should be provided.

5. **Increasing community involvement:** Permanent, effective liaison between the police, the prosecution, the courts, and the correctional systems, and Aboriginal communities should be established.

6. **Applying customary laws and practices:** The federal government should provide funding for research into Aboriginal customary law.

7. **Assessing treaty rights:** Governments should develop clear and public policies concerning the interpretation of Aboriginal and treaty rights.

8. **The police:** In order for police to be more involved in and accountable to the communities they serve, community-based policing in Aboriginal communities that desire external police services should be promoted, and federal and provincial governments should facilitate autonomous Aboriginal police forces wherever local communities so desire.

9. **Prosecutors:** Crown prosecutors should routinely provide advice to police officers on whether it is appropriate to lay charges. Special interrogation rules governing the taking of statements from Aboriginal persons should be established, including rules concerning the presence of counsel during questioning.

10. **Defence counsel:** Provincial bar associations and legal aid societies should make legal education materials, especially information about how to obtain legal aid, readily available to Aboriginal persons.

11. **The courts:** Wherever possible and desired by the community, court sittings should be held in or near the Aboriginal community where the offence was committed. Criminal procedures, such as those concerning swearing an oath, bail or requiring the attendance in court of Aboriginal persons, should be adapted in ways that are sensitive to Aboriginal needs, culture and traditions.

12. **Bail:** Bail legislation should specifically provide that, in assessing the reasonableness of any condition of release, the justice must consider an accused's occupation, place of residence and cultural background; the geographical location and size of the community to which the accused belongs; and the special requirements of traditional Aboriginal pursuits.

13. **Sentencing:** Alternatives to imprisonment should be used whenever possible. A list of factors should be enunciated which, in conjunction with other circumstances, would mitigate sentence where the offender is an Aboriginal person. The criteria governing eligibility for probation should be formulated and probation reports should be prepared so as to have proper regard for cultural differences and to meet the needs of Aboriginal offenders and communities. Incarceration for non-payment of fines should occur only upon refusal or wilful default to pay the fine, not because of inability to pay.

14. **Corrections:** A review of the design and cultural relevancy of all programs that are used as part of diversion, probation or parole should be undertaken in co-operation with Aboriginal persons and organizations. There must be appropriate education of the judiciary, Crown prosecutors and defence counsel concerning the purposes and availability of these programs. Aboriginal spirituality should, by legislation, be given the same recognition as other religions, and Aboriginal elders should be given the same status and freedom as prison chaplains. The National Parole Board and the Correctional Service of Canada should develop a national policy and guidelines concerning waiver of parole and review hearings, and information concerning waivers should be made available to correctional staff and inmates. Smaller, local correctional facilities under community control should be established.

15. **Ensuring progress:** The Task Force recommends the creation of an Aboriginal Justice Institute with a broad mandate to deal with any matters relating to Aboriginal persons in the criminal justice system, including collecting data, developing programs, providing assistance to Aboriginal communities, and developing policy options regarding Aboriginal justice systems. An Aboriginal Justice Institute should be staffed, operated and controlled by Aboriginal persons to the fullest extent possible.

▲ The Summer of 1990

AUTHOR: Standing Committee on Aboriginal Affairs, Chair, Ken Hughes, M.P.

YEAR: 1991

ABORIGINAL GROUP: First Nations

TOPICS: Federal Government/Aboriginal Relations, Provincial Government/Aboriginal Relations, Treaty Land Entitlement, Claims, Land Use, Development and Management

SUB-TOPICS: treaties, comprehensive claims, land use planning

SOURCE: House of Commons Committee

BACKGROUND

This report is the fifth report of the Standing Committee on Aboriginal Affairs. The Committee sought to examine the events surrounding the uprising at Kanesatake and Kahnawake on July 11, 1990. It addresses the evolution of the relationship between First Nations and the federal and provincial governments as well as the issues of racism and the political status of Indigenous peoples in Canada.

PURPOSE

The purpose of this report is to develop an understanding of the stand-off at Oka, Quebec, in July 1990, in order to prevent any further violence. The report's findings and conclusions are based on public hearings.

ISSUES AND FINDINGS

The major issues addressed in this report are as follows:

1. historical events and the accompanying racism experienced by Aboriginal people prior to the stand-off at Oka;

2. land issues;

3. historical governmental control over the Kanesatake community under the aegis of the *Indian Act*, with controversy both over how the *Indian Act* band council should be elected and over what constitutes band custom (a referendum, petitions, surveys and meetings were suggested to resolve the controversy);

4. events occurring from March 1987, to July 11, 1990; and

5. events following July 11, 1990.

It was established that the land status of Kanesatake does not fit within the usual pattern of reserve land, raising the question of whether Oka is an Indian reserve according to the *Indian Act*. Dispute over the region began in 1717. The 1975 comprehensive land claim that was submitted by the Mohawks was rejected by the federal government because the Mohawks had not maintained possession since time immemorial and any previous Aboriginal title had been extinguished. This land claim is distinct from most other claims in that it is one of the few Aboriginal title cases to have reached the final court of appeal. At the time of the proposed golf course expansion, the land was privately held, but formed part of the Mohawk "common lands".

In March 1987, the Club de Golf Oka Inc. tried to renew the lease of its existing golf course: this action was subsequently opposed and blocked by the Kanesatake Band Council. The appropriate system of government was also in question. The federal government proposed a referendum. It did not, however, want to get directly involved in the issue. In April 1989, 300 Mohawks peacefully marched in Oka in protest of the expansion. They were concerned that their traditional lands were being sold out without their consent. Armed barricades were erected and meetings between government officials and Mohawk representatives were set up, but the federal government would talk only about land unification, whereas the Mohawks wanted long-term solutions. An escalating pattern of conflict over the issue of land use followed. This conflict was intensified by unresolved Aboriginal grievances, inter-racial tension and the tension within the Mohawk community itself. Eventually, the controversy over land use in "The Pines" became symbolic of Mohawk land rights in general.

July 11, 1990, saw gunfire between the provincial police and the Mohawks. Negotiations followed but both parties strongly maintained their positions. The issue of land rights also encapsulated the question of sovereignty, which is seen as inseparable by many Indigenous peoples. It was concluded after the events at Oka that Canadians in general want justice for Aboriginal people, but not when accompanied by force.

RECOMMENDATIONS

The recommendations suggested by the Commission are numerous, but tend to centre on the creation of an independent inquiry, the establishment of a Royal Commission, and a change in the land claims process. The recommendations are as follows:

1. a call for an independent inquiry thoroughly to explore the facts, events and issues surrounding the 1990 Oka conflict;

2. expedient reform of Aboriginal policies in consultation with Aboriginal peoples to avoid delay and possible conflict;

3. undertaking a consultative process with Aboriginal peoples based on the Royal Commission suggested within the report;

4. establishment of a Royal Commission to inquire into and report on the relations of First Nations with other Canadians, including issues such as constitutional reforms, recognition of self-government, fiduciary responsibility, and land claims settlements;

5. granting power to the Standing Committee to appoint working groups on specific issues, with balanced representation;

6. issuance of an Order of Reference to a Committee of the House to review Part XI of the *National Defence Act;* and

7. establishment of independent bodies to review the validity of land claims and to make recommendations with regard to compensation, to monitor their implementation and to establish an independent National Mediation Service to prevent future conflict.

▲ What We Heard: Report on the Rural and Native Housing Consultation Process

AUTHOR: Canada Mortgage and Housing Corporation
YEAR: 1991
ABORIGINAL GROUP: All Aboriginal Peoples
TOPIC: Community Services and Infrastructure
SUB-TOPIC: housing
SOURCE: Federal Agency

BACKGROUND

This report is the result of the second phase of Canada Mortgage and Housing Corporation's (CMHC) Rural and Native Housing Consultation process. On April 27, 1990, minister of state for Housing, Alan Redway, released *Addressing Your Housing Needs: How We Can Help You Better? The Rural and Native Housing Consultation Paper*. The Consultation Paper contained a series of questions to provide the context for consultations with affected Canadians. This report describes the public's response to those questions.

PURPOSE

The goal of the consultation process was to develop future policy and programs based on broad public participation. The purpose of this report is "to provide a broad overview of the responses received both in the form of written briefs and during the more than 200 formal and informal meetings held across the country to discuss the consultation paper."

ISSUES AND FINDINGS

The consultation paper presented questions and *What We Heard* summarizes the responses in 10 issue areas. After collecting the initial written responses, CMHC officials attempted to clarify and refine the various positions, determining several points of consensus, then presenting additional corresponding questions to the Ottawa workshop participants in December 1990. These distilled points of agreement, along with their accompanying questions, form a subsequent section of the report. Summaries of the workshops held across the country are also provided.

The initial responses, the points of consensus, and the workshop summaries constitute the findings of this report. They are not conclusive with regard to policy, but rather indicate what CMHC officials felt was important or noteworthy in the responses they received. All three sets of findings are organized according to the original 10 issue areas identified in the consultation paper. The issue areas and a brief description of the findings are listed below.

1. Appropriateness of Rental and Ownership Tenures

The responses indicate that all forms of tenure (e.g., ownership, rental, and lease-purchase) should be made available under the Rural and Native Housing Program. Other concerns and restrictions, such as profit from sales, switching tenure from rental to ownership, ways to gain access to ownership, and additional rental options, are also presented.

2. Client Contribution Requirements

Responses address the benefits and shortcomings of the rent-geared-to-income (RGI) approach, particularly the use of gross income rather than net income as the basis for payments. Flat payments are presented as an alternative. Comments on the up-front grant demonstration program and such concerns as affordability in the North, amortization periods in non-market areas, and setting mortgage values, are also provided.

3. Native Targets (participation levels in CMHC programs)

Until Native housing needs match the level of non-Native needs, the vast majority of participants believe the national 50% target is legitimate. Provincial targets were more widely debated.

4. Client Selection

Several responses pertained to the basis for participant selection. Respondents felt that those in the worst circumstances should be selected first – generally perceived to be families with children – but seniors, the working poor, and other single people should not be ignored. The majority also felt that those receiving welfare assistance should not have an opportunity to access ownership tenure. Other responses focused on the need for local input into the selection process.

5. Client Involvement in Construction

The responses describe the benefits, requirements and limitations of self-help home construction programs. Based on the responses, CMHC officials concluded that a self-help construction option should exist and be encouraged, provided that proper support and supervision were made available.

6. Building and Servicing Standards

The respondents argued for greater input into the design of the units, and for basic facilities in each unit. They recognize, however, that strict adherence or enforcement of these conditions may lead to prohibitively high costs in certain communities and should therefore be applied flexibly. The respondents encouraged the use of prefabricated and mobile housing when appropriate, the enhancement of quality control programs, and the adoption of national quality standards.

7. Emergency Repair Assistance

Respondents felt a flexible and responsive emergency repair service with well-defined response criteria and adequate grants was necessary. Repeat assistance should also be permitted under the program, and primary residences should receive priority over secondary properties.

8. Program Delivery and Administration

In the area of program delivery and administration, a number of general responses were offered regarding timeliness, flexibility in dealing with individual situations, the adequacy of information, field staff qualities, repair programs, a two-year budget cycle, and the fee-for-service approach. Other responses addressed the possibility of greater community (particularly band) involvement in administering the programs. Respondents also argued that economic spin-offs from the program should remain in the community as much as possible.

CMHC concluded that a decentralized approach to delivery, administration and management was favourable; however, the level of interest and ability of communities (e.g., municipality, delivery agent, band council, non-profit group) is highly variable and consequently a range of approaches should exist.

9. Location Policy

According to the responses, the programs need to distinguish market from non-market and high from low cost areas, particularly with regard to ownership tenure. While responses were generally favourable, the respondents felt some changes might be necessary (particularly in non-market areas) to the current restriction of limiting program housing to communities with populations greater than 2,500.

10. Problems Within the Existing Stock

The responses addressed the problems of arrears, maintenance, and repairs within the program. Additionally, respondents discussed the role of counselling as a means to correct or improve performance in these areas.

RECOMMENDATIONS

CMHC made no recommendations in this report.

♦ *Report of the Saskatchewan Indian Justice Review Committee* (1992), see **Volume 3, Saskatchewan.**

Summaries of Reports
by Aboriginal Organizations

▲ Citizens Plus

AUTHOR: Indian Association of Alberta
YEAR: 1970
ABORIGINAL GROUP: First Nations
TOPICS: Federal/Aboriginal Relations, Provincial/Aboriginal Relations
SUB-TOPICS: policy, treaties, federal trust responsibilities
SOURCE: Provincial Aboriginal Organization

BACKGROUND

In 1969, the government of Canada presented a White Paper on Indian policy containing recommendations that would drastically alter the status of Indian people in Canadian society. The main thrust of that document was eventually to eliminate the need for a special legislative status for Indian people and to transfer most services to the provinces.

The Indian Association of Alberta (IAA) viewed this as an attempt by the federal government to renege on obligations and relationships established through treaties, and generally saw such attempts as detrimental to Indian peoples.

PURPOSE

This document outlined the reasons for the IAA's rejection of the 1969 White Paper and recommended Indian counter proposals.

ISSUES AND FINDINGS

The report addressed the six issues put forth in the White Paper. These were:

1. legal structure of Indian status;
2. Indian cultural heritage and its uniqueness;
3. delivery of programs and services;
4. enriched services;
5. claims and treaties; and
6. Indian lands.

The IAA rejected suggested changes to existing legal structures, stating that the recognition of Indian status was essential for justice. They quoted Professor L.C. Green, who found that in other countries the protection of minorities required that they be given special treatment.

With regard to the preservation of Indian cultural heritage, the report emphasized that this was dependent upon the preservation of status, rights and traditions. Since treaties provided the basis for these rights, the White Paper was simply engaging in pleasant rhetoric.

The issue that services should come from the same source as they do for all Canadians was seen as an attempt to renege on federal responsibilities as outlined in the BNA Act. The IAA emphasized that these services were not handouts, but payment for surrendering land. The report contained an historical background on the nature of agreements and relationships with the federal government.

The transfer of education to the provinces was singled out as completely unacceptable. The report contained an excerpt of a report submitted to Parliament in March 1970 concerning the Alberta Indian Education Centre. The fact the governments of Canada and Alberta continued to reach agreements on education without the formal consent of Indian people was underscored.

Reduction in the Department of Indian Affairs and Northern Development's (DIAND) mandate was rejected. It was felt that DIAND should be a persistent advocate of Indian needs, as advocated in the Hawthorn Report.

Enriched services offered in the White Paper were dismissed as bribes and attempts to divide tribes on the basis of economic status and wealth through different treatment.

The report addressed the special need for enriched services in the area of economic development. It was felt that the White Paper policy did not adequately guarantee funding since it was considered an interim measure. The IAA noted that many non-native groups, such as licensed professionals, organized labour, etc., enjoyed special legislation to ensure their economic well-being.

The report outlined an alternative solution. The immediate problem was the need to achieve a basic level of financial and social security. Two major categories of employment were to be developed:

1. performance on tasks and works that the community needs (self-government); and

2. the development of employment in private industry.

The guiding principles for economic development were to make use of the talents of private industry and to rely less on government.

With regard to the White Paper's specific policy on claims and treaties, the IAA rejected the appointment of a sole commissioner on the basis that such an appointment had already been made in the absence of consultation with Native people.

The issue of treaties was considered paramount to Indian policy. It was felt that outstanding treaty must be met, and all treaties must be recognized as binding on the federal government.

In addressing the White Paper's proposition to transfer Indian lands, the IAA report pointed out that Indian lands were not owned by the Crown but rather were held in trust. Since this arrangement ensured that Indian lands were not alienated or broken up, the IAA rejected proposals that would have permitted the sale of Indian lands by individuals.

RECOMMENDATIONS

With regard to the issue of legal structures, the IAA made two recommendations:

1. Although it rejected the repeal of the *Indian Act*, it recommended that it be reviewed to eliminate its paternalistic bent. However, it cautioned that this could only be done after the settlement of outstanding treaty issues.

2. The legal definition of registered Indians must remain.

There were no formal recommendation given on cultural heritage issues, as it was felt this was inextricably linked with treaty issues.

With regard to the delivery of programs and services, and the potential devolution to provincial and local authorities, the IAA recommended the federal government continue to meet its responsibilities, especially in the provision of education, welfare, health and economic development services.

Concerning education specifically, the IAA recommended that funds for education be offered to tribal councils, who would then decide whether to operate schools directly or contract with local public boards and education authorities.

Although against the reduction of DIAND's mandate, the IAA recommended a reduction in the size and structure of Indian Affairs to ensure an agency which was less authoritarian and more closely attuned with the needs of Indian people. The IAA also recommended a full-time minister.

With regard to economic development, the IAA made two recommendations. They were:

1. school curricula should be revised to prepare Indian people in economic affairs; and
2. private industry should be supported.

These endeavours were to be assisted by all the resources of the Alberta Indian Development System, a corporation set up by the IAA.

The document included an excerpt from a report submitted to Parliament in March 1970 concerning the Alberta Indian Development System.

Two recommendations were made regarding claims and treaties:

1. It was proposed that a Claims Commission be established in consultation with Indian people, with a mandate to modernize treaties;
2. All treaties be incorporated in updated terms in an amendment to the Canadian Constitution.

There were no formal recommendations concerning Indian lands.

1971

▲ Wahbung – Our Tomorrows

AUTHOR: Indian Tribes of Manitoba (Manitoba Indian Brotherhood)
YEAR: 1971
ABORIGINAL GROUP: First Nations
TOPICS: Federal Government/Aboriginal Relations, Self-Government, Treaty Land Entitlement, Land Use, Development and Management, Resources
SUB-TOPICS: policy, treaties, federal trust responsibilities, negotiation structures and processes
SOURCE: Provincial Aboriginal Organization

BACKGROUND

The federal government had issued the 1969 White Paper on Indian policy, a document that proved unacceptable to Aboriginal peoples across Canada.

In 1970, the Indian Association of Alberta responded with The Red Paper, or "Citizens Plus", which outlined divergences between its membership's aspirations and the intentions of the federal government. It was clear that Indian peoples and the government had very different concepts of what was implied by the federal trust relationship.

PURPOSE

The four Indian tribes of Manitoba – Cree, Ojibwa, Chipewyan and Sioux – under the auspices of the Manitoba Indian Brotherhood (MIB) presented to the federal government their position on the policies that were necessary to achieve a satisfactory relationship between the people of Canada and the Indian people of Manitoba.

ISSUES AND FINDINGS

The MIB emphasized that it was committed to the belief that both Aboriginal and treaty rights emanated from the MIB's sovereignty as a nation of peoples and as such it had a nation-to-nation relationship with the federal government.

A further implication of this was that there could be no delegation of authority or responsibility to the provinces without MIB consent.

The position paper identified seven major issues. They were:

1. treaty and Aboriginal rights;
2. land control;
3. hunting, fishing, trapping and gathering rights;
4. the *Indian Act*;
5. culture;
6. justice; and
7. reserve government.

Treaty and Aboriginal rights: The MIB declared that the grievances of Indian people, especially those involving questions of treaties and Aboriginal title, remained unacknowledged by the federal government. Specifically, it was felt that Treaties 1, 2 and 5, affecting most of Manitoba, were unconscionable agreements. The federal government was urged to recognize the need for a restructuring of the treaties.

Land control: The MIB identified three issues relating to land:

1. Continued federal control over its use and occupancy was unacceptable and the immediate transfer of such control to band councils was imperative.

2. Because the government had placed MIB peoples on meagre, substandard land, it had an obligation to ensure that the land was developed to its maximum capacity.

3. The poor quality of the lands assigned to Indian people required adjustments to meet their economic and social requirements.

Hunting, fishing, trapping and gathering rights: The fact that the federal government and provincial governments had created regulations and laws (i.e., the *Migratory Birds Act*) that restricted Indian access to traditional gathering methods was declared an unacceptable abrogation of treaty rights.

The *Indian Act*: The MIB declared that the *Indian Act* should be amended to allow for meaningful social development for Indian people, according to their own guidelines. They further stated that the Act should reflect treaty and Aboriginal rights and the protection of the Indian land base, and should be entrenched in the Constitution.

Culture: The authors noted that federal and provincial government policies regarding the preservation of Indian culture emphasized the commercial aspects of arts and crafts, and museum exhibitions, displays rather than the stimulation and growth of Indian culture.

Justice: The authors pointed out that the Canadian justice system often failed Aboriginal people because of discriminatory practices within the system as a whole, and particularly within the police forces, and because it was not based on the same value system.

Band government: The MIB stated that successive federal governments had undermined local government practices traditionally pursued under tribal customs, by forcing reserve level government to conform to the needs of national administration. This practice was inconsistent with the right of all peoples to self-determination. The MIB called on the federal government to facilitate social change and to respond to Indian needs as they were defined by Indian people, through a system of local government that was comparable to the municipal structures of the non-Indian community.

RECOMMENDATIONS

The MIB recommended that the restructuring of their treaties include the following provisions:

1. a flexible standard of compensation for losses incurred by the treaties;

2. a recovery of rights such as those of hunting and fishing, which are identified as traditional and inherent to the Indian way of life;

3. a revision of land allotment to redress the obvious quantitative and qualitative deficiencies imposed with the assignment of reserves;

4. compensation in land, money, programs, etc. for the assignment of uncultivatable land; and

5. negotiation of other issues and factors which be might be discovered through research and communication with the reserve.

With regard to control over lands, the authors asserted that the trust relationship with the government, one that protects the integrity of Indian lands, should be maintained regardless of the transfer of control to Indian people.

To bring about adjustments in the land base, the MIB recommended a joint commission be established. The principal responsibility of the commission would be to make recommendations to government for a new land adjustment policy.

In addressing the issue of traditional economies, the MIB recommended protections for hunting, fishing, trapping and gathering rights be enshrined in the constitution and reflected in the *Indian Act*.

With regard to the *Indian Act*, the authors envisioned a new Act that included:

1. the recognition of treaty and Aboriginal rights;

2. ensured federal responsibility in areas such as education, health and welfare and housing;

3. recognition that responsibility for membership decisions lie with the community;

4. recognition that reserve lands are inalienable and that the federal government is bound through the trust relationship;

5. method of election of chief and council should be left to the discretion of each community;

6. compensation for the destruction of livelihoods through flooding, pollution and industrial development; and

7. exemption from all forms of taxation.

To preserve Indian culture, the MIB recommended that a program be developed that would:

1. document and catalogue traditional expressions of Indian culture as a basis for programs designed to preserve and stimulate the growth of the Indian contributions to Canadian culture; and

2. recognize the contributions of the Indian people to the historical development of Canada.

With regard to justice, the authors proposed the creation of a reserve police forces staffed with officers of Indian heritage. These police forces would help the community solve its own problems, act as legal advisers, work with youth and explain law and legal procedures. A justice system that employed Aboriginal people and was sensitive to their needs was recommended.

The MIB recommended the establishment of a system of joint government/Aboriginal boards and commissions that would be responsible for evaluating local government submissions; examining and evaluating program applications; and providing guidance on program development and implementation.

1972

▲ Indian Control of Indian Education

AUTHOR: National Indian Brotherhood
YEAR: 1972
ABORIGINAL GROUP: First Nations
TOPIC: Education
SUB-TOPICS: pre-school/daycare, primary and secondary, post-secondary, adult, vocational/training, facilities/institutions, curriculum, fiscal relations/responsibilities, professionals/educators, student support
SOURCE: National Aboriginal Organization

BACKGROUND

The Special Committee of the Executive Council of the National Indian Brotherhood compiled this statement from provincial and territorial associations' papers or statements on education and from discussions of representatives of the associations at an Education Workshop in June 1972. The General Assembly of the National Indian Brotherhood accepted the policy in principle in August 1972, and it was presented to the minister of Indian Affairs and Northern Development in December 1972.

PURPOSE

This statement on education was prepared for the Working Committee of the Negotiating Committee of the National Indian Brotherhood. It is designed to be used for future common action in the area of education.

ISSUES AND FINDINGS

The Committee feels that it is very important that Indian children have a chance to develop a value system that is consistent with Indian culture. This was not found to be what Indian children experience in non-Indian schools, and as a result, they are experiencing withdrawal and failure. The Committee found that parental responsibility and local control of education was the way to meet this goal. The four areas that the Committee identified for attention and improvement were responsibility, programs, teachers and facilities.

1. Responsibility

The Committee found that the federal government should take the steps required to transfer to local bands the authority and funds allotted for Indian education. The band itself would then determine how the money was to be spent. The Committee also found that over 60% of Indian children are enroled in provincial/territorial schools and that there was inadequate Indian representation on these school boards.

2. Programs

In terms of programs, the Committee established that the present school system is culturally alien to Native students, and that where Indian contribution is not entirely ignored, it is often cast in an unfavourable light. Programs must be developed that maintain a balance between academic skill and Indian cultural subjects. The Committee found that specific problems in many Indian communities could be met by improved education. These problems include loss of Native languages, high school dropouts, low level of interest in adult education, and alcohol and drug abuse.

3. Teachers

In terms of teachers, the Committee found that there is a critical need for Native teachers and counsellors as well as specially trained non-Indian teachers and counsellors.

The Committee also found that the success of integration hinged on parents, teachers, pupils (both Indian and non-Indian) and curriculum. They found that Indian parents need more preparation and orientation to enable them to make informed decisions and to help their children to adjust and succeed. They also found that Indian children require help in handling the conflict of values and that Canadian classrooms need a curriculum that recognizes Indian customs and values.

4. Facilities

The Committee established that the reserve educational facilities that do exist are often unsafe and obsolete. They are not of the same standard as facilities off the reserve.

RECOMMENDATIONS

The major recommendation of the Committee is that Indian education reflect Indian values, and that it be controlled by the local Indian band and the parents of the children attending. This would require the following actions:

1. Responsibility

The report recognizes federal government responsibility for Native education and recommends that the federal government be responsible for transferring this authority to the local Indian band.

2. Programs

The Committee recommends a greater emphasis on pre-school and kindergarten programs to teach the second language in which the curriculum will be taught or to reinforce the child's image as an Indian. Alcohol and drug education programs are also suggested, as are adult education programs and cultural education centres designed to help Indian apply traditional beliefs to modern society.

3. Teachers

With respect to teachers, the report recommends, at a minimum, the hiring of teachers who are fluent in the local language; it is further hoped that Native people may be trained to be teachers and counsellors. If Indian children must go to a local school off the reserve, the report recommends that non-Indian teachers be trained in Native values and Native education and that Indian people be represented on local school boards.

4. Facilities

The report suggests that education facilities be upgraded and that high schools and vocational schools be established on some reserves.

▲ Together Today for Our Children Tomorrow: A Statement of Grievances and an Approach to Settlement by the Yukon Indian People

AUTHOR: Council for Yukon Indians
YEAR: 1973
ABORIGINAL GROUP: First Nations
TOPIC: Claims
SUB-TOPIC: comprehensive claims
SOURCE: Territorial Aboriginal Organization

BACKGROUND

This document was the result of meetings held by the Yukon Native Brotherhood to establish what kind of land claim settlement the Indian people thought would be fair for both themselves and their White brothers.

PURPOSE

In 1973, the Council for Yukon Indians (CYI) was formed to negotiate land claims settlements with the federal government. The CYI prepared this document as the basis for their land claims. The document presents a historical and descriptive account of the key settlement issues and how they have evolved.

ISSUES AND FINDINGS

The CYI found that the economic gap, the social gap and the communication gap between the Indian and the White communities were all widening, and that a lack of understanding and tolerance was developing between the groups.

1. Economic Gap

Economic inequality was seen as one of the major problems. In the Yukon, the economy is controlled by whites and the few jobs held be Indian people are those of labourers. Before 1948, the Yukon Indian people were economically independent but at the time of the report, over half the families were on welfare and the number receiving some kind of assistance was as high as eighty per cent.

2. Social Gap

In terms of social programs, the report found that all services were provided by Whites and that programs did not fit within the framework of the Indian culture.

3. Communication Gap

The Indian people felt that they could not talk to the white man as equals due to the difference in economic status. They believe, however, that a just settlement of their claims would change this situation.

The settlement discussed in the report consisted of eight parts:

1. Programs

Indian people want a settlement that allows them control over those programs that affect them so that they can make them culturally relevant.

2. Old People

Indian people want cash payments for their old people who would otherwise not benefit from the long-term impact of the claims settlements on the communities.

3. Cultural Identity

Indian people are asking for cultural programs that will help them rediscover the values of Indian religion, Indian philosophy and the Indian way of life. This includes writing their own history in the way that they remember it, and using their own language.

4. Community Development

Community development includes everything from jobs and businesses to dancing and dog races. The Yukon Indians hope to encourage natural leadership within the community to identify problems, propose solutions, and then train their own people to implement these solutions.

5. Education

Indian people feel that most of the changes in the territorial education system in recent years have not made things better for the Indian student. They are proposing many new programs for students of all ages and all levels of previous education. They also feel that there should be a university in the Yukon as well as information services where students could find out about other educational opportunities. In general, the need for Indian control of Indian education is emphasized.

6. Economic Development

Indian people believe feel that their people should play an important role in the development of the Yukon. This is the stated policy of the federal government but no workable plan has been put in place.

7. Communications

The Indian people also believe there to be an immediate need to change the communications system. Radio, television and newspapers must contain articles that are written by Indian people for Indian people.

8. Research

The Indian people feel that they need research to show them the best way to take advantage of white ways while still maintaining their own culture. They feel that they need complete control over what research is conducted and by whom.

RECOMMENDATIONS

The report makes no formal recommendations, but does present a statement of conditions for settlement that they consider acceptable. These conditions deal primarily with Indian participation in claims settlement and in Indian control:

1. the settlement must not do away with any rights of the Yukon people to programs, benefits and responsibilities that they are entitled to as Canadians;

2. Indian people do not want any Indian person who lives on lands set aside as Indian lands to pay income tax for the first 25 years;

3. the government of Canada must continue to pay all costs of health services;

4. in terms of long-range development plans, settlement must include the transfer of all programs to the Indian people;

5. the Indian people must be able to establish the qualifications for participation in the settlement and these qualifications must continue in perpetuity and include all future descendants;

6. control of their own land is a major condition of settlement, including surface and sub-surface rights, the right to hunt, trap and fish on unoccupied land, and exclusive rights on Indian lands;

7. Indian people want to receive royalties on all government ventures on all land; and

8. Indian people are asking for the negotiation of a fair and just cash settlement.

The CYI also outlines a list of programs for which the settlement funds will be used. These programs will be developed and initially controlled by the Yukon General Indian Council, but once local municipalities are developed, they will take over control.

1974

▲ The Shocking Truth About Indians in Textbooks

AUTHOR: Manitoba Indian Brotherhood
YEAR: 1974
ABORIGINAL GROUP: First Nations
TOPICS: Education, Social/Cross-Cultural Relations
SUB-TOPICS: primary, curriculum, racism
SOURCE: Provincial Aboriginal Organization

BACKGROUND

Native people have been concerned about the quality of history texts in Manitoba schools for many years. A 1971 Manitoba Indian Brotherhood study, *Wahbung – Our Tomorrows*, urged that a study be undertaken of the overall education process, and following a survey in 1972, "Education is Failing the Indian", the Brotherhood recommended that a complete study and analysis be undertaken to evaluate the treatment of Indian people in textbooks currently authorized for use in Manitoba schools. This report attempts to begin this process with an evaluation of social studies materials approved by the Department of Education for use by Grades 4, 5 and 6 in provincial classrooms.

PURPOSE

The report identifies two purposes of this evaluation:

1. to help eliminate the persistence of bias and omission in school materials by pointing out unsatisfactory areas; and

2. to introduce alternative information to provide a more balanced portrayal of Native peoples.

ISSUES AND FINDINGS

The authors relied on three approaches to evaluate the materials: content analysis of direct quotations from textbooks; evaluation coefficient analysis (i.e., an analysis of the positive or negative connotations of descriptive terms); and picture analysis. The authors articulated the following 10 forms of bias to guide their analysis of the content:

1. **Bias by omission:** selecting information that credits only one group, frequently the group to which the writer belongs;

2. **Bias by defamation:** calling attention to the Native person's faults rather than his virtues and misrepresenting his nature;

3. **Bias by disparagement:** denying or belittling the contributions of Native people to Canadian culture;

4. **Bias by cumulative implication:** constantly creating the impression that only one group is responsible for positive developments;

5. **Bias by (lack of) validity:** failing to ensure that information about issues is always accurate and unambiguous;

6. **Bias by inertia:** perpetuating legends and half-truths by failure to keep abreast of historical scholarship;

7. **Bias by obliteration:** ignoring significant aspects of Native history;

8. **Bias by disembodiment:** referring in a casual and depersonalized way to the "Indian menace" or representing the annihilation of Indian culture as part of the "march of progress";

9. **Bias by (lack of) concreteness:** dealing with a race or group in platitudes and generalizations (applying the shortcomings of an individual to a whole group), rather than being factual, objective and realistic; and

10. **Bias by (lack of) comprehensiveness:** failing to mention all relevant facts that may help to form the opinion of the student.

The report is divided into three sections, one each on content analysis and evaluation coefficient analysis of the texts, and a third on Grade 4 and 5 textbooks. Many of the Grade 4 and 5 texts did not have significant references to Native people.

The content analysis section is composed of the authors' analyses of nine textbooks and a collection of materials on Canadian history called the "the Jackdaws". The authors found that the materials suffered from many of the biased outlined above. In many cases, the authors provided an example of how the bias demonstrated in the passage could be improved upon or corrected. Often these examples come from other existing works. The authors argued that the main failure of the materials reviewed was their tendency to treat Aboriginal people as impediments to be removed so that the goals of European progress could be realized.

Evaluation coefficient analysis assigns a positive or negative value to terms commonly used to describe different groups or individuals. The words, "courageous" and "honourable", for example, are positive terms, while "savage" and "warlike" are negative in connotation. This form of analysis counts the frequency of use for these terms as they are used to describe individuals or groups. The analysis revealed that the authors of textbooks present their own bias toward Native people by the use of negative terminology. Only three texts had scores indicating a positive depiction of Native people; these scores were barely over 50%. In contrast, the depiction of Europeans in seven books was positive, with ratings above 70% and none less than 50%.

The authors of this study conclude that the textbooks used in Manitoba schools are biased, distort history, and present images of Native people as savages and barbarians. They found these works to be damaging to the productive potential of a Native child. Their effect on non-Native children was also found to be negative as it perpetuates the notion that racism and double standards are acceptable. The authors conclude that there is a need for a complete revision and re-writing of materials and textbooks.

The report addresses books and materials from Grades 4 and 5 separately from those of Grade 6, because many of those used did not discuss the history and lives of Native peoples. Those that did were addressed in the same fashion as the texts from Grade 6. For those that were devoid of Native content, the authors discussed ways in which appropriate material could be included.

RECOMMENDATIONS

The report concludes with a series of recommendations. These are summarized below.

1. that future writers of history present balanced material and various points of view;

2. that children be trained to read and observe materials in a critical manner;

3. that generalizations (e.g., the term Indian) be avoided when describing the acts of individuals or members of specific groups, and that descriptive terminology, which may offend Native people, be used carefully and with awareness;

4. that publishers and authors be cautious in their selection of material and quotes from primary sources, and when appropriate, that these sources be accompanied by prefatory material on the ethnocentrism of the writer;

5. that the Department of Education continually review new and existing textual materials and that a proper process for such review be established;

6. that handbooks and other teaching materials be developed to enable teachers to detect and fairly present biased information and attitudes;

7. that additional textbooks – a Native History Series – be developed and written by Native people; and

8. that provincial and federal governments be willing to support the efforts and wishes of Native people for improved texts.

▲ The Treaty Rights of Hunting, Fishing, Trapping and Gathering

AUTHOR: Federation of Saskatchewan Indian Nations, Manitoba Indian Brotherhood, and Indian Association of Alberta

YEAR: 1974

ABORIGINAL GROUP: First Nations

TOPIC: Resources

SUB-TOPICS: hunting/wildlife, trapping and gathering, fishing/fisheries

SOURCE: Provincial Aboriginal Organizations

BACKGROUND

This document was prepared to initiate a process of negotiation between the federal government, the provincial governments and the Treaty Indians of the prairie provinces, concerning the hunting, gathering, trapping and fishing rights of Treaty Indians.

PURPOSE

The purpose of the negotiations was twofold:

1. to affirm that the Natural Resources Agreements were not intended to alter treaty rights; and

2. to restore the treaty rights of hunting, fishing, trapping and gathering which had been abrogated by federal and provincial laws which restrict the exercise of those rights.

ISSUES AND FINDINGS

The dominant theme in the document was the incongruence between the written provisions of the treaties and the non-written agreements reached in the negotiation of the treaties. According to the report, the non-written agreements provided that Treaty Indians would be free to hunt and fish on all land included in the treaty until that land was occupied. The Treaty Indians contend that they were told that the animals would remain theirs and that the government would intervene to conserve animals for treaty Indians. They feel that these hunting and fishing rights are not restricted to domestic consumption, but instead extend to the pursuit of these activities for commercial use. Treaty Indians argue that they were assured that their hunting, fishing and trapping rights would exist as long as the sun shines and the river flows.

Since these treaties were signed, the Indian communities argue that the federal government has adopted the practice of acknowledging the right of the provinces to pass legislation affecting Indian hunting rights in the form of Natural Resource Agreements. Since 1930, these Natural Resource Agreements have been seen by jurists and government administrators as the only source of Indian hunting, trapping and fishing rights with little attention being paid to the spirit of the treaties. There has been little consultation with Indian people despite further actions by governments which have restricted the rights of Indian people. Since the Natural Resource Agreements were signed, a number of other programs, legislation, and policies have been instituted which have limited the hunting, trapping and fishing rights:

1. the federal government has adopted the position that provincial laws apply to, and therefore restrict, Indian people;

2. exemption has been provided for hunting, trapping and fishing for food but not for commercial purposes;

3. provincial governments have recognized the interests of sportsmen, non-Indian commercial fisherman, trappers, and promoters of tourism, parks and industrial projects at the expense of Treaty Indian rights;

4. the Supreme Court of Canada has stated that Parliament may unilaterally abrogate treaties and they have done so by legislating the *Migratory Birds Convention Act*, which places restrictions on Indian hunters that the government has failed to demonstrate are necessary for conservation;

5. the federal and provincial fisheries regulations require Indian people to obtain a licence which restricts their fishing to specific lakes and also places restrictions on methods used and quantities of fish taken;

6. the provincial government has failed to institute adequate measures for the conservation of fish and wildlife and the protection of the livelihood of Indian hunters, fishermen and trappers; and

7. in the treaties, the Indian people accepted the fact that the area of land open to them for hunting and trapping would be reduced by occupation but did not accept the right of any government to unilaterally declare tracts of land occupied if they were not occupied, as is the case where they have been declared national and/or provincial parks and wilderness areas.

The report argues that contrary to the spirit of these policies and programs, the treaties signed by prairie Indian nations guaranteed that their hunting, gathering and trapping rights would be distinct from and paramount to the rights of non-Indians. Furthermore, under the terms of the treaties, the federal government is obliged to take such action as is necessary to protect and conserve fish and wildlife resources for the benefit of Indian people.

The report concluded that a comprehensive program must be undertaken for review and reform of federal and provincial legislation and it should be guided by the following principles:

1. federal and provincial legislation concerning hunting, trapping and fishing should not apply to Treaty Indians;

2. all legislation and regulations concerning fish and wildlife resources should recognize the absolute priority of Treaty Indian rights to hunt, fish and trap on land which is not legitimately occupied; and

3. all legislation should recognize the priority of Treaty Indians to hunt, trap and fish for commercial purposes.

RECOMMENDATIONS

The report's recommendations are presented as proposals for the implementation of principles outlined above:

1. that the *Indian Act* and Natural Resources Agreements be amended to protect Indian hunting, fishing and trapping from the effects of federal laws of general application;

2. that any necessary restrictions to Indian hunting, fishing and trapping be made by the federal government under the *Indian Act* or a separate Act that applies to Indian hunting, trapping and fishing;

3. that an ongoing tripartite body of representatives from the federal government, the provincial governments and the Indian associations be established to investigate and recommend changes in all provincial and federal legislation affecting Indian hunting, fishing and trapping; and

4. that Indian people participate in the formulation and implementation of conservation objectives, and in changes to federal and provincial plans for the formation or expansion of parks or wilderness areas regulations where such plans would place unnecessary restriction upon land available for Indian hunting, fishing and trapping.

1977

▲ Indian Government

AUTHOR: Federation of Saskatchewan Indian Nations
YEAR: 1977
ABORIGINAL GROUP: First Nations
TOPICS: Self-Government, Federal/Aboriginal Relations
SUB-TOPICS: rights, jurisdiction, treaties, federal trust responsibilities
SOURCE: Provincial Aboriginal Organization

BACKGROUND

In the 1970s the FSIN, and other nationally, regionally and locally organized Aboriginal groups were exploring the Aboriginal rights agenda and laying the ground to articulate their positions on Aboriginal self-government, and their interpretation of historical and contemporary relationships with non-Aboriginal governments and non-Aboriginal Canadians.

This discussion paper reveals the early efforts of the Saskatchewan Indian leadership to formulate and develop positions in relation to the broader agenda of Aboriginal and treaty rights. The consistency of positions articulated in this discussion paper, with those of the Aboriginal leadership in the 1980s and 1990s is notable.

For the FSIN specifically, this document provided the basis from which future work in the area of Indian government development was launched.

PURPOSE

The discussion paper was prepared under the direction of the Executive of the FSIN to provide a basis for the development of comprehensive positions on Indian government. The paper addresses the fundamental features and foundations of Indian government and the exercise of Indian government powers, as well as relationships with Canadian governments. It questions contemporary and historical interpretations of Indian/non-Indian relationships, as they were expressed through treaties, court decisions, and the actions of the federal government, and the subsequent non-recognition of the inherent sovereignty of Indian Nations and of Indian government powers.

The purpose of the Report was to set out the major areas requiring discussion and development of positions by FSIN, First Nations, Tribal and National level organizations, and to propose ways in which Indian governments may be restored.

ISSUES AND FINDINGS

Major issues addressed in the discussion paper include: Indian sovereignty, the Federal-Indian trust relationship, Indian government jurisdiction, the treaties, the Royal Proclamation of 1763, the *British North American Act*, Indian lands, Indian government and the department of Indian Affairs, and the Indian Commission on Indian Government (FSIN).

In relation to each primary issue the discussion paper identifies the following principles and interpretations:

First Nations must be clear on their understanding of the foundations and framework within which Indian governments will be recognized and restored, i.e., positions on sovereignty, jurisdiction, relationships must be supported and understood by Indian governments themselves. Action will flow from those understandings and foundations. Indian government is achievable within the Canadian constitutional context, and will enrich national unity.

Principles of Indian Government

Indian Nations were historically self-governing. S.91(24) gave the federal government the authority to regulate relations with Indian Nations but did not, as has been interpreted by Canadian governments and officials, give the federal government authority to regulate the affairs of Indian Nations.

Indian governments and Indian government powers have been suppressed and in some cases eroded through the legislative and administrative actions of Canadian governments, through treaties and through distorted federal responses to Indian government under fundamentally different interpretations of relationships and constitutional authorities.

Indian government authority is greater than what is recognized and exercised. Indian governments must derive their mandate and authority from Indian peoples. Indian government authority is not and cannot be delegated to Indian Nations by non-Indian governments.

Treaties reserved to Indian nations a complete set of rights including the right to be self-governing, and to control Indian lands and resources without federal government interference. Furthermore, treaties take precedence over provincial and federal laws.

On the federal-Indian trust relationship, the discussion paper sets out the view that there is an implied trust relationship (though this has both passive and active features) and a fiduciary obligation on the trustee. However, the trust relationship has been mismanaged and misinterpreted; i.e., federal government has not acted in the best interests of Indian beneficiaries, there is clear conflict of interest on part of trustee (i.e., the minister of Indian Affairs and other federal departments/agents) in fulfilling responsibilities.

Although treaties did not create a trust relationship, they did imply, and have contributed to the establishment of such a relationship. The Royal Proclamation of 1763, federal legislation, policy decisions, and legal/court decisions likewise have contributed to the formulation of such a relationship, though none specifically establishes a trust relationship.

Treaties demonstrate the sovereignty of Indian nations. The inherent right of self-government was reinforced, not surrendered through the signing of treaties.

The inherent right of self-government encompasses exercisable powers in a broad range of areas, including selection of form of government, power to determine membership and regulate domestic relations, and judicial functions. The actions of Parliament and federal administrators have interfered with the internal exercise of inherent sovereignty by Indian governments and, though they have limited the exercise of such powers, they have not eliminated or extinguished inherent sovereignty and powers.

Historically Indian tribes were nations, and although many have splintered into individual bands, most still retain their national character. Arguments which deny recognition of tribal sovereignty on the basis of a small land base, physical location within the boundaries of another nation, small populations, and economic non-self-sufficiency can be rejected on the basis that there are many recognized nations in the world which exhibit those features.

On the broad question of jurisdiction, the discussion paper recognizes the source of Indian jurisdiction as resting with Indian people and the ancestors of those people. In contravention of the Royal Proclamation of 1763, which established nation to nation relationships, and as a result of misinterpretations of loosely defined federal authorities and responsibilities under the BNA Act, Indian jurisdiction has been wrongly impinged upon and eroded by federal and provincial governments.

The existence of concurrent jurisdiction of federal and Indian governments is acknowledged. For example, both federal and Indian governments may be able to exercise some jurisdiction over Indian people off-reserve, or non-Indians on-reserve. However, the jurisdictional interface must be such that each government asserts its jurisdiction in a manner which does not interfere with or impede the other government.

RECOMMENDATIONS

The report does not contain specifically focused recommendations. Rather it identifies the main points of departure for a re-assertion of Indian government authority based on Indian interpretations of the nature and extent of Indian government, the treaties and federal-Indian relations.

The discussion paper encompasses a challenge to Indian nations, tribes and organisations to begin to consider and come to some common understanding of the foundations for Indian government, and thereby to facilitate movement toward re-establishing Indian governments, and exercising authorities jurisdictions and powers according to Indian interpretations of treaties, constitutional documents and relationships with non-Indian governments.

More specifically, the paper calls for such discussions to clearly define, articulate and establish positions in relation to Indian sovereignty, the jurisdiction of Indian governments, government to government relations with non-Indian governments, and the nature and extent of the federal-Indian trust relationship.

▲ Métis and Non-Status Indian Crime and Justice Report

AUTHOR: Métis and Non-Status Indian Crime and Justice Commission, Commissioner, Harry M. Daniels

YEAR: 1977
ABORIGINAL GROUP: Métis, Non-Status
TOPIC: Administration of Justice
SUB-TOPICS: corrections, courts
SOURCE: Federal Commission

BACKGROUND

This report was a response to frustrations with previous studies and investigations which repeated the same types of recommendations especially those dealing with increased Native responsibility in staffing and programming for Native people. There was concern over the fact that, very often policies that were agreed to in principle, were not put into practice and that reiterating the same solutions to old problems left the impression that something was actually being done.

PURPOSE

The purpose of this report was to address the most pressing justice related issues and questions of the day, and to provide solutions and recommendations. More importantly, the recommendations were to be as specific as possible so that, should they be accepted, progress could be made through their implementation relatively quickly.

The Commission was asked to

1. suggest possible solutions to the high rates of involvement of Native peoples at all levels of the criminal justice system, and high rates of recidivism;

2. provide information to people working in the penal system and related fields, in Native organizations, and other interested persons;

3. provide an indication of where information gaps existed, and how these might best be dealt with without duplication or repetition.

ISSUES AND FINDINGS

The Commission looked at many issues including characteristics of the Native inmate population, court services provided for Native offenders, corrections and parole practices, community and migration trends of offenders and concerns involving Native women in corrections.

The Commission found that almost half the Native inmates were contacted were between the ages of 15 and 25 and had not progressed beyond Grade 8. Furthermore, more than half the inmates identified were in maximum security institutions. In federal institutions, it was found that most of the inmates had sentence lengths of two to five years but the third largest sentence category was "life".

With respect to court services it was found that

1. almost half the inmates said they had not been told their rights on arrest;
2. most of the inmates said they did not understand court procedures;
3. over half pleaded guilty;
4. many had been told that they would receive a lighter sentence by pleading guilty;
5. a large number said they had been told how to plea most frequently by their lawyers;
6. there were indications that many inmates had not been aware of court worker services, and court workers were "spread too thin" to be effective and
7. less than half the inmates thought their lawyers had been helpful.

In the area of corrections, the Commission discovered that the majority of inmates considered that there was no point in lodging grievances within the institution, because it was unlikely improvements would be made. In addition almost half of the inmates had difficulties in gaining access to their lawyers although there was a perceived need for legal services to assist in obtaining transfers, parole and arranging appeals.

It was also found that Native inmates were generally less likely to receive parole or temporary absence passes. Moreover, there were few Native people in pre-release centres, and there was a great need for Native halfway houses.

Some interesting facts were discovered by the Commission in respect of Native communities. For example, it was found that almost half of all inmates had been brought up on-reserve and over half came from areas where more than half of the work force was unemployed (and employment that was available was either unskilled or semi-skilled at best). Lack of employment opportunities was one of the most frequent reasons cited for the inmates originally leaving home. Some other interesting findings were that the average family size of inmates was between nine and eleven people, and almost half of the inmates had relatives who had been in jail when they were growing up.

In the area of migration, it was found that over half of the inmates had left home by the time they were 16 and more than three-quarters had been arrested by the time they were 16. As well, over half had been first convicted of a property related offence and a large proportion had received jail sentences after they had first been released. Finally, almost half the inmates who answered questions had been in trouble with the police before they had been arrested.

In the area of women inmates, it was found that most Native women had been convicted of offences "against the person" and these offences were more likely to have been committed in a group. As well, it was found that there was a high level of unemployment and alcohol abuse and that existing programs for women inmates were totally inadequate.

RECOMMENDATIONS

The Commission made recommendations in two areas. The first recommendation was for structural changes within the existing system. Some of these recommendations included the modification of existing advisory councils. More specifically representation needed to be improved.

It was also recommended that within the penitentiary system more Native input was needed at all levels of the system. As well, sensitization to Native needs and concerns should be a requirement for all staff working with Native people and should be carried out and designed on an ongoing basis by a Native person.

One of the most important recommendations made by the Commission was that the Canadian advisory council should be abandoned and substituted with broadly based and provincially funded provincial justice councils. Only after receiving provincial funding and incorporating Native representation should an application be made by a provincial justice council to join the federal advisory council.

Other recommendations made by the Commission involved incremental changes to the existing system. These changes included recommendations in the fields of Native brotherhoods and sisterhoods, Native liaison staff, northern development, women inmates, parole and policing. The underlying and overlapping concerns in these areas involved more sensitivity to and education in respect of Native culture, more participation and increased involvement by Native people in existing processes, and educational services for Native people before and after incarceration.

This report dealt with only a sample of inmates who were incarcerated in federal penitentiaries. As a result the Commission identified several areas that required further investigation including Native juveniles and their relationship with the criminal justice system, provincial correctional systems and the evaluation of new and active programs.

◆ *Indian Commission of Ontario: Terms of Reference* (1978), see **Volume 3, Ontario.**

1979

▲ Indian: The Spirit and Intent of Treaty

AUTHOR: Federation of Saskatchewan Indian Nations
YEAR: 1979
ABORIGINAL GROUP: First Nations
TOPIC: Treaty Land Entitlement
SUB-TOPIC: claims
SOURCE: Provincial Aboriginal Organization

BACKGROUND

Between 1817 and 1929, over 20 major international treaties were signed between the British government (or Canada in the right of the Crown), and the Indian/Dene Nations. As a result of this process, the Indian Nations agreed to cede certain lands for use and settlement in return for specific guarantees, or treaty rights. During treaty negotiations, the Indian leadership guaranteed:

1. all powers of Indian Nationhood;

2. Indian jurisdiction;

3. the right to be born, and live, an Indian; and

4. socio-economic rights.

PURPOSE

This report provides an account of what treaty rights were guaranteed and an interpretation of what these rights mean today.

ISSUES AND FINDINGS

The following represents a brief summary of each of the rights guaranteed in the treaties and their significance. They include the right to:

1. **Indian/Dene government and nationhood:** The treaties established the sovereign relationships between Indian Nations and Canada.

2. **Indian institutions and administration:** A full range of social, economic, spiritual, cultural and educational institutions are guaranteed as necessary elements for any sovereign nation to govern.

3. **Indian lands, water and resources:** The treaties established reserved Indian land. It should be recognized that anything not specifically ceded by the Indian Nations by the articles of treaty remains under Indian jurisdiction.

4. **Education:** It was agreed in treaty negotiations that the government of Canada, under the authority and direction of the Indian government, is responsible for the establishment of the necessary facilities and the required resources.

5. **Health:** The government agreed to supply and maintain all types of health services.

6. **Social assistance:** Indian negotiators, foreseeing the difficulties facing Indian people until sufficient economic advancement could occur, were intent on securing the assistance required to achieve the quality of life promised.

7. **Police protection and the extradition process:** Offences, other than *Criminal Code* offences, are defined by Indian law and punishable by Indian courts with right of appeal through the Canadian court system. Federal and provincial laws do not apply on Indian land except where the Indian government involved has passed a law expressly adopting a specific law.

8. **Economics:** The Indian Nations are guaranteed the following: exclusive Indian ownership, jurisdiction and management of economic resources on Indian land; financial and technical support for the establishment of a self-sufficient Indian economy; Indian economic institutions for development and banking; and support for Indian businesses, industrial and resource development.

9. **Hunting, fishing, trapping and gathering:** Indian people have the right to hunt and fish on their lands.

10. **Exemption from taxation:** The treaties granted Canada access to the resources upon which much of the national economy and wealth is built. The treaties, therefore, represented prepayment by Indian people for services guaranteed to them in perpetuity.

11. **Exemption from war services:** Indian people cannot be forced to fight in any war in which Canada, or any other nation, becomes involved.

12. **Meet in council:** The Indian people and the federal government were to meet to review the treaties at least once annually.

13. **Cross international boundaries:** The Jay Treaty of 1794 recognized the right of Indian people to travel freely across North America to conduct trade and commerce without paying any form of taxes or duties.

RECOMMENDATIONS

There are no recommendations presented in this document.

▲ To Have What is One's Own

AUTHOR: National Indian Socio-Economic Development Committee
YEAR: 1979
ABORIGINAL GROUP: First Nations
TOPICS: Economic Development, Employment Development
SUB-TOPIC: economic development on-reserve
SOURCE: Aboriginal/Federal Commission

BACKGROUND

This is a report of the National Indian Socio-Economic Development Committee (NISEDC). The committee was established in 1978 for a three-year period, under the joint sponsorship of the Department of Indian Affairs and Northern Development (DIAND) and the National Indian Brotherhood (NIB).

NISEDC's three-year mandate was not completed as a result of the dismissal of the special adviser, Mr. J. Beaver, on the request of the NIB in 1979, and the subsequent dissolution of the NISEDC.

PURPOSE

The committee was asked to review the recommendations of the NIB/DIAND Strategy Report, assess existing government programs and policies, and develop policy recommendations with respect to Indian socio-economic development.

ISSUES AND FINDINGS

The economic situation of Indian communities is one of under-development. This situation has not improved, even with increased government expenditures. The report identifies lack of control of economic resources by Indian communities as a primary contributor to poor economic circumstances. This situation is in part a result of government policies and Indian organizations.

The under-development of the Indian communities is linked with the under-utilization of economic resources in activities of direct benefit to the community, and to limited access to financial capital, as a result of constraints imposed by the legal status of reserve lands. The direct consequence of economic under-development is high unemployment on-reserve, further aggravated by limited labour force participation by Indian peoples outside the reserve community.

The report argues that neither government nor Indian bands have addressed the problem. Bands have not been successful in effecting needed policy and program changes, mainly because:

1. DIAND and NIB have different understanding with respect to their roles and functions in the process of policy development; and

2. there is a level of political tension and confrontation between government and the NIB.

A major obstacle to the development of policies to address the socio-economic under-development of Indian communities is the inability of the government and the NIB to work together.

Efforts by DIAND to develop policy have failed to incorporate Indian participation. Current policies fail to understand both the fundamental nature of problems faced by the Indian bands. This misunderstanding has resulted in a lack of consistent policy measures to address the problem.

The report argues that revision of the *Indian Act* is vital to the evolution of Indian self-government and that self-government is essential to controlling the resources necessary for socio-economic development.

In particular, the report proposes three funding options for Indian bands:

1. bands receive capital funds held in trust, plus a per-capita amount equivalent to that provided by the federal government to the provinces;

2. bands receive direct funds equivalent to amounts received for national programs (health/education/public works); and

3. bands receive funds based on a funding formula.

The report calls for a change in government funding approaches, from one of "funding", to one which emphasizes "investment" in Indian communities. This would reduce the cost of remedial services and create an environment of Indian control of economic development.

RECOMMENDATIONS

The report's recommendations focus on two elements which are seen as essential to Indian economic development:

1. Indian self-government; and

2. community-based planning and development.

The report also recommends the creation of an independent organization, either within or outside DIAND, with a mandate to assist and advise Indian communities in economic development.

1980

▲ Freedom to Live Our Own Way in Our Own Land

AUTHOR: Conne River Indian Band Council (Jerry Wetzel, Pat Anderson, Douglas Sanders, Huguette Giard, and Pamela White)

YEAR: 1980

ABORIGINAL GROUP: First Nations

TOPIC: Claims

SUB-TOPIC: comprehensive claims

SOURCE: Local Aboriginal Organization

BACKGROUND

In 1977, the Inuit and the Naskapi-Montagnais of Labrador submitted their land claims to the federal government. These claims were assessed and were deemed valid by both the premier of Newfoundland and Labrador and the minister of Indian Affairs and Northern Development.

In 1978, the Micmac Association of Newfoundland submitted an interim report setting out their basis for a land claim on insular Newfoundland. This report, as well as two additional documents submitted a year later, were rejected by the federal government on the grounds that they did not contain enough evidence to support a land claim. In 1980, a revised claim, argued in *Freedom to Live Our Own Way in Our Own Land*, was submitted to the federal and provincial governments.

PURPOSE

The purpose of *Freedom to Live Our Own Way in Our Own Land* was to outline the facts of Micmac and European use and occupancy in Newfoundland. In order to complete this task, pre-contact and pre-colonial Micmac occupancy of Newfoundland was documented. Accounts of Micmacs, non-Native writers, and observations and references to Micmacs in the early European records of Newfoundland, were used.

The research was designed to refute the federal government's position concerning Aboriginal occupancy of Newfoundland. In doing so, it was deemed necessary to demonstrate that there had in fact been so little European use and occupancy of the southern coast and interior, that neither the French nor the English were in a position to document the Micmac existence in this area. As well, the research was designed to dispel myths concerning the relationship between the Micmacs and the Beothuks; this relationship had been previously described as hostile, and some had argued that the French paid the Micmacs to kill the Beothuks. According to the report, these notions are unfounded.

ISSUES AND FINDINGS

The evidence presented in the report indicates that the Micmacs had used the southern and southwestern shores of Newfoundland long before 1600. The report also contends that the Micmac people had occupied and used the south central interior of Newfoundland exclusively for several hundred years prior to European contact in the sixteenth century. The document further asserts that the Micmacs were killed by the English in the course of their quest for the fishery on the northeastern coast. Contact with the Europeans was determined to have taken place in the 1860s.

RECOMMENDATIONS

There are no formal recommendations presented in this document.

▲ Indian Nations: Self-Determination or Termination

AUTHOR: Union of British Columbia Indian Chiefs
YEAR: 1980
ABORIGINAL GROUP: First Nations
TOPICS: Self-Government, Constitution, Federal Government/Aboriginal Relations, Claims
SUB-TOPICS: rights, development, treaties, jurisdiction, federal trust responsibilities, policy
SOURCE: Provincial Aboriginal Organization

BACKGROUND

This report, prepared by the Union of British Columbia Indian Chiefs (UBCIC), contends that Indian Nations are in a state of emergency across Canada. A major impetus to this crisis has been the transfer of British control of the British North America Act to Canada, which has threatened termination of the rights of Indian people.

PURPOSE

This report was prepared as a proposal for immediate action to prevent the Canadian and British governments from terminating the British Trusteeship over Indian Nations, and thereby to prevent political and cultural absorption of Indian Nations and peoples into an independent Canada.

ISSUES AND FINDINGS

The UBCIC raises issues in four principal areas:

1. Canadian Constitution and the BNA Act

The BNA Act, while delegating provincial and federal authority, does not create or delegate authority to Indian governments. Instead, it delegates administrative duties empowering the Canadian government to protect Indian national lands, Indian government, and provide financial and technical assistance to Indian governments in the fulfilment of British treaty responsibilities.

The UBCIC contends that Britain's and Canada's responsibilities toward Indian Nations are a result of international law, not Canadian domestic law. They found the BNA Act to be partly based on treaties and agreements between Indian Nations and Britain, and these agreements are seen as the foundation upon which the international rights of Indian Nations are based. Despite this relationship, however, Indian Nations have not been consulted or included in the patriation of the BNA Act. They seek direct participation in discussions with both Canada and Britain to ensure their political integrity with Britain and their security from absorption within Canada.

2. Patriation

Patriation is viewed as a significant set of constitutional amendments having serious implications for all Indian Nations:

(a) the amendments release Canada from all administrative responsibilities toward Indian Nations performed on behalf of the British government;

(b) the lack of Indian participation can be interpreted to mean that Canada will not recognize a place for Indian Nations in its federation;

(c) traditional Indian rights and freedoms could be considered "discriminatory" and therefore illegal under the Canadian Constitution; and

(d) equalization payments could lead to the termination of the special relationship between the federal government and Indian Nations.

3. Federal Intentions

The UBCIC believes that Canada remains intent on achieving total assimilation of Indian peoples and a complete destruction of Indian government. This policy toward termination is consistent with long-standing Canadian objectives and practices.

The report presents some historical evidence to support their belief concerning the federal government's assimilationist intentions. According to the UBCIC, the federal "game plan" remained essentially the same from Confederation (when Canada's stated policy was to "civilize" the Indian Nations) to the White Paper in 1969 (which advocated the end to special status and Indian rights) to the establishment of the Office of Native Claims and the development of a specific claims policy in the 1970s (which were designed to accelerate the termination of special status) to the present, 1980.

4. Reserving Indian Political Rights

The UBCIC also raised the issue of reserving Indian political rights. They found that Indian rights to land, resources, culture, language, a livelihood, and self-government are pre-existing rights and are inviolable. The report established that the authority of Indian Nations does not depend on the Canadian Constitution; the Constitution cannot diminish, alter or eliminate the rights of Indian peoples, as this power rests only with the citizens of various Indian Nations.

RECOMMENDATIONS

The UBCIC concluded that a new Canadian Constitution could result in either of two scenarios for Indian Nations; it could have the effect of entrenching poverty, dependency and alienation, or the effect of re-opening avenues to Indian national growth and development. In order to enable the latter to be realized, the Union felt that a positive approach would be required which would elevate constitutional patriation to an exercise in nation-building. As such, they made the following recommendations, aimed at resolving and preventing serious conflict:

1. that representatives of Indian Nations, Britain, and Canada enter into internationally supervised discussions in Oslo, Norway, to settle a number of questions, including:

    (a) defining boundaries of Indian Nations and Canada;

    (b) establishing mechanisms for resolving future conflicts;

    (c) defining the terms of political coexistence;

    (d) designing methods of financial aid;

    (e) determining the measures for exercising full self-government; and

    (f) agreeing upon the formation of an International Indigenous Trust Council within the United Nations to oversee future relations between Indigenous peoples and countries.

2. that Canada notify the Indigenous provisional government that it will not finalize constitutional patriation until the above-mentioned trilateral conference has concluded;

3. that the Indigenous provisional government also be notified of Canada's intent not to violate the political or territorial integrity of the Indian Nations at any time;

4. that the Canadian and British governments share equally in the costs to support the Indigenous government in the trilateral conference; and

5. that Britain notify the Indigenous government of her intent to fulfil its trust responsibilities to the Indian Nations.

▲ National Indian Brotherhood National Indian Health Policy: A Compilation of Health Policy Papers

AUTHOR: National Commission Inquiry on Indian Health, NIB Health Development Program

YEAR: 1980

ABORIGINAL GROUP: First Nations

TOPIC: Health

SUB-TOPICS: non-insured health services, fiscal relations/responsibilities

SOURCE: National Aboriginal Organization

BACKGROUND

In October, 1977, the Commission was formed in response to a National Indian Brotherhood Executive Council resolution; it functions as a technical sub-committee of the NIB Executive Council. It held several sessions (seven commission meetings and one ad hoc meeting) in an attempt to discuss a number of Indian health issues. The Commission was mandated to investigate the steps necessary for Indian control of Indian health services.

PURPOSE

The Commission investigated the fundamental issues in Indian health. It addressed the root causes of Indian ill-health and potential administrative and structural cures.

ISSUES AND FINDINGS

Many issues are presented in the numerous policy papers contained within the report.

1. The first paper, the Statement of Policy, National Commission Inquiry on Indian Health Services, deals with the issue of Indian control over Indian health services. The Commission addresses the point that health has been a federal responsibility, administered by the Department of Indian and Northern Affairs (DIAND), and then by the Department of National Health and Welfare; the services were found to have been inadequate since they were initiated.

2. The second paper, the History of Indian Health, the Documentation of the Causes of the Decline in Indian Health, examines the issue of Indian health history. The Commission found that Indian people were in good health when living by their traditional lifestyle and when they had minimal contact with the Europeans. The major sources of disease were (1) trauma, (2) acute starvation (occurring occasionally and increasing with the frequency of contact with Europeans), and (3) some eye disorders. Most infectious diseases and chronic degenerative diseases were absent or rare prior to European contact. Eventually, Indian people incorporated the European refined foods as a significant part of their diet, thereby increasing the incidence of disease not associated with their traditional foods. Declining Indian health was exacerbated by several factors: (1) their nomadic lifestyle which did not accommodate long periods of recovery, resulting in frequent starvation; (2) confinement to reserve life on land which was frequently not arable or of sufficient size; (3) degenerative diseases caused by the lack of physical work resulting from high unemployment; (4) the suppression of traditional medicine and the medicine man, combined with the introduction of western medicines in an inadequate manner; (5) lack of funds and the development of a professionalised monopoly; and (6) government paternalism which has demoralized the Indian people and has contributed to the increase of poor health.

3. The third paper, A Brief Summary of Rights and Priorities in Indian Health, deals with the issue of Indian rights to health care. Included in previous treaties is the clause that the "medicine chest" would be kept by the Indian people. From 1876 onward, however, medical services were supplied to Treaty Indians, and health care was a federal responsibility. The paper deals with the priorities for Indian health care, which include the following: (1) adequate services for off-reserve Indian people; (2) a co-ordinated approach to the environmental causes of disease, and to the administration of Indian health by DIAND; (3) a community health representative program; (4) nutrition and health education; (5) mental and spiritual health; and (6) a return to the traditional Indian medicines.

4. The fourth paper, Priorities for Indian Health Care, examines the priorities for Indian health care set out in the third paper. It asserts that the present approach is inadequate and that many changes are required. It urges that unacceptable environmental conditions, including water and sanitation, be brought up to a level of parity. It suggests that the responsibility of community health representative programs should rest with the community. According to the paper, present nutrition programs are inadequate and must be changed to reflect Indian needs.

5. The fifth paper, Indian Control of Indian Health, looks at the failure of the federal government in the area of Indian health. It states that the federal government is masking its true agenda and is waiting for an appropriate time to transfer responsibility, particularly financial responsibility, to territorial or provincial governments. It suggests that there is a need for self-determination, since federal programs fail when the people directly affected are not involved, and it recognizes Indian health as a top priority. It also addresses the issue of the role of the federal government, recommending less interference but more assistance. The paper makes a key distinction between Indian control of Indian health and Indian management of federally determined health programs; funding alone is considered inadequate.

6. The sixth paper, The Role of Indian Organizations in the Development of Indian Health Councils, examines the issue of participation by Indian people, and finds it essential to the effective provision of health care services to Indian people.

7. The seventh paper, the Presentation to the All Ontario Chiefs Conference, deals with the issue of the Ontario Regional Liaison Council. It finds it to be too politicized in structure, and to function predominantly as a rubber stamp. It also deals with the inadequacies of Native housing.

8. The eighth paper, A Resource Paper for the Development of Indian Health Councils, examines various alternative approaches for developing Indian Health Councils. It sees benefits to band councils of a health council that can act as a resource to band councils, and can facilitate the organization of community-based health programs. The paper contends that these councils must have the support of various interest groups in the community to be effective.

RECOMMENDATIONS

Each paper makes its own recommendations, dealing with the issue it has examined. There is however, a common recommendation that control over Indian health care should be given to the Indian people.

1. The first paper recommends a suspension of the Policy Directive for uninsured services.

2. The second paper advocates a holistic approach, incorporating health care with community development.

3. The third paper suggests returning the administration of medical services to DIAND in order to ensure efficiency.

4. The fourth paper recommends that the gap between the quality of Indian health and of Canadian health be narrowed within a specified time frame. It also recommends the establishment of Indian health boards.

5. The fifth paper asserts the continued importance of Indian self-determination and communal decision making. It recommends the redirection of national health goals, in an effort to recognize the health and welfare needs of the country as a whole, with Indian health requiring top priority. It further recommends Indian control of services and movement toward self-determination.

6. The sixth paper recommends meaningful participation and involvement, at all levels, by Indian people in order for health care services to be effective. It is suggested that a national forum for consultation be established.

7. The seventh paper makes no relevant recommendations.

8. The eighth paper suggests that single-dimension approaches to health councils tend to limit their effectiveness; therefore, co-ordination between the activities of the councils and health-related activities outside the health care system must occur.

▲ The Nature of Aboriginal Title – Is It Transferable or Assignable?

AUTHOR: Association of Métis and Non-Status Indians of Saskatchewan

YEAR: 1980

ABORIGINAL GROUP: All Aboriginal Peoples

TOPICS: Treaty Land Entitlement, Claims, Federal Government/Aboriginal Relations, Provincial Government/Aboriginal Relations

SUB-TOPICS: claims, treaties, federal trust responsibilities, legislation, Crown lands, resources

SOURCE: Provincial Aboriginal Organization

BACKGROUND

This paper provides a historical assessment of significant court decisions addressing the issue of Aboriginal title. It includes discussions of British colonial practice, and pursues the possibility that the benefits derived from the extinguishment of Aboriginal title can be assigned or transferred.

PURPOSE

The purpose of this paper is to examine the nature of Aboriginal rights, and to answer the question of whether the right to title is transferable or assignable.

ISSUES AND FINDINGS

The paper is divided into two sections. The first examines the historical record regarding the assignment or transfer of Aboriginal title. In the second section, the report examines the cases and the history pertaining to the transfer or assignment of the benefits derived from the extinguishment of Aboriginal title. The report's examination focuses on the legality of transfer or assignment of benefits under treaties, halfbreed grants, and scrip.

In section I of the paper, the report refers to a progression of court cases and historical documents to support his finding that Aboriginal title cannot be assigned or transferred, that it is a personal right and can only be alienated to the Crown.

The report cites *Johnson* v. *McIntosh* (a case argued before the United States Supreme Court in 1823), in concert with the Royal Proclamation of 1763, and submits that this decision places the right of purchase (extinguishment) of Indian lands only with the Crown and not with individuals. The report follows with reference to the *British North America Act* of 1867 (particularly sections 91 and 109) and its relevance in the *St. Catharines Milling Case* (1889), to support this assertion.

The *St. Catharines* decision was to establish the tenure of Indian title for Canada through its conclusion that the Crown maintained the absolute fee and Indian people a "personal and usufructuary right" to the land. Thus the Crown was established as the single entity to which Indian people could surrender or extinguish their right or title to their land.

The report looks to *Calder* v. *Attorney General of British Columbia* (1973), and the Caveat Case (1973) in the Northwest Territories as the modern expression of the Crown's (federal government's) interest underlying the Aboriginal title. These cases upheld the principle that Aboriginal title is inalienable; it cannot be transferred but rather can only be terminated by reversion to the Crown. These cases provided a finer distinction of the nature of Aboriginal Title. They assert the characteristic of communal possession of the right to occupy and enjoy the fruits of the land and waters by those who descend from the Aboriginal peoples of Canada, excluding those who do not have a valid legal claim based on possession from time immemorial (or at least prior to Colonial entry into the country and region). Therefore Aboriginal title cannot be transferred or assigned to those individuals or groups who do not possess this characteristic of communal possession.

In the second section of the paper, the report explores the possibility that the benefits derived from the extinguishment of Aboriginal title can be assigned or transferred. The report examines this possibility under treaties, and the issuance of halfbreed grants and scrip.

Treaties

The report finds that by treaty, any benefits derived from the extinguishment of Indian title can only be enjoyed by those people covered by the treaty. The report refers to the *Provincial Wildlife Act* of Saskatchewan in conjunction with the Natural Resources Transfer Agreement of 1930 in support of this position.

Halfbreed Grants and Scrip

The report concludes that the Indian title of halfbreeds cannot be assigned or transferred. According to the judiciary (in addition to legislation and Orders-in-Council), however, the sale benefit (i.e., land that was acquired by halfbreeds in the purported extinguishment of Indian title) can be assigned or transferred.

The report raises, but does not answer, the question of whether this form of extinguishment is legally valid and whether the federal government has breached its trust obligation. In conclusion, the report argues that it is still possible to demand restitution of the sale benefit, even if the halfbreed's Indian title has been legally extinguished.

RECOMMENDATIONS

This discussion paper contains no recommendations.

1981

▲ Native People and the Constitution of Canada: The Report of the Métis and Non-Status Indian Constitutional Review Commission

AUTHOR: Métis and Non-Status Indian Constitutional Review, Commissioner, Harry W. Daniels

YEAR: 1981

ABORIGINAL GROUP: Métis, Non-Status

TOPICS: Constitution, Federal Government/Aboriginal Relations, Provincial Government/Aboriginal Relations, Intergovernmental Relations, Treaty Land Entitlement, Claims, Resources, Economic Development, Administration of Justice, Education, Child Welfare, Family/Family Relations, Language, Cultural Affairs, Membership/Citizenship/Constituency, Communications

SOURCE: National Aboriginal Organization

BACKGROUND

This report was commissioned at a time when the federal government was seeking input into the development of a new constitution for Canada. Input was sought from many areas, including the many Aboriginal organizations throughout the country.

PURPOSE

The Métis and Non-Status Indian Constitutional Review Commission was established by the Native Council of Canada in July 1980, to canvass the views of Métis and non-status Indians across Canada on the subject of a new constitution. It provided an opportunity for broad participation by these Native groups in the formulation of policy initiatives with respect to Aboriginal peoples and their status within a new constitution.

ISSUES AND FINDINGS

The report was divided into six broad areas for consideration:

1. Native collectivities;
2. Native rights in Canada;
3. Native people and the polity;
4. culture and communications;
5. Métis land claims and;
6. Native people and the economy.

Each of these subject areas was dealt with extensively throughout the report. Within the recommendations section of this summary, each of these areas is dealt with separately. In terms of the report's issues and findings, however, a number of general themes are developed that are common to all of the areas of study.

One such theme addresses the lack of participation by Native peoples within the decision-making institutions of our country. Historically, the treatment of Native peoples has been poor in this country and the desire to change this record is quite strong.

Many who made presentations to the Commission felt that the opportunity to entrench Aboriginal rights within the constitution was the first step toward ensuring that Aboriginal peoples would be recognized for their important contribution to Canadian history. They argued that Aboriginal peoples were not proportionately represented in the institutions that govern this country and that decisions made on their behalf were made without their input. The report highlighted the lack of representation in the House of Commons and the Senate and the desire of Native peoples to be part of these institutions.

As well, it was argued that the traditional values and cultures of Native peoples were not reflected in either the institutions or programs that governed them. The report refers to both the educational and legal systems as examples of institutions that do not encourage or reflect the uniqueness of Native peoples and their traditions. The report highlights the lack of understanding by non-Native Canadians of Native culture and its importance to the identity of this country. As well, the report illustrates the need for the creation of new programs that would allow Native peoples to educate and promote their traditions and values within their communities.

The report also looks at the economic disparities of the Native communities and the lack of financial programs to address this problem. This issue is intrinsically related to that of land claims. Many argued that all levels of government need to address the land claim issue quickly so that a resolution to the economic problems could be achieved. The Native peoples see the advantages of having their own land base and the ability to have a voice in how the land might be used for the betterment of their communities.

RECOMMENDATIONS

The report makes 53 recommendations which cover each of the areas of study. They are summarized as follows:

1. Native Collectivities

The report insists that the constitution should recognize the existence of Indian, Métis and Inuit collectivities and their right to develop in accordance with their own aspirations. It calls on the government to accurately enumerate Canada's Métis and non-status Indian population through the administration of the decennial census.

The report also calls for an end to the many biases within the *Indian Act* that discriminate against women and men who have lost their status and wish to regain it. It calls on the federal government to enter into agreements with various bands to allow non-status Native people to return if they so choose, to expand both the land size and budgets of reserves to accommodate any increase in population, and to ensure the same rights and privileges for non-status Indians living off-reserve as those Status Indians living on-reserve.

With respect to the education system, the report calls for the increased participation of Native peoples. More spaces should be made available to Native people to enter teachers' college, and more places should be reserved on school boards and administrations where the numbers warrant. As well, Métis and non-status Indian students should be allowed to receive the same financial assistance from the federal government as that of Status Indian students.

The report also recommends that the federal government should have jurisdiction in those areas of family law where particular provision is made for the interests of Native children. Changes should be made to the current family law legislation that could better reflect the traditional customs, values and practices of the Native communities.

2. Native Rights in Canada

The report recommends that Native peoples be recognized as founding peoples in a preamble to the constitution and that a Charter of Native Rights be added to the proposed Constitution Act. The report also proposes the adoption of a new amending formula for those sections of the constitution which would directly affect the rights of Native peoples. The amending formula should require the consent of Native groups and the support of the Parliament of Canada for constitutional amendments that would affect Native rights.

3. Native People and the Polity

The report recommends that the constitution confirm the jurisdiction of the federal government over Métis and non-status Indians. It also calls for the removal of provincial authority over Métis and non-status Indians.

The report recommends the creation of a Métis National Council as the non-sovereign governing body of the national community of Métis and non-status Indians. A separate secretariat should be developed by the federal government to co-ordinate existing and future federal policies that would affect this population of Native peoples.

The Commission also calls for increased participation and representation of Native peoples within the political institutions that govern our country.

The report calls for the creation of Native constituencies as well as the allocation of existing seats in the House of Commons to increase representation within government. The report also calls for a change in the voting system to reflect the language and geographical concerns of the Native peoples across Canada, including the creation of a separate voting list. Guarantees should also be made for similar representation in provincial and territorial legislatures as well as in the Senate of Canada; such provisions should be based on the size of the Native population.

With respect to the legal system, the report again calls for greater participation by Native peoples within the system. More Native lawyers and para-legal personnel such as court workers should be trained to make the court system more responsive to the needs of Native peoples. Language barriers should be addressed and changes should be made to incorporate the cultural and traditional ways of this population within the system.

4. Culture and Communication

According to the report, the constitution should recognize the Aboriginal heritage of Canada as an integral part of the national culture. Public cultural institutions should ensure that the Native dimension of Canadian identity is portrayed.

All levels of government should work to ensure that Native history, languages and culture is taught within the education system. Furthermore, the federal government should support the creation of Native-run educational institutions and the development of Native studies programs at Canadian universities.

Native communications programs should be developed through the federal government and the CRTC. The establishment of greater participation by Native peoples in the CBC and the National Film Board should be encouraged by the federal government. Financial assistance should be provided to Native communities to set up their own broadcasting facilities and to develop their own programming.

5. Land Claims

The report recommends, through the constitution, the creation of a special Court of Aboriginal Claims to deal with past and future disputes arising out of the various land claims before the federal government.

6. Native People and the Economy

The Commission recommends that the federal government and Métis and non-status Indian representatives enter into negotiations with provincial governments to settle the land titles of Native peoples and that the federal government be prepared to compensate the provinces for lands transferred to Native peoples.

The report calls for the creation of equalization payments for Native communities to lessen disparities in the different regions of the country and to allow for the governing bodies of the Aboriginal peoples to have sufficient revenues to promote economic development within their own communities.

The report also calls upon the federal government to recognize that hunting, fishing, trapping and other renewable resource rights should be considered Aboriginal rights and should be included in the constitution.

◆ *Native Women – Labour Force Development* (1981),
see **Reports by Federal Bodies.**

◆ *Report of the Tripartite Local Government Committee Respecting Indian Local Government in British Columbia* (1981),
see **Volume 3, British Columbia.**

1982

▲ The Newfoundland Government's Rejection of the Micmac Land Claim

AUTHOR: The Indian and Inuit Support Group of Newfoundland and Labrador

YEAR: 1982

ABORIGINAL GROUP: First Nations

TOPIC: Claims

SUB-TOPIC: comprehensive claims

SOURCE: Provincial Aboriginal Organization

BACKGROUND

This report was prepared in response to a 1982 report for the government of Newfoundland and Labrador, *Assessment and Analysis of the Micmac Land Claim in Newfoundland* (the Jones Report), which argued that the Micmac claim was invalid. Premier Peckford rejected the claim on the basis of the findings of the Jones Report.

PURPOSE

The general purpose of the report is to voice the concerns of the Indian and Inuit Support Group with regard to the arguments contained within the Jones Report. To this end, the report argues that the Premier's intervention was inappropriate, and that the arguments contained within the Jones Report are flawed.

ISSUES AND FINDINGS

The Support Group identifies four issues that are critical to the provincial government's treatment of the Micmac land claim. The first issue addresses the inappropriateness of Premier Peckford's rejection of the claim before the federal government had made its decision. Because claims are submitted to the federal government, it is unprecedented and unconstitutional for the provincial government to pass judgement on the claim prior to the federal government's response. The report indicated that there was some speculation that the Premier might have rejected the claim due to public opposition. The Support Group views his intervention as an obstruction of justice.

A second issue of concern to the Support Group is the validity of the criteria used in the Jones report. The report claims that the arguments contained within the Jones report were based on narrow, legal principles, derived from the case of the Inuit of Baker Lake, Northwest Territories. The Office of Native Claims had requested only a non-legalistic, common-sense demonstration of long-term occupation, not legal principles. The Support Group asserts, however, that even if the Baker Lake Criteria were one day required, the Micmac would be able to present a convincing case.

A third issue relates to the validation of an Aboriginal claim by showing title to the territory before European contact. The Jones report conducted no original research into this subject area. The Support Group contends that not only did the Jones report not take Micmac research into consideration, but it dismissed all oral history accounts, even those dating back to information collected between 1839 and 1922. There is still archaeological research and historical evidence being collected that is relevant to the Micmac land claim.

A fourth issue deals directly with historical evidence. According to the Support Group, Jones overlooked the major historians specializing in the region and the time period. Jones may have interpreted seasonal use of the land as not constituting genuine occupation; this seasonal use, however, by no means weakens the claim, as it is considered a basic element of the hunters' land tenure system. Jones also overlooked archival sources indicating historical evidence of occupation.

RECOMMENDATIONS

The Support Group recommends that the government of Newfoundland examine key archival evidence indicating historical Micmac occupation and that more research be undertaken to determine occupancy.

▲ Public Government for the People of the North

AUTHOR: Dene Nation and Métis Association of the Northwest Territories

YEAR: 1982

ABORIGINAL GROUP: First Nations, Métis

TOPICS: Self-Government, Constitution, Constitutional Development, Political Development/Relationships

SUB-TOPICS: rights, structures/institutions, jurisdiction, development

SOURCE: Territorial Aboriginal Organizations

BACKGROUND

This position paper outlines the views of the Dene and Métis Nations on self-government and constitutional change at a time when the federal government was in the process of renewing Canada's Constitution.

PURPOSE

The purpose of the paper was to outline a political system that would embody Dene values and that would reflect the Dene style and form of political organization. The goal was to provide a just and efficient government for both

Dene and other Canadians in the western part of the Northwest Territories (N.W.T.).

ISSUES AND FINDINGS

The document sets out a model of public government in which powers are divided between a provincial system of government and community government. The political system proposed is based on recognition that the Dene are the original inhabitants of the territories and still comprise the majority of permanent residents in the western part of the N.W.T.; they are therefore entitled to a form of public government that reflects their majority. The paper emphasizes that it is essential that the future political system recognize the rights of Aboriginal peoples, and that certain lands be designated for the exclusive use by the Aboriginal communities so that they can continue to enjoy their way of life.

According to the report, the present system has produced a dependency by Native people on the federal government. In addition to this dependency, the report identifies a number of important issues facing the Dene and Métis Nations:

1. immense social problems;
2. the lack of control over natural resources;
3. the lack of control of public utilities;
4. the rapidly rising cost of living; and
5. the dominance of the federal government, which makes all but the most trivial decisions.

The report contends that the most important issues for the Native communities are reaching an agreement on Aboriginal rights, and creating political jurisdictions in the North that will enhance the ability of all northerners to govern their own lives.

RECOMMENDATIONS

The report proposes a new system of government for the western part of the N.W.T. to be controlled by the Dene Nation. The report offers a detailed description of the proposed structure and operation of the government. A brief outline is presented below.

1. Division of Powers

A clear division of powers between Denendeh (land of the people and the name given to the Dene Nation government) and the federal government would be necessary. The goal is to make Denendeh a political jurisdiction with powers similar, but not identical, to those of other provinces. Denendeh might even have some powers which other provinces do not have.

The Dene Nation report also recognizes the Inuvialuit in the Mackenzie Delta region and their desire to form a regional government. The Dene Nation would negotiate to include a form of Inuvialuit regional government within Denendeh.

The Denendeh system of government would share constitutional powers similar to those of other provinces, such as those regarding institutions of government, administration of justice, health and welfare, local trade, and commerce. The Dene government would want the transfer of power from the federal government to their government to include areas such as navigation and fisheries, family relations, communications, labour and employment, areas of shared powers, and regulations with other Aboriginal nations.

2. Charter of Principles

The Denendeh system of government would establish a Charter of Founding Principles similar to the Canadian Charter. The Charter would establish institutions and services which reflect the values and ways of Aboriginal peoples in areas such as education, health services, social services, arts, media, recreation and games, and training in traditional skills and crafts. The Charter would also contain rights and freedoms similar to those included in sections 18, 19, 21 and 22 of the International Covenant on Civil and Political Rights, including freedom of thought, conscience, and religion, as well as language rights.

3. Land and Resources Ownership in Denendeh

This aspect of government would provide for exclusive Dene land, land and resources controlled by the government of Denendeh, and private property for members of Dene communities.

4. Sharing of Powers

Within the new political system, there would be two levels of government – a provincial level of government and community government.

5. Community Government

A community government would have powers in areas (with some limitations) such as natural resources, services (health, education, social services, policing, recreation, etc.), finances (community budget, issuing of licences, management of funds), and operations (water, sewage, retail goods, construction and maintenance, public goods,etc). The structure of the community government would include a community assembly open to all residents (with some limitations, such as a two-year residency in the community, and a ten-year residency in Denendeh) and would have the power through referendum to decide on broad policy direction for the community. A community council would be established, made up of a chief and councillors who would be elected by the community assembly and whose power to make decisions would be derived from the community. Length of office and structure would also be determined by the community assembly.

6. Provincial Level of Government

The provincial level of government would be responsible for broad policy issues in the areas of jurisdiction that were once the responsibility of the federal government. The provincial level of government would also have responsibility in the area of intergovernmental relations, particularly relations with the federal government and other regions across Canada.

The Dene government at the provincial level would also have a national assembly fashioned after current provincial systems with the Aboriginal people deciding the composition and terms of office for their elected representatives. An executive level of government with a cabinet would also exist, as would a Dene Senate with veto powers over legislation passed at either the community or provincial level that adversely affect Aboriginal rights or freedoms based on tradition. The composition and structure of the Senate would be determined by the Dene.

7. Fiscal Viability of Denendeh

The report proposes that the Dene government be treated like any other jurisdiction in Canada and that it be eligible for transfer payments from the federal government in addition to powers of taxation currently held by provinces. The report acknowledges the rich resource base of the North and concludes that economic self-sufficiency could be achieved.

8. Transition of Power

The report offers a detailed outline of the process of consultation that would occur within the Dene Nation and with the federal government in order to move toward a new system of government in the North. The report stresses the need for all members of the Dene Nation to be represented and for all views to be heard in order to create a system of government truly representative of Aboriginal people.

▲ What Does the Future Hold for Native Women – Aboriginal Entitlement

AUTHOR: Ontario Native Women's Association
YEAR: 1982
ABORIGINAL GROUP: All Aboriginal Peoples, Aboriginal Women
TOPICS: Political Participation, Constitution
SUB-TOPICS: documents, rights
SOURCE: Provincial Aboriginal Organization

BACKGROUND

A conference of the Ontario Native Women's Association was held on March 7, 1982. The conference was organized around the theme of "what does the future hold for Native women?". One of the main purposes of the conference was to decide on the future course of action for Native women.

PURPOSE

The purpose of this paper is to report the findings and issues raised at the conference.

ISSUES AND FINDINGS

The primary issues raised at the conference were those concerning the Constitution and the *Indian Act*.

The Native Women's Association addressed a number of issues related to the Constitution. They focused primarily on those sections of the Constitution affecting Aboriginal peoples and women, particularly section 91(24) of the *Constitution Act, 1867*, section 15 of the Charter, and other provisions of the Charter and the *Constitution Act, 1982* which affect Aboriginal women. Section 25, which deals with Aboriginal and treaty rights not affected by the Charter, was controversial; although it recognizes existing Aboriginal and treaty rights, it does not go so far as to define these rights. In essence, the participants found that question of whether or not Indian women's rights are protected under the Constitution is still subject to legal interpretation.

The conference participants also raised the issue of the document known as "the Memorandum to Cabinet – amendments to remove the discriminatory sections of the *Indian Act*", which was released in draft form in 1981. The action was prompted by the finding by the United Nations that the *Indian Act* was discriminatory. The purpose of the memorandum was to determine what changes were necessary to remove the discriminatory clauses from the *Indian Act*.

The report also outlines the position of the Aboriginal women on other topics. Specifically, the report indicates support for the following:

1. the education of their children, families and communities as to their distinct way of life;

2. the promotion of the concept of Nationhood within a Nation;

3. the belief that the treatment of existing Aboriginal and treaty rights by the courts is biased in favour of the federal government;

4. the fundamental principle, philosophy, and concept of the inherent right to self-government;

5. the role of women in providing opportunities to develop the awareness, knowledge, and skills required to effectively perform management and administration; and

6. the need for a balance between the traditional forms of government and modern concepts of government.

RECOMMENDATIONS

The Ontario Native Women's Association made several recommendations regarding the future of Aboriginal women's participation:

1. that participation of Native women be increased by attending the First Nations conference in Penticton, British Columbia, and the World Council of First Nations Conference in 1982;

2. that Native women make representation on this conference to other Canadian Aboriginal organizations;

3. that Native women be assured of direct input in all constitutional discussions;

4. that Native women articulate their definition of rights to government and Aboriginal organizations;

5. that the Association locals be encouraged to hold workshops on cultural awareness; and

6. that the Association publicize its recognition of one Nation of people which includes Métis, non-status, Status and Inuit, and its dismissal of legal classifications which divide Aboriginal peoples, which have characterized the practices and applications of law by the federal government.

1983

▲ Le besoin de réévaluer et d'améliorer les relations Québec-Inuit

AUTHOR: Société Makivik

YEAR: 1983

ABORIGINAL GROUP: Inuit

TOPICS: Claims, Land Use, Development and Management, Resources, Environmental Protection, Economic Development, Education, Administration of Justice, Social Development, Community Services and Infrastructure

SUB-TOPICS: comprehensive claims, commission/institutions, land use planning, zoning, development, management

SOURCE: Local/Regional Aboriginal Organization

BACKGROUND

This report was presented as a general information memorandum to a National Assembly committee on the constitution. La Société Makivik, or the Makivik Corporation, created under Quebec law at the time of the James Bay and Northern Quebec Agreement in 1975, represents the Inuit of Northern Quebec in all economic, social and constitutional matters related to the Agreement.

PURPOSE

The purpose of the report is to present an overview of the goals and aspirations of the Northern Quebec Inuit, and their current preoccupations. The recommendations of the Makivik Corporation are based on their experience with the James Bay Agreement.

244

ISSUES AND FINDINGS

Three areas of concerns were studied: economy and society; culture; and political systems.

1. Economy and Society

In the area of economy and society, problems related to funding, program implementation, infrastructure, and economic development projects were cited by the Makivik Corporation:

(a) regional budgets allocated under the Convention were found to be inadequate to meet the mandate they had been given, as evidenced by problems of underfunding experienced by both the Kativik school board and the Kativik regional municipality;

(b) existing programs were found to be inefficiently implemented, with such provisions as compulsory employment of 25% Native people in construction projects, and priority procurement contracts to Northern Quebec companies, inhibiting effective program implementation;

(c) poorly developed infrastructure and essential services were also cited by the Corporation, as seen for instance by the lack of fire fighters, the need for professional training of Inuit in health services, and the inability of community centres to meet the high demand for leisure and sports; and

(d) there was found to be a need for more frequent economic development programs, but particularly those sensitive to the needs of the local peoples (i.e., the Northern Quebec Inuit favoured activities such as tourism or commercial hunting and fishing over the mega-projects approach of Hydro-Québec which tends to impose environmental pressures, as well as economic disturbances on a region that already has a price level twice that of other Quebec regions).

2. Culture

In the area of culture, the document reports problems in the areas of education, telecommunications, justice, and environmental conservation:

(a) the need to adapt teaching services to promote and protect Inuit culture was identified by the Corporation;

(b) Inuit culture was found to be poorly represented in communication services such as television;

(c) the report found that most of the provisions of the James Bay Agreement regarding the institutions and the management of justice (police training, access to legal services, incarceration) for and by the Inuit had not been implemented at the time of the report; and

(d) the Corporation argued that more scientific research needs to be performed to adapt southern practices to Northern Quebec conditions in order to ensure that environmental conservation efforts are effective.

3. Political Systems

The last area reviewed by the memorandum is political systems. The Corporation identified the need for the reform of electoral districts, fiscal administration, and legislation:

(a) the report found that electoral districts need to be reformed to increase Inuit representation in the National Assembly;

(b) the fiscal administration practices imposed on Inuit should be adapted to their own context, especially with regard to municipal planning; and

(c) the James Bay Agreement should be made a dynamic institution, with the participation of the Inuit in its evolution, and should be updated regularly to reflect the evolution of political systems in Northern Quebec.

RECOMMENDATIONS

Five recommendations were put forth in the memorandum:

1. that a tripartite committee (Quebec-Canada-Inuit) be established to ensure the proper implementation of the James Bay Agreement;

2. that a permanent parliamentary committee for Aboriginal people be created in order to have a unified policy toward Aboriginal people, including Inuit;

3. that Northern Quebec institutions become more independent of Quebec authorities by retaining sufficient funding and by entering into agreements to share tax revenues in the region;

4. that a special parliamentary committee be established to plan and increase the number of economic development programs in Northern Quebec, with special attention being given to the economic costs and benefits from both large and small projects; and

5. that the James Bay and Northern Quebec Agreement be updated every two years.

▲ Manitoba Métis Rights: Constitutional Consultations: Final Report

AUTHOR: Manitoba Métis Federation, Constitution and Land Claims Secretariat

YEAR: 1983

ABORIGINAL GROUP: Métis

TOPICS: Self-Government, Constitution, Financial Arrangements/Responsibilities/Public Finance, Taxation and Customs, Land Use, Development and Management, Economic Development

SUB-TOPICS: rights, financial arrangements/mechanisms, revenue generation, non-reserve lands/traditional lands, development, regional Aboriginal

SOURCE: Provincial Aboriginal Organization

BACKGROUND

The Métis National Council (MNC) was formed when the Native Council of Canada (NCC) reversed a decision to allow the Métis Constitutional Committee to have one of the two seats allocated to the Native Council of Canada for the constitutional talks. The Métis National Council sought its own seat, from which it could fight for constitutional recognition of a Métis land base and other rights, and represent itself rather than depending of the NCC or the provincial delegation to speak on behalf of the interests of Métis people.

PURPOSE

The Métis National Council engaged in extensive consultations across the province for the purpose of developing a position paper on Métis rights for presentation at the First Ministers' Constitutional Conference on the Rights of Aboriginal Peoples in 1983. The resulting document continues to be used by the Manitoba Métis Federation (MMF) as a guiding document for future constitutional work. This report contains the MNC position paper as well as detailed information yielded from a consultative process undertaken by the MMF and the documents of the government's delegation to the First Ministers' Conference.

ISSUES AND FINDINGS

The position paper discusses a number of issues, including recognition of Métis rights and the constitution, the need for a Métis land base, program and service delivery, the economic situation of Métis people, and the financing of Métis communities.

The position paper on Métis rights which is included in this report calls for amendments to the Constitution which would protect the rights of the Métis people to exist and develop as a nation, to use their own languages, to preserve and enhance their cultural heritage, to own land collectively and resources, to hunt, fish and trap, to establish their own forms of self-government, and to design and operate their own social and economic programs.

There is a general agreement expressed in this report that the Métis require a land base, as well as the technological assistance to develop this land, in order to realize the economic and political independence outlined in the rights which they are claiming. The position paper argues that colonial attitudes held toward Métis communities must be altered and the Métis must be given general municipal powers as well as the authority to administer their land bases, provide economic and social services, and control their own economic development. Employment, income security, child care, health, education, justice, housing, and communications are examples of services which the Métis must begin to administer if they are to exist and develop as a nation.

The majority of the report outlines the detailed results of community consultations which were conducted by the Manitoba Métis Federation. During these meetings, community representatives were asked to answer a survey which dealt with issues of nationhood and culture, land and natural resource rights, political rights, economic and social rights, and constitutional rights. The responses are reproduced in full, organized by region and community. It should be noted that there was a high degree of consensus in the answers given by Métis people in all regions of the province.

According to the responses, the Métis people felt they were not being properly represented in many of the other more broadly based Native forums. Programs designed for the benefit of Native people that do not contain portions earmarked for Métis often do not benefit the Métis people. Frustration has developed within Métis communities because of their exclusion from many programs and resources which are provided to other Indian bands by the government.

The report contends that the current landless status of Métis people ensures that they will not be able to survive as an Aboriginal people. The provision of a land base, owned and controlled by the Métis people (but with some shared aspects of land management such as conservation policies) is seen to be at the root of all the demands which are made in this document. The provision of such land would provide a basis for self-government, self-sufficiency and political representation. The Métis would be able to raise and collect taxes, and exercise political autonomy with guaranteed participation in the larger political system. Individual land grants, on the other hand, do not ensure the development of the land for the benefit of those to whom the land was allotted, but rather prevents the exercise of a collective jurisdiction and the development of self-governing structures.

The consultative process which preceded the First Ministers' Conference depicted the economic situation of Métis communities, including 85% unemployment in many Métis communities, as a significant barrier to improving the social and political situation of the Métis people. With increased control over natural resources such as lumber, mining and hydro development, Métis communities would be able not only to support themselves economically through the development of employment opportunities both on and off the land base, but also to give purpose to the lives of its people.

Many of the services currently provided to Métis communities were found to be ineffective for various reasons. The paper contends that only by exercising control over the implementation of services, having access to service resources, and setting the priorities which apply to these resources, will the Métis be able to improve their situation and integrate service planning and delivery as part of an overall thrust toward self-government.

The position paper argues that Aboriginal people should not have to pay taxes but should still have the right to levy taxes on their own lands because their lands receive no services from other levels of government. Fiscal transfers to Aboriginal communities are necessary, given that Aboriginal people pay Canada Pension Plan (CPP), Unemployment Insurance (UI), road taxes, licensing fees, etc. The Métis National Council suggests that these fiscal arrangements be similar to those currently in place for transfers and equalization payments to provincial and municipal governments.

RECOMMENDATIONS

The primary recommendations which emerged from the consultations are summarized in the policy position paper:

1. that the right of Métis people to exist and develop as a nation, collectively to own land and resources, to establish forms of self-government and to design and operate social and economic programs be recognized; and

2. that fiscal financial responsibility permit the exercise of these rights.

Other recommendations are discussed in further detail in the submissions of the Métis National Council and the Manitoba government to the First Ministers' Conference on Aboriginal Constitutional Matters which are reprinted in this report. These documents make specific recommendations regarding a land base, self-government, economic development, service provision and fiscal arrangements. All parties agree that Aboriginal consent to any amendments is fundamental to the legitimacy of the process.

The consultations also resulted in unanimous opposition to the Garrison Diversion plan which would involve diverting waterways for the purpose of developing an irrigation scheme in North Dakota.

▲ The Métis People and Aboriginal Rights

AUTHOR: Association of Métis and Non-Status Indians of Saskatchewan

YEAR: 1983

ABORIGINAL GROUP: Métis

TOPIC: Claims

SUB-TOPIC: comprehensive claims

SOURCE: Provincial Aboriginal Organization

BACKGROUND

This report by the Association of Métis and Non-Status Indians of Saskatchewan was designed to set the background for the positions presented in the constitutional negotiations with the federal government.

PURPOSE

This report is a one-chapter extract from a larger submission in which the Association of Métis and Non-Status Indians of Saskatchewan argue their case in support of an Aboriginal Claim. This portion of the report contains much of the historical background which provides the rationale for the rights the Association would like included in a reformed Canadian Constitution.

ISSUES AND FINDINGS

This paper examines the emergence of the Métis as a distinct people in Rupert's Land, including the role of the Métis in the social, economic, and political life and development of the area; the growth of Métis nationalism; and factors which shaped that growth and which led to the Red River resistance and the Northwest Rebellion. In addition, the report examines the question of Métis rights as perceived by the Métis, and as recognized by the provincial and federal governments. It is the presentation of the history itself which the Métis suggest will be sufficient to make the argument for their current claims.

According to the report, in the mid-1800s when the West was being settled, the Métis had disagreed with the government regarding their status as Aboriginal people. Because of their mixed blood, many considered them to be Europeans. Nonetheless, the first *Indian Act* in 1850 did not distinguish between full-blood and mixed-blood Native people. It was not until 1870 that the federal government changed its definition of "Indian" to exclude halfbreeds covered under the *Manitoba Act*.

The report contends that the Métis were an important factor in the settlement of the Northwest. Acting as guides, independent traders and freighters, they often worked at the trading posts as an important liaison between the traders and Indian people. Traders often took Indian wives. Children were then raised at or near the trading posts and as they grew were used as a valuable Indigenous work force for the expansion of their companies. As settlers came to the West, the Métis became a more cohesive group, dedicated to the protection of their land and their way of life. Communities of farmers, labourers and hunters sprung up in the Red River area. The Métis were key players in the western economy, serving as labourers, as markets for the trade in furs and manufactured goods, and as a military patrol for the plains. They developed a vibrant social life and played a critical role in the development of politics, education and religion distinct from both Indian people and Europeans.

The Association argues that the right to claim a specific plot of land and to free access to the common land was recognized in the laws of the Council of Assiniboia. Additional rights of the Métis included the right to local self-government, control over the public domain, language rights, the right to vote and the right not to be taxed without permission. These rights were claimed on the basis of the Métis position both as the first settlers of the Northwest and as decedents of the Aboriginal peoples.

According to the report, it was in 1869 that the Hudson's Bay Company transferred Rupert's Land and the Northwest Territory to Canada. This agreement stipulated that Canada would be responsible for dealing with any land claims of Indian people. The policy of the Canadian government was to view Aboriginal people either as full citizens or as Indian people. The Métis were therefore given no claims as Aboriginal people unless they joined an Indian band.

The report recounts how the federal government began surveying the land acquired from the Hudson's Bay Company only to be driven off the land by the Métis led by Louis Riel. The Métis took immediate action to put the territory under their control, arming themselves, setting up a provisional government, drafting a bill of rights, and organizing forces to block the roads into and out of the settlement. The settlers of this area claimed the rights of a province, consistent with the provisions made for other provinces. While some agreement was achieved, when the bill was drafted and passed it read that Indian title to the land would be extinguished in exchange for a one-time land grant to the families of half-breeds. Once this action was complete, the government began to implement assimilationist policies, forcing halfbreeds either to sign treaties or receive land.

The Association argued that at this time, a Métis Nation existed in the sense of a community of people with a common language, purpose, customs, traditions and institutions. The *Manitoba Act* recognized a wide range of national rights including the rights of local government, rights with respect to denominational schools, language rights, as well as the guarantee of local laws, customs and usages.

In 1885, an Order in Council was passed which explicitly provided for the issue of scrip to satisfy claims existing in connection with the extinguishment of the Indian title preferred by the halfbreeds. According to this policy, the Métis were forced to either sign treaties or receive land. Government policy was seen as inconsistent; i.e., they acknowledged the legitimate claims of the halfbreeds but preferred to evade their responsibility in exchange for land grants.

RECOMMENDATIONS

No recommendations are presented in this report.

◆ *Report of the MacEwan Joint Métis-Government Committee to Review the Métis Betterment Act and Regulations Order* (1984), see **Volume 3, Alberta.**

1985

▲ An Amended Proposal for Planning and Development of the Ontario Native Business Corporation

AUTHOR: Ontario Métis and Non-Status Indian Association
YEAR: 1985
ABORIGINAL GROUP: Métis, Non-Status
TOPICS: Economic Development, Programs and Services
SUB-TOPICS: business development/entrepreneurship, institutions
SOURCE: Provincial Aboriginal Organization

BACKGROUND

Consultations with Native and non-Native business people indicated there was a need for an institution to support the business development needs of Native people in Ontario. Discussions had also been held with senior Ontario government officials, professional business and financial analysts, and the federal government. The Ontario Métis and Non-Status Indian Association (OMNSIA) wished to establish a mechanism for involving Native people in the economic/business sectors of their communities. OMNSIA had previously incorporated a limited economic development component as part of its organizational structure.

PURPOSE

The purpose of the proposal was to undertake the necessary research, consultations, analysis, and developmental process leading to the establishment and capitalization of either a viable and self-sustaining institution, or several institutions serving the business, financial and technical needs of Métis, non-status Indians and off-reserve Indian people living in Ontario.

ISSUES AND FINDINGS

Although there is some dispute over the actual number of Métis and non-status Indians living in Ontario, OMNSIA claims to represent 185,000 Métis and non-status Indians. In addition, there are an estimated 27,000 Status Indians living off-reserve whose economic plight is similar to that of the Métis and non-status Indian population.

Existing demographic data, although limited, indicates that the Métis and non-status Indian population are significantly disadvantaged groups. In 1978, due to the youth of this group, the dependency ratio was 80% greater than that of the Ontario population as a whole. In the same year, only 5% of the Métis and non-status group had any post-secondary education, compared to one-third of the Ontario population. The unemployment rate for Métis and non-status Indians was 23.1% while the provincial average was 7.2%. Other conditions faced by Métis and non-status Indians include poor or insufficient housing, lack of community infrastructure, high out-migration from communities, and high levels of social assistance.

The Métis and non-status Indian communities of Ontario generally lack natural and human resource bases and economic development activity. The report notes that there is a need for an accelerated process for determining areas of economic need and opportunities in order to create jobs and enhance the social circumstances of the client base.

The off-reserve Native population has limited access to, and benefit from, existing Native economic development programs, job creation programs, and training funds. Provincial economic development assistance is mainly in the form of loan guarantees, term loans, and export support lines of credit for business and industry. There is no money provided for capacity development. Ontario's Native peoples, therefore, have had little opportunity to take advantage of economic opportunities existing in urban, rural and remote areas throughout the province.

RECOMMENDATIONS

The proposal recommends that an institution or institutions be planned and developed in Ontario to facilitate the involvement of Native people in the identification of economic/business development needs and opportunities in their communities.

▲ Canadian-Indian Nation Relationships

AUTHOR: Prairie Treaty Nations Alliance

YEAR: 1985

ABORIGINAL GROUP: First Nations

TOPICS: Federal Government/Aboriginal Relations, Treaty Land Entitlement

SUB-TOPICS: treaties, jurisdiction, federal trust responsibilities, claims
SOURCE: Regional Aboriginal Organization

BACKGROUND

Treaty-making power in Canada is part of the royal prerogative. Canada is bound by the terms of treaties that it enters into and breech thereof may give rise to international claims. Since the signing of the treaties, the policies of the former British Colonial governments and the subsequent Canadian governments have either been in conflict with the terms and intent of treaty or have been inadequate as a genuine response to treaty obligations.

PURPOSE

This document outlines a Terms of Reference to guide a bilateral undertaking between the Prairie Treaty Nations Alliance and the government of Canada on major Canada-Indian Nations Relationships.

ISSUES AND FINDINGS

The report examines the relationships between Canada and Indian Nations in six different contexts:

1. Canada-Indian Nations Political Relationships

According to the terms of reference outlined in the document, the Prairie Treaty Nations Alliance and the prime minister of Canada must enter into a formal process for renewal, clarification and affirmation of the true relationships between Canadian and Indian Nations governments in a number of fundamental areas. The undertaking shall be governed by the spirit and intent of treaty and inherent rights and shall take into account all factors and components of the Canada-Indian Nations government relationships.

2. Canada-Indian Nations Government and Fiscal Relationships

According to the document, the provision by the Crown of financial resources for the support of Indian government political structures is an obligation of the Crown under treaty, inherent rights and title.

3. Canadian-Indian Nations Economic Relationships

Socio-economic development is the primary controlling instrument for community self-sufficiency. Indian reserves in Canada have been restricted from attaining this degree of independence through foreign exploitation of lands and resources. With the establishment of Indian reserves, imposed social programming took precedence over long-term plans for the economic development of national resources to sustain the communities. It is now imperative that Canadian-Indian economic relationships be established which will support the socio-economic development of Indian reserves.

4. Canadian-Indian Nations Constitutional Relationships

A new constitutional relationship and process shall be governed by the spirit and intent of treaty and inherent rights and shall take into account all factors and components of the Canada-Indian government relationships. The process will not be limited by narrow legislative interpretations by any party.

5. Canada-Indian Nations Treaty Relationships

The British Crown, as opposed to any one department or ministry, entered into the treaties. The negotiations leading to their conclusion were conducted on the basis of mutual sovereignty. Acceptance of the treaty provisions was solemnly accompanied by ceremonies appropriate to the conclusion of international treaties. Furthermore, there have been adhesions to these treaties; this is presented as the appropriate method for later participation by other parties in international treaties.

6. Canada-Indian Nations Bilateral Relationships

There is evidence that the interest of Treaty Indian Nations are not being satisfactorily represented. The Prairie Treaty Nations Alliance was formed based on the premise that Indian Nations, by virtue of bilateral international treaties, maintain a special status and relationship with the Crown of Canada. This structure will reinforce the Crown/Canada/Indian Nations relationship, emphasizing the integrity of nationhood, the exercise of the jurisdiction of Indian Nations government, and the recognition, enforcement and administration of treaty provisions.

RECOMMENDATIONS

There are no recommendations presented in this document.

▲ Denendeh Public Government

AUTHOR: Dene Nation

YEAR: 1985

ABORIGINAL GROUP: All Aboriginal Peoples

TOPICS: Self-Government, Constitutional Development, Political Development/Relationships

SUB-TOPICS: implementation, structures/institutions

SOURCE: Territorial Aboriginal Organization

BACKGROUND

In 1981, the Denendeh document was made public. This document proposed the creation of a province-like jurisdiction called Denendeh to be the homeland of the Dene and the Métis, with provisions for the Inuvialuit. In the document, the Dene/Métis proposed a system of public government in which power was to be divided between a provincial type of government and community governments. Within the Inuvialuit Settlement region, a regional government for the Beaufort Sea-Mackenzie Delta was contemplated.

On April 14, 1982, a plebiscite was held at which the people of the Northwest Territories gave their support to the concept of the division of the N.W.T. With the possibility of division in the near future, this document is an expression of the form of government which would be acceptable to and which would safeguard the rights and interests of both Aboriginal and non-Aboriginal people.

PURPOSE

Since the Denendeh document, the Dene/Métis have begun to consider that the Inuvialuit and some Inuit may also be citizens of an extended Denendeh; as a result, the Dene and Métis, without abandoning the principles and objectives which underlie the Denendeh document seek to take the discussion beyond the model originally presented. This document is an attempt to foster discussion concerning the development of a form of government which will ensure that all peoples and their cultures will be protected and respected.

ISSUES AND FINDINGS

The underlying approach to government suggested in the report is one of partnership among the different communities, both Aboriginal and non-Aboriginal. The form of government discussed in one in which:

1. the constitutional partnership agreement would recognize that all citizens have certain basic rights due to their Canadian citizenship;

2. certain citizens would have Aboriginal and treaty rights which would be included in the constitutional partnership agreement;

3. the Dene, Métis, Inuvialuit and Inuit, whose communities and Aboriginal lands are within the boundaries of the territory, would have some rights of self-government;

4. non-Aboriginal people would have certain collective rights included in the constitutional partnership agreement; and

5. the relationship of Aboriginal peoples to the land would be recognized and protected in the constitution of the new province.

The report outlines eight objectives of the proposed public government:

1. accountability, where the provincial and community governments are required to keep their promises to the electorate;

2. citizen participation, in which constructive ways would be devised for citizens to voice their opinions and participate in decision making directly as well as through their elected representatives;

3. community-based government, in which the Dene and Métis would continue to see the communities as the basic political units and as building blocks for the provincial-type government of the Denendeh province;

4. single community government, in which band, local and municipal elected bodies and councils would form a single community government in every hamlet, settlement, town and city;

5. authority of community governments, in which the jurisdiction of community, regional and provincial levels of government would be clearly defined;

6. flexibility of community government structures, in which community and/or regional government structures would enable adequate representation of voting residents whatever their population and composition;

7. statute review, in which current laws would be reviewed and amended at both the territorial and community (by-law) levels in order to serve the peoples of the Denendeh province and communities; and

8. non-Aboriginal participation, in which non-Aboriginal communities would be adequately represented in government.

Given these objectives, the Dene and Métis put forward the following mechanisms for public government:

1. a reasonable residency requirement before a resident is entitled to vote or run for office;

2. provisions to guarantee representation to cultural communities;

3. recognition of the right of Aboriginal peoples to administer Aboriginal lands transferred through claims legislation and of mechanisms to enable them to do so;

4. recognition that elected members are delegates, not autonomous representatives;

5. a review mechanism to determine whether a cultural or Aboriginal right is at issue;

6. a constitutional amending formula which would require the agreement of the founding partners through elected representatives of their cultural communities;

7. a royalty and/or resource revenue sharing formula for Aboriginal peoples whose lands form part of the new province; and

8. regional government where necessary, with mechanisms for their creation to lie with the community governments, although the law creating them might be passed by the provincial government.

A possible model for public government is proposed in the report. The model, discussed at the Western Constitutional Forum, is based on the idea of "partnership of consociation". This concept is based on two principles: that the system of democracy be based on majority rule; and that the rights of minority cultural communities be protected.

This model assumes that there will be certain matters that are under the control of particular cultural communities (specifically, the Dene, Métis, Inuvialuit, Inuit and non-Aboriginal cultural communities, as defined in the constitution) and others that will be handled exclusively on the basis of majority rule. The constitution would set out issues to be decided by each cultural community. In addition, those forming a particularly cultural community would be able to elect people from their own list of electors directly to the Legislative Assembly or community council, thereby ensuring that the Dene, Métis, Inuvialuit, Inuit and non-Aboriginal peoples would be represented. When legislation arose that affected the rights of a particular cultural community, this legislation would not pass if a majority of the representatives from the affected cultural community were opposed.

This type of model, "direct consociation" or direct partnership, makes possible the following guarantees:

1. a charter of rights defining the fundamental rights of both Aboriginal and non-Aboriginal communities;

2. a mechanism whereby these fundamental rights could not be changed without a two-thirds majority within each cultural caucus;

3. a mechanisms whereby legislation that affects the charter rights of Aboriginal and non-Aboriginal communities could be subjected to the same multiple majority;

4. a mechanisms to ensure guaranteed cultural community representation in the Assembly; and

5. a mechanism to ensure guaranteed cultural community representation on the Executive Council.

RECOMMENDATIONS

The report outlines specific provisions for proposed government structures, including community councils, the legislative assembly, cultural councils, and regional councils, according to the model presented above.

In conclusion, the report presents the consociation model as a different expression of the principles and objectives embodied in the earlier Denendeh model. The model is put forth as one which might better serve the needs and interests of a variety of cultural communities, and balance the interests of the Dene, Métis, Inuvialuit, Inuit and non-Aboriginal peoples who may be residents of the proposed Denendeh or Western Arctic province.

▲ Education Proposal

AUTHOR: Ontario Métis and Non-Status Indian Association
YEAR: 1985
ABORIGINAL GROUP: Métis, Non-Status
TOPIC: Education
SUB-TOPICS: primary and secondary education, adult education
SOURCE: Provincial Aboriginal Organization

BACKGROUND

The Ontario Métis and Non-Status Indian Association (OMNSIA) was incorporated in June 1971 to represent the interests of Métis and non-status Indians in the province. One its objectives was to further the educational opportunities of its members. In 1976, the Task Force on the Educational Needs of Native People issued a report identifying the major problems common to all Native people in Ontario. In its introduction, this proposal remarks that some of the Task Force's recommendations have been implemented since that time. The report points out, however, that generally the actions were directed toward Status Indians without addressing the needs of the Métis and non-status people of the province of Ontario.

The intention of this proposal is to develop education strategies that emphasize the needs of Métis and non-status Indians, to organize and orient the Association, the communities, the provincial and the federal governments to address this issue, and to develop an educational plan that combines the heritage of the Native peoples of Ontario and the mainstream requirements.

PURPOSE

The purpose of this proposal is to find appropriate measures for the short and long term education of the Ontario Métis and Non-Status Indian Association membership. The report lists short- and long-term objectives as follows.

Short-Term

1. the development in the first year of an operational plan, operating system and provincial network;

2. the identification, at the community, zone and Association level, the special educational requirements for the development of the long-term plan; and

3. the development of a management information system for information flow from the communities to the zones and thereafter to the Association.

Long-Term

1. the development and implementation of a plan for improving the education of Métis and non-status Indians of Ontario based on the decentralization plan (i.e., placing education into the hands of the Native people).

ISSUES AND FINDINGS

The proposal divides the task of developing and carrying out a plan for the improvement of Native education into three phases to be carried out over three years.

Phase One: Design and Development of Plan

In this phase OMNSIA will take the following actions:

1. engage the appropriate staff;
2. establish the structural/organizational linkages from the community to zones and to OMNSIA;
3. develop an activity plan;
4. establish performance standards;
5. organize zone workshops;
6. develop training schedules (for the OMNSIA education co-ordinator, the zone project directors, and the community education advocates); and
7. prepare a financing plan to determine the source and application of funds (operational and capital), the allocation of funds by OMNSIA zones, and the accounting systems and procedures for accountability of funds.

Phase Two: Project Implementation Study

The measures OMNSIA plans to undertake in this phase are as follows:

1. engage and train community education advocates (3 for each zone, 15 in total);
2. determine the local community needs;
3. develop programs;
4. set goals and priorities; and
5. undertake community work.

Phase Three: Pilot Project, Review, Analysis and Recommendations for Change

In this final phase, OMNSIA is to take the following actions:

1. review the up-to-date performance of the plan and programs established;
2. analyze input from community groups;
3. review communication systems;

4. review liaison with Native groups, schools, universities, boards of education, and government education authorities;

5. analyze financial performance and accountability; and

6. prepare a report of changes and recommendations for the program.

RECOMMENDATIONS

The purpose of this document was not to provide recommendations but to determine the requirements and the specific steps necessary to set up an organization to improve the education of Métis and non-status Indians in Ontario. The education proposal is in its entirety and in its detail a recommendation for a plan of action.

▲ National Association of Friendship Centres Urban Research Project, Phase I & II: Alcohol, Drug and Solvent Abuse: Final Report

AUTHOR: National Association of Friendship Centres

YEAR: 1985

ABORIGINAL GROUP: Urban Aboriginal People

TOPICS: Programs and Services, Health

SUB-TOPIC: substance abuse

SOURCE: National Aboriginal Organization

BACKGROUND

In 1984, the Research Committee of the National Native Advisory Council approved a contribution to the National Association of Friendship Centres (NAFC) to undertake the Urban Research Project. This report addresses the problems and needs of urban Native peoples as they relate to substance abuse.

PURPOSE

The purpose of this report is to provide solid data regarding the scope and nature of existing and proposed alcohol, solvent and drug abuse relevant to urban Native people. It is intended for use by the NAFC and/or provincial/territorial associations in the initiation, design, development or implementation of policies and programs at the federal, provincial and territorial levels of government.

ISSUES AND FINDINGS

The issues examined within the study consist of the following:

1. existing programs, services and activities;
2. types and levels of abuse;
3. community referral workers;
4. court work program services;
5. project proposals; and
6. government programs, services and resources.

1. Existing Programs, Services and Activities

The report outlines the availability of services, their appropriateness, adequacy and accessibility. The services identified include counselling, public education and awareness, school curriculum, recreational programs, spiritual/cultural programs, Native self-help groups, follow-up activities/treatment, outreach, and liaison meetings.

The report's findings were provincially targeted. In the Yukon and Northwest Territories, it was found that most centres provided a "just adequate" level of services, despite a number of problem areas. In British Columbia, all centres attempted to provide acceptable levels of service, but all were found to be experiencing major problems. The majority of the centres in Alberta are limited to making referrals for assistance as they are not equipped to provide services themselves; as a result, the report found that they encounter major problems with other agencies and that the existing level of services is inadequate. In Saskatchewan and Manitoba, the centres did provide some assistance for those with substance abuse problems, but identified major problems in the quality of their services as well as those offered by other agencies. Centres in Ontario, Quebec and the Maritimes were also found to provide limited services in the area of substance abuse, and were forced to rely on other agencies for assistance.

2. Types and Levels of Abuse

The general finding was that abuse is widespread and occurs at very serious levels. Target groups include children, teenagers, young adults, pregnant women, single women, unemployed men, chronic alcoholics, treatment clients, and the elderly. While alcohol was the most widely used substance abused, others identified include solvents, chewing tobacco, glue, gasoline, cigarettes, marijuana, plastic wood, white-out, nail polish remover, lysol, hashish, acid, pills, LSD, cocaine, shaving lotion, antifreeze, heroin, street drugs, and other chemicals. The stages of abuse were identified as light, occasional, chronic, severe, out-of-control, and life-threatening; people from most target groups were found to abuse substances at all of these stages. This pattern was relatively consistent across Canada.

3. Community Referral Workers

Community referral workers are the primary contacts who work within the centres assisting people with substance abuse-related problems. According to the community referral workers, the major problems encountered by substance abusers were unemployment, housing, education and health.

4. Court Work Program Services

It was found that the majority of offences by urban Native people are alcohol-related, and that offenders are primarily male.

5. Project Proposals

It was found that friendship centres and provincial/territorial associations wanted to implement their own projects, but have met with only limited success in acquiring provincial or federal funding.

6. Government Programs, Services and Resources

It was found that none of the provincial or territorial governments had a Native-specific mandate regarding substance abuse. There was also found to be a general attitude that the issue of Native substance abuse is a federal responsibility.

RECOMMENDATIONS

The report makes a number of recommendations regarding Native substance abuse. It recommends the reconsideration of applications for funding for centres to allow them to address their stated needs. It also recommends that the minister of National Health and Welfare form working groups composed in part of representatives of national Native organizations in order to discuss issues related to substance abuse. Furthermore, the report suggests that there be concrete efforts by education authorities to place alcohol/drug education on the curricula. Graduate fellowships should be provided to Native people training as alcohol/drug counsellors. Finally, financial resources must be provided for the development of community-based treatment facilities, such as urban Native-specific programs within existing centres. This requires the establishment of agreements with provincial/territorial governments for the development of these programs.

▲ Native Family Violence Study: A Discussion Paper

AUTHOR: Native Counselling Services of Alberta
YEAR: 1985
ABORIGINAL GROUP: All Aboriginal Peoples
TOPIC: Family/Family Relations
SUB-TOPIC: family violence
SOURCE: Aboriginal Service Provider

BACKGROUND

The report is based on interviews with 31 staff members of the Native Counselling Services of Alberta (NCSA), chosen from each NCSA regional office across the province. These staff all had experience dealing with situations involving family violence.

PURPOSE

The purpose of the study was to collect information on family violence in Native communities.

ISSUES AND FINDINGS

There were 17 questions asked of each respondent. The main issues and concerns expressed were as follows:

1. respondents estimated that approximately 70% of Native people have experienced family violence;

2. the loss of traditional values and of identity, were perceived by two-thirds of respondents to play a major role in family violence;

3. many felt that violence was first learned by Native people in residential schools where corporal punishment was the norm;

4. the study suggested that many issues pertaining to Native family violence may be comparable to non-Native issues;

5. most respondents agreed that alcohol played a major role in family violence, not as the cause of the problem but as a symptom of existing problems;

6. respondents noted that there appeared to be a relationship in some Native people between a lack of self-expression and interpersonal skills and a tendency toward violence;

7. unemployment was considered an important factor contributing to family violence; and

8. it was suggested that confusion associated with family roles among Native people may be another factor contributing to family violence.

RECOMMENDATIONS

The report presented the following recommendations:

1. that more services be provided by Native agencies to serve those Native persons who are unlikely to use other services;

2. that agencies develop programs aimed at working with the whole family;

3. that awareness of the problem be enhanced through public education efforts;

4. that there be more intervention by Native organizations; and

5. that programs be designed to help offenders with their problems.

◆ *Reflecting Indian Concerns and Values in the Justice System* (1985), see **Volume 3, Saskatchewan.**

▲ Submission to the Council of Maritime Premiers

AUTHOR: Maritime Aboriginal Peoples Council
YEAR: 1985
ABORIGINAL GROUP: All Aboriginal Peoples
TOPICS: Provincial Government/Aboriginal Relations, Constitution
SUB-TOPICS: institutions, political representation/participation
SOURCE: Regional Aboriginal Organization

BACKGROUND

The Council of Maritime Premiers was established in 1971 and since then, has played a role in facilitating regional dialogue between the citizens of the three Maritime provinces. Aboriginal peoples, however, have not been a part of this process. The Submission to the Council of Maritime Premiers by the Maritime Aboriginal Peoples Council (MAPC) reflects a desire, on the part of Aboriginal organizations, to begin the task of working with governments to address the problems faced by Aboriginal peoples in the Maritimes. The MAPC comprises the New Brunswick Association of Métis and Non-Status Indians, the Native Council of Nova Scotia and the Native Council of Prince Edward Island.

PURPOSE

The purpose of this Submission is to address regional concerns expressed by the members of the MAPC in order to ensure that Aboriginal Maritimers enjoy the same standard of living and quality of life as other citizens of the Maritimes.

ISSUES AND FINDINGS

There are three principal topics addressed in the submission:

1. the reasons why Aboriginal peoples are not progressing at the same pace as the rest of the Maritimes;

2. the value of regional dialogue between Aboriginal peoples and governments of the Maritime provinces; and

3. the Constitutional process as a means of resolving the concerns of Aboriginal peoples in the Maritimes.

The submission first discusses why Aboriginal peoples have not been able to obtain the standard of living characteristic of non-Aboriginal people in the Maritimes. By way of explanation, the MAPC asserts that the marginal existence of Aboriginal peoples in the Maritimes dates back to Confederation, and the lack of dialogue between the federal government and the political governments of the Maritimes within whose boundaries the Micmac and Malecite lived and associated.

The MAPC suggests in the submission that a regional forum for dialogue between Aboriginal peoples of the Maritimes and their provincial governments should be established. Such a forum would greatly enhance the work being done to resolve the situation of Aboriginal peoples in the Maritimes by sharing and assisting in the development of regional solutions.

The Constitutional process was identified by the MAPC as the primary means through which Aboriginal Maritimers could improve their quality of life, address Aboriginal rights issues, and achieve socio-economic self-determination. By working through a Constitutional process, an obligation is placed on the governments to learn about and to consult with the Aboriginal peoples of the Maritimes.

RECOMMENDATIONS

The MAPC recommends that a Maritime Aboriginal Affairs Committee (MAAC) be established by the Council of Maritime Premiers (CMP) in order to facilitate dialogue between the Aboriginal communities and the provincial governments. Each provincial government and each provincial Aboriginal association would appoint a Governor to the Board of the MAAC, and the Governors could recommend to the CMP that specific study or research projects be conducted. Project staff would submit their reports to the Board of Governors, who in turn would report to CMP with conclusions and recommendations for action.

▲ Suicides, Violent and Accidental Deaths Among Treaty Indians in Saskatchewan: Analysis and Recommendations for Change

AUTHOR: Federation of Saskatchewan Indian Nations
YEAR: 1985
ABORIGINAL GROUP: First Nations, Aboriginal Youth
TOPICS: Health, Social/Cross-Cultural Relations, Elders, Substance Abuse, Suicide
SUB-TOPICS: suicide, racism, roles, participation
SOURCE: Provincial Aboriginal Organization

BACKGROUND

This research project was initiated by the Health and Social Development Commission of the Federation of Saskatchewan Indian Nations through funding from the National Native Alcohol and Drug Abuse Program (NNADAP) of Health and Welfare Canada. The study was perceived as a necessary response to a crisis situation faced by Indian communities experiencing high numbers of suicides, violent and accidental deaths. The problem of youth suicide was a particularly strong catalyst in the decision to conduct this research.

PURPOSE

This portion of the research project was intended to examine the problems and issues of unnatural deaths in Indian communities through extensive consultation at the community level with Indian leaders, elders and human service workers.

ISSUES AND FINDINGS

According to the report, the situation of suicide, accidental and violent deaths in Indian communities has reached crisis proportions. Traditional Indian beliefs of the role of the Creator in the life cycle make suicide unacceptable. Suicide rates among Saskatchewan Indians, however, are significantly higher than amongst the non-Indian population. Statistics on other accidental and violent death rates provide similar results, often with seventy to eighty percent of incidents involving alcohol and/or drugs. The report found that accidents, violence and suicide are the most common causes of death for the Saskatchewan Indian population, especially among Indian youth, as compared to heart disease, which is the most common cause of death in the non-Indian population.

Several general arguments are presented in this report:

1. that racism is a dominant factor in the analyses of contemporary Indian suicides, violent and accidental deaths; and

2. that a balanced approach, using both traditional Indian holistic methods and western science, is required to combat the negative effects of racism and alcohol/drug abuse within Indian communities.

The research contained in this report adopts the perspective that racism is an important and pervasive dimension from which the analysis of Indian problems and issues must be examined; this approach contrasts with those that view Indian problems as problems of poverty, alcohol/drug abuse, acculturation, and/or of a disadvantaged minority. As a result, the report is concerned primarily with the situation of Indian people who are defined in social terms as Indians by their features and skin colour, and excludes those who lack physical Indian characteristics and can therefore pass as white and may choose to do so.

The research identified a number of variables associated with the high incidence of suicides, violent and accidental deaths among the Treaty Indian population:

1. contact with the dominant white society;

2. cultural disintegration;

3. acculturation;

4. alcoholism;

5. the effects of boarding schools;

6. high frequency of contact with the justice system;

7. loss of role definition;

8. widespread unemployment; and

9. geographical isolation.

All of these factors were found to contribute to a high level of stress, but most of these variables were found to be symptoms, rather than causes of the problem. According to the report, this misdiagnosis is why so many former studies have failed to identify actions and programs to improve the situation; i.e., they have not focused on the structural and institutional forces that maintain dominance based on race.

According to the report, the self-proclaimed mission of the European nations to civilize and christianize the people of the "discovered" land reflects a cultural racism which is reflected through religious ideology and supported by theories of Social Darwinism which became popular in the nineteenth century. Cultural differences were seen as evidence of a biological superiority, justifying the subjugation of, and policies of wardship toward, Indigenous people.

The report contends that eventually policies attempted to eradicate Indian ways and values through new education, religious, economic and political systems. Traditional ceremonies were banned and Indian leadership was replaced. The biological perspective changed at the beginning of the twentieth century to recognize issues related to culture. According to this cultural perspective, Indians could become civilized, but only if they abandoned their Indian ways and were assimilated into white society. It was believed that it was their special status that was responsible for their degradation and their poverty. The reserve environment was seen to perpetuate dependency, apathy and other psychological and social symptoms which could be resolved through complete assimilation.

The report recounts how the dominant Euro-Canadian image of Indian people slowly changed from one of backward children to one of aggressive challengers of the status quo. The current system is seen as one of neo-colonialism with the maintenance of central control in order to perpetuate and maintain domination. Programs are constantly threatened as government priorities and fiscal restraints change, continuing the pattern of paternal control.

According to the report, differential power is a necessary prerequisite for the emergence of racial stratification. The report is critical of current programs designed to facilitate integration while preserving ethnic identity, rather than establishing constitutional and structural recognition of Indian governments within the present political system. These policies are seen to perpetuate the belief that Indian people have been given every opportunity to attain equality but still socio-economic problems remain because of reasons inherent to their culture.

The report contends that racist attitudes toward individuals compound the problems faced by Indian people. The problem, however, is not prejudice or discrimination but domination through institutional racism. Indian children who attend white institutions experience the negative influences that exist in a society in which the Indian is perceived as inferior and uncivilized. The lack of positive Indian cultural realities coupled with a socialization process which equates white ways as successful, progressive, and civilized, presents special problems and stresses for Indian children. The report cites evidence that both white and Indian children from three to seven years of age have negative images of Indian people and positive images of whites. School experiences therefore tend to accentuate rather than resolve identity problems, resulting in increased behavioral and disciplinary difficulties and eventual failure in academic achievement.

The report also addresses the relationship between substance abuse and domination. Feelings of low self-worth become internalized into depressive symptomology, from which substance abuse often provides a temporary escape. Psycho-social factors combine to continue the substance abuse among Indian people and even for those who escape this trap there are few social, recreational, educational, cultural or economic programs to help them remain "clean". Substance abuse, seen in this way, is a form of "chronic suicide" manifested in self-destructive tendencies.

The report also describes the situation of Indian people caught between two cultures. With the loss of their own culture and the refusal to accept the dominant culture, feelings of disorientation, negative self-image, anger, shame, apathy, and dependency result. If these feelings are not dealt with, a pattern of negative behaviours tended to develop that manifested itself internally and/or externally.

The paradox of being caught between two cultures and its related crisis identity problem appear to have had a more marked effect on Indian people in southern Saskatchewan. These groups were found to have greater and more frequent exposure to Canadian institutions, exacerbating the paradox of identity crisis; as a result, suicide rates are more prevalent in the southern regions of Saskatchewan.

According to the report, pre-packaged government solutions can never bring acceptable approaches to "solving Indian problems". Unless Indian people themselves can shape their own policies and priorities, and have opportunities not only to participate but to take control and administer their own programs and services, attempts at solutions will fail.

Action within the last 20 years has resulted in the relaxing of the neocolonial mentality, increasing transfer of control, power and authority to Indian people and governments. Along with this approach has been an emphasis on greater self-sufficiency, technological sophistication, management and control of an expanding number and scope of programs and services. There has been a movement toward recognizing that social change is not only a question of intellect and rationality but of spirit, intuition and subjectivity. It is believed that the re-establishment of a positive identity and the reorientation of Indian people toward their culture and beliefs will release Indian human potential.

Such a holistic approach recognizes that the physical and the spiritual components of existence are interrelated, interdependent, complete and equal. This approach represents long term hope. Given that it has taken Indian people five generations to reach this stage of disintegration, a reconnection with the Indian way of life will not happen overnight. The increased use of elders as guidance counsellors, spiritual advisers and consensus builders will aid in the long process of becoming conscious, finding meaning, and healing.

RECOMMENDATIONS

The report recommends a number of changes in the provision of services in order to make them more culturally relevant:

1. that health centres change the way they practice medicine to ensure that the person as a whole is considered;

2. that the holistic promotion of human development and growth be introduced into the current curriculum of schools with a predominant Indian population;

3. that special support programs be developed to meet the cultural, social, emotional and psychological disadvantages that Indian students experience;

4. that training programs for Indian para-professionals be developed;

5. that Indian leaders be used in substance abuse awareness and self development workshops;

6. that Indian bands take over social assistance programs on their reserves;

7. that a code of ethics be put into place for Indian leaders;

8. that more activities for Indian youth be developed; and

9. that additional resources be made available to implement these recommendations.

1986

▲ Bill C-31 Project: Final Report

AUTHOR: Nova Scotia Native Women's Association
YEAR: 1986
ABORIGINAL GROUP: First Nations, Aboriginal Women
TOPIC: Membership
SOURCE: Provincial Aboriginal Organization

BACKGROUND

Prior to the implementation of Bill C-31, section 12(1)(b) of the *Indian Act* provided that Native women lost their Indian status upon marriage to non-Indian men, while Indian men not only retained their Indian status, but passed this status on to their non-Indian spouses and their children.

One woman, Sandra Lovelace, brought her case before the United Nations (U.N.) Human Rights Committee, charging that these provisions violated Canada's international human rights obligations. The U.N. Human Rights Committee agreed that these provisions of the *Indian Act* did indeed violate Lovelace's right to practise her culture with other members of her tribe.

Shortly thereafter, the Constitution was repatriated and the Charter of Rights entrenched. Section 15, the Equality Clause, was to become effective in 1985, giving the Canadian government three years to amend discriminatory legislation such as the provisions of the *Indian Act* which conferred loss of status.

On June 28, 1985, the minister of Indian Affairs announced the passage of Bill C-31, an Act to Amend the *Indian Act*. The purpose of the amendment was to end discrimination against Indian women, restore Indian rights to those who had lost them and enhance the jurisdiction of Indian band governments.

Subsequently, a reinstatement process was developed to restore Indian status and band membership to individuals who had lost their status as a result of sexual discrimination, as well as to the children who were band members at the time their mothers' rights were lost. The number of people in this category had already, by the time of this report in 1986, exceeded the previously estimated figure of 18,000.

The minister of Indian Affairs made funding available to Native organizations to establish programs to inform people of the changes to the *Indian Act* in order to ensure that the reinstatement process would be effectively employed. The Native Women's Association of Canada received $1,062,372 to assist them in their promotional efforts. The Association in turn awarded a portion of this funding to each of its provincial and territorial member associations, including $45,000 to the Nova Scotia Native Women's Association for the implementation of a six-month Bill C-31 Implementation Project. The Nova Scotia Native Women's Association hired two Native women, one for the mainland of Nova Scotia and one for Cape Breton Island. These women assisted individuals in filling out applications for reinstatement and held Bill C-31 information workshops on reserves.

PURPOSE

The main objectives of the project were:

1. to examine, review and clarify the contents of Bill C-31, determine its impact and effects on Native women and assess its deficiencies;

2. to ensure that the Nova Scotia Native Women population is made aware of the contents and meaning of Bill C-31;

3. to review proposed changes to the *Indian Act*, which resulted in the implementation of Bill C-31, and the implications of approved changes for Native women;

4. to review the proposed changes to Bill C-31 – both those that are supported and those that are opposed by the Native Women's Association of Canada;

5. to assist those Native women who want to apply for reinstatement; and

6. to prepare an action plan, recommendations and resolutions to address the existing discriminatory sections in the *Indian Act*, and the deficiencies in Bill C-31.

ISSUES AND FINDINGS

According to the Nova Scotia Native Women's Association, Bill C-31 is still a discriminatory piece of legislation and the Department of Indian Affairs still controls who will be registered as a Status Indian. Two groups in particularly are discriminated against by the legislation:

1. Indian Children

The legislation provides for non-Indians to gain both status and band membership through legal adoptions by Status Indians; however, there will be some Indian children who will not be eligible for Indian status.

2. Single Mothers and their Children

Because of Bill C-31, a mother must name the father of her children to ensure that the father was registered as a Status Indian, and if she does not do so, then the father will be assumed, by the Registrar, to be non-Indian. As a result, some children with Status Indian fathers will never be recognized as Indians.

Non-Indian women who gained status through marriage to Indian men are still protected in the *Indian Act*. Moreover, if she divorces her Indian husband after April 17, 1985, she retains her Indian status.

The Nova Scotia Native Women's Association held a number of workshops on Bill C-31. Emanating from these workshops were a number of recommendations and concerns which may be summarized as follows:

1. that amendments be made to Bill C-31 to address the discriminatory sections against children and single mothers;

2. that more information workshops on Bill C-31 be held on the reserves and that it be made mandatory for the Chiefs and Councillors to attend all the meetings;

3. that the department of Indian Affairs not determine the status of unborn Native children nor have the right to decide who is eligible for Indian status;

4. that mothers and children not be faced with red tape when applying for registration;

5. that bands delay establishing membership codes to decide who their members will be until they receive increased funding to accommodate the influx of new band members;

6. that reserve residency, housing benefits and voting rights be addressed by the chiefs and their membership, and that their decisions be respected through band council resolutions. They should also decide whether or not to include non-Indians on the reserves. A 51% vote by band members either in favour or against the inclusion of non-Indian spouses should decide the issue;

7. that if Indian Affairs retains the right to decide who is eligible for Indian status, they also be responsible for court cases and increased funding for new members;

8. that the media be used to spread the concerns on Bill C-31;

9. that non-Indian women lose their status after they divorce their Indian husbands; and

10. that non-Indian children who gain Indian status through adoption lose their Indian status when they reach the age of eighteen.

RECOMMENDATIONS

The following are recommendations are put forth by the Nova Scotia Native Women's Association:

1. that the Nova Scotia Native Women's Association present the final report on the Bill C-31 Project to the Chiefs in Nova Scotia, the President of Union of Nova Scotia Indians, the Native Women's Association of Canada, and the Native Council of Nova Scotia, and request a meeting with the groups to discuss the project's concerns and recommendations;

2. that the final report be submitted to the Native Women's Association of Canada (NWAC) who would, with the consensus of all Native women's provincial and territorial associations, develop a position on Bill C-31;

3. that the contents of Bill C-31 be reviewed and that discriminatory sections deleted;

4. that the Registrar retract the directive which states that both parents have to be named; and

5. that the definition of "child" be amended to read "a child born in or out of wedlock, a legally adopted Indian child, and a child adopted in accordance with Indian custom."

▲ **"By Means of Conferences and Negotiations" We Ensure Our Rights: Background Principles for New Legislation Linking Métis Aboriginal Rights to "A Resolution Concerning an Amendment to the *Alberta Act*"**

AUTHOR: Alberta Federation of Métis Settlement Associations

YEAR: 1986

ABORIGINAL GROUP: Métis

TOPICS: Self-Government, Provincial Government/Aboriginal Relations, Land Use, Development, and Management

SUB-TOPICS: structures/institutions, legislation, institutions, non-reserve land/traditional lands, land use planning, zoning, development, management

SOURCE: Provincial Aboriginal Organization

BACKGROUND

This report was prepared by the Federation of Métis Settlement Associations in response to the conditions prescribed in "A Resolution Concerning An Amendment to the *Alberta Act*" which was unanimously passed in the Alberta Legislature in June 1985. The resolution called for the Métis to define and propose fair and democratic criteria for membership in settlement associations, for the allocation of settlement lands to individual members of settlement associations, and for the composition of governing bodies to manage Métis settlements.

PURPOSE

This report acts as a first step in the response to the Alberta Legislature. The overall goal is to amend the *Alberta Act* in such a way as to effectively entrench

Métis settlement lands in the Canadian Constitution, as was originally recommended by the Ewing Royal Commission in 1936. In so doing, the government would ensure a Métis land base and demonstrate the viability of a new, unprecedented approach to recognizing and affirming Métis Aboriginal rights.

ISSUES AND FINDINGS

In the adoption of "A Resolution Concerning an Amendment to the *Alberta Act*", the provincial government committed itself to proposing a revised *Métis Betterment Act* (first enacted in 1938) once appropriate criteria were established for settlement membership, land allocation and the composition of governing bodies capable of holding land. The province would then amend the *Alberta Act* to entrench Métis ownership of existing Métis settlement lands.

This report outlines the Westlock resolution which was passed by all settlement councils, and which proposed guiding principles to govern the granting of membership and the allocation of interests in Métis settlement lands. The Métis maintain their position that the existing Settlement Associations are capable of holding land and therefore new governing bodies are not required.

In addition to fulfilling its commitment to outline appropriate criteria for membership, land allocation and governing bodies, this report outlines the Métis Federation's desire for a new *Métis Betterment Act* to be renamed the *Métis Settlement Act* in fulfilment of section 3 of the resolution. This Act would firmly place the major responsibility for the political, social, economic and cultural development of the settlements on the settlements themselves. This proposal is designed as a compromise between the government's need to maintain legislative authority and the settlements' need to have the capacity to protect their culture and lands.

The proposed *Métis Settlement Act* would provide for four bodies: elected Settlement Councils and appointed Elders Committees which would be permanent institutions functioning on each settlement, as well as Métis arbitration tribunals and an elected Métis governing council which would collectively represent the settlements. The proposed Act sets out details for the election or appointment and functioning of such bodies (i.e., terms in office, disqualification of candidates, by-elections, budgets, conflict of interest, and the powers of the various bodies).

Other clauses in the proposed Act deal with the procedure for membership application, including considerations, an appeal procedure and provisions for the suspension or termination of membership. Provisions for Land Applications are similarly set out, allowing for several different levels of land "ownership", the from a memorandum of allocation to a certificate of occupancy.

The proposed Act also provides for the establishment of a Métis Settlements Resources Trust Fund to be administered by the Métis Governing Council. The Council would take all moneys accrued from the sale or lease of natural resources and place these in a Trust Fund whose income would be used for the benefit of individual settlements.

Assuming that this proposed legislation established "appropriate criteria", the next step in the legislative process outlined in the resolution would lie with the government of Alberta. It would be the government's responsibility pursuant to section 5, to "introduce, once a revised *Métis Betterment Act* has been enacted, a resolution to amend the *Alberta Act*". The report then sets out proposals for the resolution to the *Alberta Act* which would recognize and affirm the Métis settlement lands.

RECOMMENDATIONS

The Westlock resolution is reprinted in full, outlining in detail the guiding principles to govern the granting of membership and the allocation of interests in Métis settlement lands. This resolution provides for any Métis who is a long-term resident of Alberta (five years) to apply for membership in a Métis settlement. It also establishes that allocation of land would be governed by by-laws which would specify the requirements for the productive use of land.

This report also includes a draft of a proposed *Métis Settlement Act* to replace the *Métis Betterment Act*. The next step would be for the provincial government to convene a joint process to prepare the required legislation. The Federation proposes that this task be completed by the spring of 1987 so that the new Acts can be tabled at the First Ministers' Conference on Aboriginal Rights.

◆ *Speaking Out: Consultations and Survey of Yukon Native Languages: Planning, Visibility and Growth* (1986), see **Volume 3, Yukon.**

◆ *Kwiya: Towards a New Partnership in Education* (1987),
see **Volume 3, Yukon.**

▲ **Our Land, Our Culture, Our Future**

AUTHOR: Council for Yukon Indians
YEAR: 1987
ABORIGINAL GROUP: First Nations
TOPICS: Resources, Land and Resources, Economic/Social
   Development
SUB-TOPIC: trapping and gathering
SOURCE: Territorial Aboriginal Organization

BACKGROUND

The Council for Yukon Indians (CYI) represents the 14 First Nations in the
Yukon. The report discusses the history, culture, and current situation of the
peoples represented by the CYI.

PURPOSE

This paper was prepared to present the issues and the realities facing the Yukon
Indians today, especially those regarding trapping. It was produced as a
result of co-operative efforts between the CYI and the government of Yukon.

ISSUES AND FINDINGS

The report describes how the First Nations of the Yukon have lived off of
the land for over 40,000 years, and how this way of life, which is centred on
the land, constitutes their culture. Policies of non-Aboriginal people, however,
have destroyed that way of life, policies such as:

1. the European boycott on sealskin, which undermined trapping as their
   primary economic activity and traditional way of life;

2. the Klondike gold rush of 1898, which caused dislocation and disease
   among them;

3. missionaries and residential schools, which destroyed part of their culture;

4. World War II, which brought soldiers and a highway to the North; and

5. the anti-trapping campaign, which condemns leg-hold traps, but does not contribute to humane trap research and development.

The report emphasizes the important of trapping in the Yukon, not only in terms of its cultural importance, but also as one of the few ways to make a living in the North. In order to fight the anti-trapping movement, involvement in organizations such as the Fur Institute of Canada and Indigenous Survival International is supported throughout the North. Another effort to sustain this way of life in the Yukon has been through trapper education.

RECOMMENDATIONS

No recommendations are presented in the document.

1988

▲ Dene/Métis Child Care Study

AUTHOR: Dene Nation, Metis Association of the Northwest Territories, and Native Women's Association of the Northwest Territories (Thomas M. Palakkamanil)

YEAR: 1988

ABORIGINAL GROUP: First Nations, Métis

TOPICS: Social Development, Child Welfare, Economic/Social Development

SUB-TOPICS: child care, adoption/foster homes

SOURCE: Territorial Aboriginal Organization

BACKGROUND

In 1978, the *Indian Child Welfare Act* became law in the United States. This legislation was drafted in response to a situation similar to the one in Canada; specifically, evidence collected in the 1960s and 1970s indicated that a highly disproportionate number of Indian children were involved in the child welfare system in the United States. The objective of the United States legislation was to reduce the number of Indian children being taken from their families and placed in non-Indian homes. The legislation authorized the transfer of jurisdiction for the welfare of both on-reserve and off-reserve Indian children from the state to Indian tribes.

In the 1950s, the traditional way of assisting Native children and their families through the extended family was considered to be inadequate. In the 1960s, Indian and Northern Affairs Canada developed agreements with all the provinces under which the federal government funded the extension of existing provincial child welfare services into Indian communities; it soon became obvious, however, that simply extending provincial services into Native communities was not the answer. The fundamental problem was that social workers/child care workers often employed their own customs and values in their efforts to protect Native children, rather than the customs and values of the Native people they were serving.

Since the early 1970s, child welfare programs and procedures have evolved due to initiatives undertaken by Indian bands to design and operate their own community-based services. At the time of the report, approximately one-third of the 592 Canadian Indian bands were delivering a full range of child welfare and family services through community-based agencies. The provision of these services recognizes that Canadian Indian communities have distinctive social and cultural needs which must be realized in any effort to protect and preserve their children and their families.

Purpose

The objectives of the Child Care Study were

1. to consult with the Dene/Métis people in the Western Arctic on child care issues relating to families, substitute families and residential facilities;

2. to determine concerns and develop recommendations for a comprehensive, community-based child care program in the Northwest Territories; and

3. to present a summary of this report to the Department of Social Services for their consideration in future child care services and facilities to serve the Dene/Métis population of the Western Arctic.

Issues and Findings

Three primary issues were examined in the study:

1. whether family and child welfare services delivered by the Department of Social Services were culturally appropriate for Native people;

2. whether the services met the needs of the Native population of the Western Arctic; and

3. whether there was sufficient Native involvement and consultation in the process of decision making, program delivery and administration.

The report found that the characteristics of the current child welfare policy echo the characteristics of the former Indian residential schools of the North. Such policies and programs devalue the status of the Native in relation to the dominant culture.

The author established that there is a direct relationship between poverty and the child welfare system as low-income families tend to have dealings with the system more often than higher-income families. Native families tend to be among the poorest in Canada and have the highest unemployment rate, and these situations tend to place considerable hardships on Native families and their children.

While poverty was found to be one of the major causes of crisis with Native families, it was not the only one identified. The present child welfare legislation and policy was criticized for failing to recognize the culture, special needs and special status of Native people. Community social workers and administrators tend to use middle class criteria in deciding on the Native child's best interest. This use of non-Native values in deciding on the well-being of the child often leads to the removal of the child from his/her natural environment; this removal affects the mental well-being of the child and causes problems for family relationships.

Furthermore, the natural system within the Native communities – the extended family – was found to have been largely ignored by the child welfare workers. The child is removed from the family, community and culture and placed in a completely alien and conflicting environment. This has a direct effect upon personal growth and development.

RECOMMENDATIONS

The report makes a number of recommendations, including a strategy for protecting children outside their own homes through the extensive use of foster care. The recommendations are summarized as follows:

1. that the Department of Social Services review the present *Child Welfare Act of the Northwest Territories*, the *Young Offenders Act*, the *Northwest Territories Child Daycare Act* and the *Northwest Territories Child Daycare Facilities Act* and revise them as necessary;

2. that the Department of Social Services review concerns expressed in the study with regard to foster parents, foster homes, and communication links between the social worker, the foster parents, the child and the biological parents;

3. that the Department of Social Services preserve the traditional custom adoption/private adoption practices among the Dene and Métis population;

4. that the Department of Social Services establish community-based family support services at each of the Western Arctic communities;

5. that there be greater co-ordination between the various departments of the government of the Northwest Territories in program planning and delivery;

6. that the Department of Social Services increase and improve the services its offers, such as goal-oriented treatment programs for young offenders, support services at the community level for unwed mothers, and appropriate services to children with special needs;

7. that the Department of Social Services hire Native workers whenever possible, and provide cultural orientation and training to every newly hired non-Native worker;

8. that the Department of Social Services keep the community informed of its various programs and encourage community participation;

9. that the Department of Social Services review very carefully the present family allowance and welfare systems, to ensure that it is proportionate to the cost of living, which is extremely high in isolated communities; and

10. that the Department of Social Services treat family violence as a community problem.

▲ Tradition and Education: Towards a Vision of our Future

AUTHOR: Assembly of First Nations
YEAR: 1988
ABORIGINAL GROUP: First Nations
TOPIC: Education
SUB-TOPICS: fiscal relations/responsibilities, facilities/institutions, professionals/educators, curriculum
SOURCE: National Aboriginal Organization

BACKGROUND

The 1973 Policy Paper "Indian Control of Indian Education" recommended the devolution of responsibility for education to First Nations. By the mid-

1980s these recommendations still had not been addressed. The federal government subsequently agreed to a three-year study to review the status of First Nations education, with this study to be undertaken by the Education Secretariat of the Assembly of First Nations. This report has become more commonly known as the National Review of First Nations Education.

PURPOSE

The purpose of the study was to review the impact of the 1973 Policy Paper, survey all provincial and territorial research in the area of education since 1972, examine First Nations jurisdiction over education and recommend improvements in education legislation and policy.

ISSUES AND FINDINGS

Four major issues are discussed throughout the three volumes:

1. jurisdiction;

2. quality;

3. management; and

4. resourcing.

Each is examined in the context of the research review in Volume 1 and the school and policy development review contained in Volume 2. Volume 3 is an executive summary of the first two volumes.

Jurisdiction: The study of jurisdiction examined:

1. different patterns of jurisdiction of First Nations education which have emerged in response to the transfer of administrative responsibilities from the federal government to First Nations;

2. obstacles to First Nations control; and

3. First Nations influence on provincial and territorial schools and the relationship of First Nations education to other educational institutions and other jurisdictions.

First Nations are best able to deal with matters that affect them. In education this is reflected in the readiness of First Nations to establish educational structures and processes to assist in reaching the goal of self-sufficiency. The opposition of provincial and territorial school staff to First Nations exercise of local jurisdiction over education is indicative of the lack of sympathy and understanding of non-First Nations educators. First Nations children cannot learn from those who do not have an understanding of self-government.

Each First Nation should be able to make laws in the area of education. The cornerstone of local jurisdiction is community involvement and awareness. It was found that many First Nations community members were unaware of the nature of inherent Aboriginal rights, and that their support was critical to ensuring successful First Nations programs.

There were two primary conclusions in the area of jurisdiction:

1. education is an inherent right, and that people must understand that self-government and self-sufficiency are related; and

2. First Nations-controlled school systems must incorporate contemporary First Nations issues (self-government) in curriculum.

Volume 1 recommends new legislation to empower First Nations in education, and a withdrawal by federal and provincial governments and agencies from the field. These governments would continue to act as funding agencies. Any new legislation, or a constitutional expression of First Nations jurisdiction would need to recognize the primary responsibility of governments in supporting First Nations education.

Volume 2 examines how education is dealt with both in the treaties and through the *Indian Act*. It was emphasized that amendments to the Indian would not provide a sufficient basis for the exercise of First Nations authority in education. Among other things, new legislation would need to recognize treaty and inherent Aboriginal rights over First Nations jurisdiction over education.

Quality: In its examination of the issue of quality in education, the report examines the following indicators: recent evaluations of First Nations programs, components of a First Nations educational system, characteristics of successful education systems, relevance of current programs vis-à-vis First Nations objectives in education, present needs of the educational system, First Nations expectations of the educational system and, critiques of the present system, and models for identifying objectives in education.

Cultural education programs are necessary for quality education for First Nations students. First Nations schools should be a cultural resource centre for the whole community.

Language is also an important cultural issue as it provides a link to the past and hope for the future. The report found that the First Nations languages should be given official status. Further, the report pointed to a need for new and improved administrative policies, procedures and personnel to create a unified approach to language teaching. In this vein, post-secondary institutions should be encouraged to implement teacher training programs aimed at cross-cultural education.

The quality of First Nations education is based upon traditional values. Quality could be improved through the active involvement of parents, elders, local political leaders and educators.

Volume 2 looks First Nations students' status in the present education process, and determines that success or failure is closely associated with the quality of education delivered and related educational programs and services.

In summary, the report emphasizes that the quality of First Nations education will be influenced by several factors; parental and community involvement, integration of culture and language in curriculum, cultural education centres, early childhood education, special education as part of the regular system, competency of education staff, student performance, student support services, school facilities and transportation.

Management: With respect to management, Volume 1 focuses on the existing management structures of DIAND, provincial, territorial and First Nations education systems and, options for the future management of First Nations education.

Each First Nations educational needs and objectives will be unique. Each First Nation will require sufficient local authority and resources to reach stated educational goals. The management of First Nations schools must be improved through the provision of resources equal to those transferred to the provinces.

First Nations should have control over education from early childhood education through to post-secondary and adult education. Parents, elders and local educators should be involved in the development of programs and policies. First Nations must develop mechanisms for to evaluate the progress of each community.

Research indicates there is a great need for more First Nations personnel working within the educational system, and that professional training for educators should be made available at the community level.

Volume 2 studies also emphasized that responsibility for the management of First Nations education must reside in the community. Further, the changing role of educational authorities points to a real need for policy development.

First Nations education authorities must have the power to review and establish priorities, goals, and management policies and to negotiate with other governments.

Resourcing: A transfer of jurisdiction means a transfer of resources. The issue of how the federal government interprets the concept of transfer of jurisdiction and how First Nations view this concept must be clearly defined and resolved by both parties.

In the area of resourcing, the Volume 1 study contained a review of federal, provincial and territorial approaches to funding First Nations education.

Research found that funding arrangements were complex and failed to perceive regional and local variations. The lack of multi-year capital budgets, has meant that local communities can not undertake long range capital planning. The report suggests DIAND develop and implement plans which will clear the backlog of education capital projects.

Alternative methods considered of funding included direct resourcing from Treasury Board, zero-based budgeting, block grants and program cost model resourcing.

Resourcing problems identified included a shortage of school supplies, lack of equipment, space and human resources.

Volume 2 also examined present funding arrangements, including the current Data Base system (DIAND) and the Nominal Roll system. It was agreed that these systems were ineffective and inaccurate because of poor updating procedures and appropriate definitions.

RECOMMENDATIONS

Recommendations in the area of jurisdiction include recognition by all levels of government of the right of First Nations to resume jurisdiction over education affecting First Nations students in federal, First Nations and other public schools.

It was also recommended that national level efforts be directed at increasing public awareness of First Nations educational philosophy and goals.

The final recommendation was for the development of education policies and programs for First Nations people residing off-reserve.

With respect to quality in education, the report recommends recognition of the right of First Nations students to education programs and services of the highest quality, incorporating culturally relevant content and academic skills.

It was recommended that First Nations educators be well paid, members of the First Nations, allowed to update their training and evaluated annually. Funding for Early Childhood Education, adult training, special need life skills and counselling should be increased dramatically.

In the area of management its was recommended that First Nations have the capacity to establish educational systems that meet local First Nations community needs, priorities, and long-range goals.

It was also recommended that First Nations education systems have access to financial, human and material resources equivalent to those available in public school systems. Additional funding should be allotted for the acknowledged special needs of First Nations education.

First Nations should be able to exercise complete control over all aspects of financial management.

The First Nations should have the capacity to negotiate new fiscal arrangements in education with the federal government. All governments should be more accountable to First Nations for how monies for Aboriginal education are spent.

Resources for staffing, curriculum and adult education should be increased. It was also recommended there be no more cut backs in the area of post-secondary education.

1989

▲ Aboriginal Title and Rights Position Paper

AUTHOR: Union of British Columbia Indian Chiefs
YEAR: 1989
ABORIGINAL GROUP: First Nations
TOPICS: Self-Government, Constitution, Federal Government/Aboriginal Relations
SUB-TOPICS: rights, federal trust responsibilities
SOURCE: Provincial Aboriginal Organization

BACKGROUND

This report was prepared in celebration of the twentieth anniversary of the Union of British Columbia Indian Chiefs.

PURPOSE

This report sets out the foundation upon which First Nations in British Columbia are prepared to negotiate a co-existing relationship with Canada.

In the view of the Union of British Columbia Indian Chiefs (UBCIC), the effective implementation of their position would resolve current political, economic, legal and social conflicts facing their people, and would ensure that, for the first time, Indian people would share in the wealth of Canada.

ISSUES AND FINDINGS

The report presents an argument in favour of the inherent Aboriginal right to self-government, based on Aboriginal title and rights, international human rights, and the provisions of the Canadian constitution. It first discusses the tradition of First Nations Aboriginal title and rights, and the history of the co-existence of Indian and European institutions in Canada. The report then calls for the decolonization of the First Nations and a return to an atmosphere of mutual recognition and respect.

The UBCIC argues that because each First Nation collectively maintains title to the lands in its respective traditional territory, it should have the following additional rights:

1. the right to choose and determine the authority they wish to exercise through Indian governments;

2. the right to exercise jurisdiction to maintain their sacred connection to Mother Earth; and

3. the right to share the governing powers over their land only by informed consent.

The UBCIC also looks to the international arena for support for self-government. The report quotes from the International Covenant on Economic, Social and Cultural Rights, and the International Covenant on Civil and Political Rights, in making its case for a right to self-determination and inherent sovereignty.

As the final basis for inherent self-government, the UBCIC employs an argument based on the Canadian Constitution. It asserts that the Canadian Constitution was patriated on the condition that Canada forever protect its Crown obligations to the First Nations. The UBCIC claims, therefore, that Canadian sovereignty is conditional upon the assurance that self-determination of First Nations becomes a reality.

RECOMMENDATIONS

The UBCIC makes no specific recommendations, but instead presents a case in support of self-determination.

▲ Breaking Free: A Proposal for Change to Aboriginal Family Violence

AUTHOR: Ontario Native Women's Association

YEAR: 1989

ABORIGINAL GROUP: First Nations, Métis, Aboriginal Women

TOPICS: Administration of Justice, Health, Social Development, Child Welfare, Family/Family Relations, Cultural Affairs

SUB-TOPICS: system (integrated vs. separate), courts (structures and procedures), sentencing and remedies, mental health, substance abuse, family violence, religion/spirituality

SOURCE: Provincial Aboriginal Organization

BACKGROUND

The Ontario Native Women's Association was formed in 1972. It is a non-profit Aboriginal women's organization, incorporated in the province of Ontario, whose mandate is to represent and develop the leadership potential of Métis and First Nations women. In 1987, a special committee of the Board of Directors, called the Native Child and Family Support Services Committee, was formed to study the issue of family violence among Aboriginal people. This report is the result of the work of that committee.

PURPOSE

The report expresses the views of First Nations and Métis women. It looks at the problem of family violence, the reasons behind it and proposals for change.

ISSUES AND FINDINGS

The findings were based on 104 completed questionnaires (688 questionnaires were sent) and 167 telephone and personal interviews with representatives from agencies and organizations and with Aboriginal people.

The responses indicated to the Committee that the level of family violence in Aboriginal communities is more severe than had previously been suggested. Eighty-four per cent of respondents indicated that family violence occurs in their communities, 15% stated that they did not know and only 1 respondent stated that it didn't occur. Eighty per cent of respondents stated that they had personally experienced family violence. (The incidence in Canadian society is considered to be approximately 10%). In 90% of the cases, women indicated that alcohol abuse was an immediate cause of the problem. The Committee found that the awareness and availability of services is limited and the severity of injuries sustained is dangerously high.

The Committee believes that at the core of many of these problems is the absence of self-government. They believe that the inability of people to establish their destiny based upon their own cultural beliefs has stifled Aboriginal culture, creating a sense of confusion and loss of many of the traditional values that were predicated on respect and dignity of the individual.

The Committee found that the availability of shelter services or safe homes for Aboriginal women in Ontario is scarce. They also found that non-Aboriginal shelters have little awareness of the plight or cultural experience of Aboriginal women.

The Committee established that there is a definite need for more highly qualified Aboriginal persons in the medical professions. They need to be trained to identify family violence, to treat the victim and refer her and her family to a holistic program which includes treatment for alcohol abuse and other psychological and medical problems related to family violence. The Committee also identified the need for services directed exclusively at members of the Aboriginal family who have been exposed to violence.

The report found that the response of the Ontario government to family violence has been one of enhanced criminalization and law enforcement. The Committee questioned the usefulness of this approach due to cultural differences that see abuse as a community problem. The court system is often seen as alien and fraught with institutional racism. The example the Committee described dealt with access to matrimonial property; due to certain clauses in the *Indian Act*, it is very difficult for women to gain interim occupancy of matrimonial property on a reserve during family violence situations.

When interviewing service providers to Aboriginal communities, the Committee found that the respondents were almost unanimous in their desire for more training with regard to family violence. This included academic as well as cultural sensitivity training.

The survey found that there was a drastic need for services in rural and isolated communities (i.e., Métis communities, non-status bands, or status bands without reserves) that are often overlooked by the federal government.

The Committee found that these people as well as other groups must be given funds so that they can develop their own intervention and prevention programs to suit their special needs.

RECOMMENDATIONS

The Committee presented 13 recommendations. They may be categorized under the headings of services, education, justice and training.

1. Services

In the area of services, the Committee recommends that the provincial and federal governments pursue a policy of equality of access, create a network of Healing Lodges, create a program for male batterers, and children and develop programs for alcohol and drug abuse. The Committee found that a community response team is necessary for every Aboriginal community as is an increase in medical services. They also recommended a toll free telephone line specifically for victims of Aboriginal family violence.

2. Education

With respect to education, the Committee found that an immediate education program based on their findings should be developed for Aboriginal people. Its purpose would be to educate the communities on the causes and nature of family violence and the needs of Aboriginal families and to encourage the communities to start their own treatment and prevention programs.

3. Justice

In the area of justice, the Committee suggested that the province support the creation of an Aboriginal justice system involving elders and community leaders, and that it address the issue of matrimonial property.

4. Training

The Committee also recommended a training package for medical personnel to help them identify family violence and to assist Aboriginal families in a culturally sensitive manner. The establishment of a clearinghouse or organizational centre specifically on Aboriginal family violence was also recommended.

▲ Comprehensive Housing Study: Housing and Poverty

AUTHOR: New Brunswick Aboriginal Peoples Council
YEAR: 1989
ABORIGINAL GROUP: Métis, Non-Status
TOPICS: Community Services and Infrastructure, Social Development
SUB-TOPICS: housing, income support/poverty
SOURCE: Provincial Aboriginal Organization

BACKGROUND

The predecessor of the New Brunswick Aboriginal Peoples Council (NBAPC), the New Brunswick and Prince Edward Island Association of Métis and Non-Status Indians, undertook a housing survey in 1973. They identified sub-standard housing conditions among the Métis and non-status Indians in their jurisdiction, and established a non-profit housing corporation to deal with the problems. Since that time, the NBAPC has been involved in a number of housing projects, and consequently, it felt it necessary to conduct a comprehensive review of housing conditions to direct it in its attempts to ensure a better quality of life for the residents.

PURPOSE

This report was prepared by the NBAPC, and supported by the New Brunswick Housing Corporation and the Canada Mortgage and Housing Corporation. Its purpose was to study the records of the housing programs of the NBAPC, the provincial and federal governments in order to ensure that the current programs will meet the needs of the 1990s. The NBAPC examined the housing problem from the perspective of Aboriginal residents. It hoped that the report would complement the report of the Minister's Task Force on Housing by examining housing as a social tool in the struggle against poverty.

ISSUES AND FINDINGS

The issues identified in the report were based on an examination of the history of NBAPC's housing initiatives, a literature review which explored the characteristics of poverty, and a survey of Aboriginal households.

The review of NBAPC's housing initiatives recognized that many efforts had been made to pressure the federal government into addressing the inadequate housing conditions in which many Aboriginal people live. The report also outlined the shifting responsibility for housing, from provincial to federal to joint endeavours.

Based on a review of the literature, the report identified a number of characteristics of poverty. These characteristics illustrate the magnitude of poverty in New Brunswick, and act as a basis for the NBAPC to understand future housing needs and to assess the amount of resources which will be needed to improve the quality of life for off-reserve Aboriginal people in New Brunswick.

The analysis and summary of the survey indicated that housing services had improved greatly since the 1973 survey. Unfortunately, there is still much to be done to integrate social and economic policies in a way which will free these families from the cycle of poverty. The survey found that inadequate housing is highly correlated with a lack of money, and consequently, affordability was the largest problem identified by the respondents. Also reported in the survey was the unusually large number of houses headed by a single parent.

Based on the review of NBAPC initiatives, the literature review, and the survey, the NBAPC concluded that housing, although a key aspect of quality of life, is not the sole tool required to dismantle the poverty cycle. Instead, a more comprehensive approach, of which housing is but one element, is needed.

RECOMMENDATIONS

The Housing Study conducted by the NBAPC concluded with 27 recommendations. In general terms, the study recommended that housing programs be used as a social tool (i.e., a means to an end rather than an end in and of itself), as part of more comprehensive approach to poverty, and that this comprehensive approach be upheld even if it means that fewer housing units will be available.

Despite this emphasis on a comprehensive approach, the report recommended a number of changes to the current housing programs, which would improve housing as one aspect of the fight against poverty:

1. that social and economic policy be integrated among all levels of government;

2. that para-professionals and professionals be hired to offer pre- and post-occupancy counselling;

3. that housing programs be located in close proximity to residents' support groups;

4. that a maintenance and repair program be established;

5. that a small loans program and a fire and contents insurance plan be developed for low income families;

6. that families entering a housing program be charged a fixed monthly payment for approximately five years, in order to provide an incentive to break the cycle of poverty; and

7. that training in marketable skills be a requirement for targeted groups, given that a permanent well-paying job was seen to offer the greatest assistance to a family living in poverty.

By following these recommendations, the NBAPC believes that the quality of life for the Aboriginal people affected by housing programs could be greatly improved.

▲ A Comprehensive Plan to Increase Native Participation in the British Columbia Fishing Industry

AUTHOR: Native Brotherhood of British Columbia and Native Fishing Association
YEAR: 1989
ABORIGINAL GROUP: First Nations
TOPICS: Resources, Employment Development
SUB-TOPIC: fishing/fisheries
SOURCE: Provincial Aboriginal Organizations

BACKGROUND

The Native Brotherhood of British Columbia (NBBC) and the Native Fishing Association (NFA) produced this report in response to declining Indian participation in the fishing industry. This decline was attributed largely to regulatory changes made under the Davis Plan which adversely affected Indian people relative to non-Indians in the fishing industry. These changes included the introduction of limited entry licensing in 1969, and of vessel quality standards in 1970, both of which served to exclude Native people from the British Columbia fishery. The Native Brotherhood was also concerned that Native participation was being compromised because Indian people did not understand the value of licences and subsequently sold them to non-Indians during economic downturns or when a fisherman left the fishery.

This report was also generated with the knowledge that past attempts to increase Native participation in the fishery had failed. These programs included the introduction of Indian only fishing licences for salmon and herring (1971), the Indian Fishermen's Assistance Program (1968-79), the Indian Fishermen's Emergency Assistance Program (1981), the establishment of the Northern Native Fishing Corporation (1982), and the creation of the Native Fishing Association (1986). The Native Fishing Association was established to provide loans to Native fishermen from funds set aside under the Indian Fishermen's Economic Development Program, and according to the report, it has been strikingly successful in stabilizing Native participation in the British Columbia commercial fishing industry.

PURPOSE

The purpose of this report is to present a comprehensive plan to increase Native participation in the fishing industry, which will allow for the creation of a solid base on which to develop continued sustainable economic growth for British Columbia's Native people. It is based on the idea of increasing Indian ownership of commercial fishing licences. The plan fulfils the two criteria that had been identified by the rest of the fishing industry as fundamental to any plan to increase Native ownership of fishing licences and participation in the fishery:

1. that the increase in Native licences be accomplished by purchasing existing licences, not reinstating ones or creating new ones; and

2. that it not disrupt the fishery.

This plan is intended as the first phase of a long-term program to provide economic opportunities to Indian people by increasing their involvement in all aspects of the Pacific fishery. The plan is supported by many fishing industry organizations, including the Fisheries Council of BC, the Pacific Fishermen's Alliance, the United Fisherman and Allied Workers Union, and the Sport Fishing Advisory Board.

ISSUES AND FINDINGS

The report examines past efforts by the NBBC and the NFA to increase Native participation in the fishing industry focusing on the 1987 report, "Analysis of Impacts of Federal Government Commercial Fisheries Licensing Policy and Regulations on Indian Fishing Communities" (the Licensing Study). The Licensing Study recommended the creation of Indian only licences for each fishing licence category and the establishment of an Indian Licence Advisory Board.

This study also served as a basis for the development of a "Proposal for an Indian Licensing System". The proposal argued that past efforts to redress declining Native participation in the fishery caused by the Department of Fisheries and Oceans (DFO) licensing policies and practices have failed for a variety of reasons:

1. an emphasis on grants rather than loans to assist Native fishermen;
2. a lack of training programs for Indian fishermen on how to conduct a successful, profitable fishing business;
3. a lack of a funding mechanism to make "Indian only" licences obtainable;
4. a lack of clear definition of "Indian only" fishing licences;
5. the administration and control of programs were maintained by the federal government rather than by the Indian community; and
6. there was no means to consolidate and secure short term gains in Native participation.

The report concludes that owning fishing licences is the key to Indian economic wealth and stability, without which there can be no increase in employment or income for Indian people in the fishing industry.

Based on these findings, the NBBC and NFA present a comprehensive plan to increase the participation of Native people in the fishery. The objective is to increase Native ownership of licences to 30% over the next 10 years without issuing new licences or disrupting the industry. This objective would be accomplished by following the recommendations made in the Licensing Study and Licensing Proposal as outlined below. The report emphasizes the benefits that the implementation of this plan would have for Indian people in British Columbia, speculating that over 2,000 jobs and more than 1,000 person-years of employment would be created for Native people through these measures.

RECOMMENDATIONS

The comprehensive plan pursues the recommendations made by the Licensing Study and the Licensing Proposal. It includes the following elements:

1. the extension of Indian only categories for all fishing licences, and the purchase of existing fishing licences for conversion into new Indian only categories;
2. the creation of an Indian Licence Advisory Board to establish targets and monitor Native participation, and to provide a vehicle through which the Indian community can provide policy advice in a co-management context with DFO;

299

3. the prohibition of beneficial ownership of Indian-only licences by non-Indians;

4. changing Indian only herring licences from personal to vessel licences; and

5. the provision of capital funding to finance the purchase of fishing licences and vessels by Indian fishermen.

▲ National Inquiry into First Nations Child Care

AUTHOR: Assembly of First Nations
YEAR: 1989
ABORIGINAL GROUP: First Nations
TOPICS: Education, Social Development
SUB-TOPIC: child care/daycare
SOURCE: National Aboriginal Organization

BACKGROUND

At the time of this report's preparation, wrangling between the federal and provincial governments had contributed to a breakdown in family and social structures in First Nations communities. There was limited day and child care facilities and programs to meet the particular needs of First Nations communities, and fewer services were provided to Indian children than for any other group of children in Canada.

PURPOSE

The purpose of the Inquiry was to undertake research and make recommendations for action on child care issues. It was to investigate the major concerns and policy preferences of Aboriginal people and to discover the most urgent needs of children in First Nations communities.

ISSUES AND FINDINGS

Three prevalent issues are addressed in the report. These are:

1. the traditions of First Nations child-rearing and the history of child welfare and education in First Nations communities;

2. the agencies and child care programs established by First Nations and what they can do; and

3. the jurisdictional, financial, cultural and societal problems faced by First Nations child care programs.

Traditional systems of raising children involved the extended family and community. Traditionally, children were included in all adult activities and learned through observation and emulation. Residential, provincial and federal school systems contributed to the erosion of these values. Under the *Indian Act* (1951), provinces were given authority to extend their child welfare services to Indian communities, allowing social workers to remove children from their homes. The removal of children from their families and communities began in the early 1960s.

In the area of child care programs and agencies, First Nations favour preventive systems over the protective systems imposed by federal and provincial governments. The success of First Nations-run agencies has demonstrated that the First Nations people have the ability to solve their own problems. Existing First Nations agencies and programs rely on the extended family, preventive care, and are based on an understanding of local culture and community. Legislative barriers present obstacles to greater First Nations control and the extension of such First Nations-run programs and agencies.

First Nations child care programs face many problems in relation to

1. jurisdiction: both provincial and federal governments deny responsibilities in this field, yet neither is willing to give surrender control and responsibility to First Nations;

2. inappropriate standards for existing child care programs: provincial standards are designed to meet the needs of white, middle-class, urban Canadians;

3. inappropriate licensing and teaching requirements which make it difficult for First Nations to establish programs and to staff them with culturally sensitive care givers;

4. lack of financial resources: at the time of the Inquiry, $60 million targeted for First Nations child care was eliminated.

The root cause of many of the social problems that contribute to the need for increased child care is cited to be the interaction of structural and cultural colonialism and subordination within Canada. First Nations see a major role for child care in helping to reverse the damage already inflicted, and prevent the perpetuation of an unacceptable situation. First Nations child care centres are expected to benefit the community as well as First Nations children. It is hoped that such centres will offer family care to facilitate family healing and promotion of community well-being.

RECOMMENDATIONS

The report contains 45 recommendations, most of which fall into one of five major areas. These are:

1. child care as a cultural issue;
2. First Nations vision of child care;
3. policy and jurisdiction;
4. funding; and
5. training and programs.

By emphasizing child care as a cultural issue, the report reflects the view that any new systems must encompass Indian values and traditions, and embrace comprehensive, community based care.

The First Nations vision of child care is that this should be offered as a basic social service, and that child care should reflect the unique needs of the First Nations community.

First Nations government jurisdictions, power and responsibilities and the inherent right to develop and control First Nations child care systems must be recognized. Also in respect of jurisdiction and policy issues, First Nations recommended the federal government consider a national First Nations Child Care Act, similar to that of the United States.

The Report recommended flexible funding be made available immediately and that capital expenditures be controlled by First Nations. The report contains related recommendations concerning the application for grants under the Child Care Initiatives Fund (Health and Welfare Canada) to begin planning for the implementation of First Nations child care.

As for training and programs, the report emphasized the need for alternatives to traditional Early Childhood Education programs and suggested the implementation of programs designed to increase cultural sensitivity by care givers, and enhance capacity of professionals to address local problems.

First Nations also recommended that First Nations child care be extended to urban First Nations families and not limited to on-reserve members.

Finally, First Nations endorsed constitutional recognition and protection of First Nations' rights to control their lives and lands.

◆ *Native Advisory Committee on Heritage, Language and Culture: Committee Report* (1989), see **Volume 3, British Columbia.**

▲ Native Council of Nova Scotia Health Demonstration Project: Final Project Report

AUTHOR: Native Council of Nova Scotia (Theresa Martin)
YEAR: 1989
ABORIGINAL GROUP: Métis, Non-Status, Urban Aboriginal People
TOPICS: Health, Programs and Services
SUB-TOPICS: primary and secondary health care, substance abuse, health care professionals
SOURCE: Provincial Aboriginal Organization

BACKGROUND

The Native Council of Nova Scotia (NCNS) contends that many services, including health care, are inaccessible to Native people living off-reserve. These people are most at risk because of the inter-jurisdictional dispute between the federal Department of Indian Affairs and Northern Development and the provincial government over who is responsible for Native health care. The NCNS felt that in order to address this problem, a study supported by Health and Welfare Canada, needed to be conducted in order to address the health care concerns of the members of the NCNS.

PURPOSE

This project entailed the administration of a needs assessment survey in an attempt to identify and document the alcohol and drug concerns of the Council's membership. The needs assessment survey was supplemented by a services questionnaire aimed at determining the effectiveness of various service agencies in serving Native people off-reserve and a leaders' questionnaire, the purpose of which was to solicit the responses of Native leaders regarding health care. The purpose of the project was to educate, inform, and sensitize people to the health care needs of the NCNS members.

ISSUES AND FINDINGS

The needs assessment found that Native people off-reserve face more problems and emotional downfalls than those living on-reserve. Causal factors which might explain this distinction include the displacement of cultural beliefs, feelings of segregation, and distrust of non-Native services. Social and community concerns include unemployment, alcohol and drug abuse, housing, education, recreation, youth, crime, health (quality of care), suicide, child abuse, sanitation, sexual abuse, heart disease, cancer, and AIDS.

With regard to servicing, it was found that there were rarely Native representatives or staff in service agencies; as a result, many NCNS members feel that there is a need for a facility that is organized and run by Native people. It was further found that Native people off-reserve are sometimes treated as though they are non-Native and expected to integrate into mainstream society. Finally, the services questionnaire revealed that many Native people are not knowledgeable about health services and programs available to them off-reserve.

RECOMMENDATIONS

The NCNS Health Demonstration Project offered the following recommendations:

1. that a provincial health care task force be established, which would include Native representatives, to develop strategies to secure long-term funding for Native health care programs that would reflect the needs of Native people off-reserve;

2. that health care programs receiving long-term funding have a built-in evaluation component;

3. that policies and strategies for dealing with alcohol and drug abuse be developed, along with educational materials for Native people off-reserve;

4. that there be increased liaison with service agencies, health departments, addiction centres, etc., to increase the sensitivity toward the health care concerns of Native people off-reserve; and

5. that the Health Demonstration Advisory Board, established under this project, be further developed to provide a stronger voice in future health care initiatives.

By following these recommendations it is anticipated that the health concerns of Native people off-reserve can be better addressed.

▲ Peace and Good Order: Recognition of First Nations Jurisdiction in the Administration of Justice in Manitoba

AUTHOR: Manitoba Assembly of Chiefs
YEAR: 1989
ABORIGINAL GROUP: All Aboriginal Peoples
TOPIC: Administration of Justice
SUB-TOPICS: justice system, law enforcement, legal representation, courts
SOURCE: Provincial Aboriginal Organization

BACKGROUND

The Manitoba Assembly of Chiefs presented this report as a brief to the Manitoba Aboriginal Justice Inquiry. The inquiry was mandated to determine the effect of the justice system on Aboriginal people, the extent to which Aboriginal people are dealt with differently than non-Aboriginal people, and the changes needed to improve the system.

In preparing this study, the Chiefs contacted other Aboriginal people in Canada and the United States as well as many non-Aboriginal people. Based on this process, the Chiefs proposed the restoration of two fundamental concepts:

1. the traditional system of Aboriginal justice, which serves the needs of its society based on the principles of healing, reconciliation and the re-establishment of the community in situations where the peace and harmony of the community is disrupted; and

2. that the same object of peace and harmony be employed when conflicts between two societies arise.

PURPOSE

The purpose of the study was to examine the impact of the justice system on Aboriginal peoples and to propose changes to bring about reform in the system.

ISSUES AND FINDINGS

The report addresses the major problems of Aboriginal people vis-à-vis the justice system, and found that

1. there is widespread mistrust of the Canadian justice system by Aboriginal people which leads them to avoid using the system when they need it;

2. the Canadian adversarial system is antithetical to the traditional Aboriginal system of conflict resolution;

3. Aboriginal people are generally unfamiliar with the system and process and with their rights within the process;

4. there is little representation of Aboriginal people within the system, including judges, lawyers and police officers;

5. it is difficult for Aboriginal people to obtain competent legal representation because of costs or, in the case of legal aid, because it may not be available in cases where treaty or Aboriginal rights issues are involved; and

6. Aboriginal people experience great frustration over the length of time involved in resolving a matter in the justice system.

RECOMMENDATIONS

In making recommendations, two objectives are identified: to improve the image of the justice system as it affects Aboriginal people and to provide a better quality of justice for Aboriginal people. To this end, the Assembly of Manitoba Chiefs recommends the development of Aboriginal control of their own justice system. This position is based on the distinctiveness of Aboriginal peoples, and on the inherent right to Aboriginal self-government. Specific recommendations are summarized as follows:

1. that an Indian Tribal Court with civil and criminal jurisdiction over Indian people and Indian land be established, and that alternative judicial arrangements be considered for Indian people not living on reserves;

2. that all parties (Indian peoples, the province and Canada) commit themselves to seeking and applying solutions to the problems in the current judicial system; and

3. that a Framework Agreement, involving political and technical representatives of the Assembly of Manitoba Chiefs, the province of Manitoba and the government of Canada, be established to outline the process for reform.

▲ Women and Development: The Effects of Militarization

AUTHOR: Conference on Women and Development, Conference
    Committee
YEAR: 1989
ABORIGINAL GROUP: All Aboriginal Peoples, Aboriginal Women
TOPICS: Political Participation, Economic Development, Land Use,
    Development and Management
SUB-TOPICS: development, non-reserve lands
SOURCE: Other Aboriginal Organization

BACKGROUND

The Conference on Women and Development took place in North West River,
Labrador, from May 5 to 7, 1989. The conference served as a vehicle for
fulfilling the needs of a number of different organizations:

1. the Labrador Native Women's Association's annual meeting;
2. Oxfam-St. John's follow-up conference to the 1988 Women and
   Development Conference;
3. the Mokami Status of Women Council's need to report the findings of
   their telephone survey on Labrador women's attitudes to military expansion
   in Labrador and Quebec; and
4. the Sheshatshit Women's Group's desire to present to Innu women a guest
   speaker on Filipino women's experiences with U.S. military bases.

Conference planners blended these purposes to create a single agenda for the
conference. This document is a report of the proceedings of the conference.

PURPOSE

One purpose of the conference was to inform the women of Labrador and
elsewhere of existing and proposed plans for NATO military activities in the
region. The conference was also intended to provide a vehicle for sharing
experiences regarding militarization and local development. Conference
planners hoped that the participants would leave the conference with an
understanding of how they might experience and cope with the developments,
both individually and collectively.

ISSUES AND FINDINGS

The conference was composed of sessions, each addressing a different theme. The first session was a storytelling session, with presentations by women who have had experience with the presence of military bases in their communities and countries. Although some related positive experiences or consequences from contact with the military bases, such as cultural exchange or the initial flow of money into the community via construction or other jobs, most related negative experiences and negative social consequences. Stories of prostitution, drugs, and crime were common, but the women also spoke of the instability and artificiality of the base economy.

The objective of the second session was to find out what the participants knew about the military bases in Labrador and Quebec, and to provide them with information about what was being proposed. The participants ultimately formed groups to produce lists of questions that the group wanted answered. The questions generally dealt with the following concerns: control; decision making and communication; impacts on people and the environment; military facts and information; and employment and development.

The next session dealt with who is in control of this development (i.e., the military, the government, big business, or the people) and what the impact would be on the people of Labrador. Through skits, the participants played out their perceptions of how the military development might occur, who the players might be, and what changes the people might experience. The group concluded that the people possess the power to counter the power of government, the military, and business, but they must stand together to be successful. Participants argued that greater information and education efforts are needed for local people. They also concluded that the military development would ultimately be short-term and leave the region.

The fourth session explored the participants' visions for future development in their communities and on their land. Many envisioned control by local people, and emphasized small craft businesses and traditional activities. They emphasized the importance of preserving natural resources and the health of the people in order for these visions to be achieved.

The final session was conducted in an effort to develop action plans for the participants to present to their communities. The process began with a presentation of possible courses of action and the identification of areas where action was needed based on previous discussions. The list included efforts in the areas of education, communication, information and networking, as well as proposed actions to cope with expansion, control development, and the involvement of silent voices in development decisions.

During the discussion on action, three dominant themes emerged:

1. something should be done to support the Innu as they deal with the military expansion;

2. the concerns about alternative economic developments must be addressed; and

3. there is a need for more effective communication between the different affected groups.

RECOMMENDATIONS

The conference produced no official recommendations. The main result of the conference was to provide people with connections to people and ideas, and perhaps to provide the impetus for action with the support of their new contacts.

In response to the three themes identified, the participants suggested that the following actions be taken:

1. Innu Support

(a) that participants report on the conference to their communities;

(b) that participants write letters to the politicians and newspaper editors;

(c) that participants arouse popular support, particularly from Labrador people, by holding meetings with different groups;

(d) that participants lobby the government; and

(e) that participants examine why more Labradorians are not involved.

2. Alternative Development

(a) that the people of Labrador find alternative jobs;

(b) that participants lobby provincial government for alternatives; and

(c) that participants lobby government to get equal funding for all Labradorians.

3. Communication

(a) that exchanges between students and women be developed;

(b) that participants engage in teleconferencing;

(c) that information centres be established for information gathering and distribution;

(d) that participants seek funding to minimize their reliance on volunteers;

(e) that participants establish follow-up committees to this conference; and

(f) that annual women's conferences be held.

▲ A Community Perspective on Health Promotion and Substance Abuse

AUTHOR: Pauktuutit (Inuit Women's Association)
YEAR: 1990
ABORIGINAL GROUP: Inuit
TOPIC: Health
SUB-TOPIC: substance abuse
SOURCE: National Aboriginal Organization

BACKGROUND

Substance abuse has long been recognized as a major problem in Inuit communities. Pauktuutit (the Inuit Women's Association) works from the perspective that a wide variety of personal, social, economic and political circumstances both contribute to, and are exacerbated by, the problem of substance abuse. The best approach for addressing substance abuse must therefore be capable of responding to other serious community problems, such as housing, unemployment, poverty, family violence, and the lack of recreational activities.

PURPOSE

In December, 1989, Pauktuutit received funds from the National Native Alcohol and Drug Abuse Program (NNADAP) to conduct research into alcohol, drug and solvent abuse in Inuit communities. The research was conducted through a survey distributed to 186 individuals and organizations involved in the alcohol and drug abuse and health care fields in 39 communities in the Northwest Territories, Nunavik (Northern Quebec), and Labrador. A shorter version of the questionnaire was also distributed to individuals, Inuit women's committees and organizations throughout the North. Based on the results of the survey, Pauktuutit explored the need for programs and services to address the problems of substance abuse identified by the research; this report outlines the results of this task.

ISSUES AND FINDINGS

The questionnaire asked respondents to identify what they felt were the primary problems faced by Inuit communities. Substance abuse was the most frequently identified problem. Drug abuse was also considered to be a major concern, viewed as more serious than either alcohol or solvent abuse in some regions. Other problems identified included housing shortages and substandard housing, unemployment, lack of education, particularly the high drop-out rate, and suicide.

The report found that a comprehensive and co-ordinated approach to health promotion throughout the North was needed to address these problems. The research also indicated that there were significant regional differences in the problems identified. To accommodate these differences, the report recommended that substance abuse prevention programs be developed at the regional level.

RECOMMENDATIONS

Based on the results of the survey, the report recommended that the NNADAP, and its counterpart in the Northwest Territories, begin funding a pilot project in an Inuit community in each of the provincial/territorial jurisdictions. This project would be aimed at co-ordinating existing community services and facilitating the development of a co-operative approach to problem-solving at the community level. A Community Animator should be hired in each pilot project to foster co-operation and co-ordination among the different organizations.

The report recognized that this type of approach would require a long-term commitment by the community. It recommended that the project span three years, and that there be a degree of national co-ordination to help start the pilot projects, to provide information, and to facilitate the opting-in of other communities. Pauktuutit proposed that it provide the national co-ordination as part of a proposed National Inuit Substance Abuse Co-ordination Project. In addition to co-ordinating the community pilot projects, the proposed Project would also develop and maintain a resource library on current issues in the prevention and treatment of substance abuse, provide the Inuit with information in both Inuktitut and English on substance abuse and related issues, and act as an ongoing resource to Inuit communities by providing information, resources, and general assistance.

◆ *Discussion Paper Regarding First Nation Land Claims* (1990),
see **Volume 3, Ontario.**

▲ **The Lieutenant-Governor's Conference – Celebrating
Alberta's Families: Métis Families**

AUTHOR: Métis Nation of Alberta and Métis Children's Services
Society (Fred Anderson and Carolyn Pettifer)
YEAR: 1990
ABORIGINAL GROUP: Métis
TOPICS: Child Welfare, Family/Family Relations
SOURCE: Provincial Aboriginal Organizations

BACKGROUND

The Lieutenant Governor's Conference, Celebrating Alberta's Families, was
held in Edmonton from February 19-21, 1990. The Conference participants
included 19 Métis delegates from across the province and represented the first
time representatives nominated by each of the six zones had been brought
together to discuss the future direction for Métis families.

The workshop on Métis Families, which ran concurrent to the Conference,
was organized in anticipation of concerns that the Conference would not
provide an adequate forum to educate government and the general public on
issues affecting Métis families.

PURPOSE

The study paper and research project presented in this report were intended
to stimulate discussions and begin the process for future resolutions on
issues affecting Métis families. The report was submitted to the President of
the Métis Association of Alberta by Fred Anderson, Social Services, Métis
Association of Alberta, and Carolyn Pettifer of Métis Children's Services.

ISSUES AND FINDINGS

The report is divided into three principal sections:

1. Study Examining the Impact of a Changing Society on the Métis Family

The study recounted the history of the Métis, including the role of the Métis in the fur trade, the impact of mission schools on the cultural identity of the Métis, and the development of the Métis movement in the early 1930s, as the Métis began to petition the provincial government for land, and for their own Métis organizations. Also discussed was the 1987 Framework Agreement between the government of Alberta and the Métis Association of Alberta. This Agreement was a political accord designed to ensure participation of the Métis in government decision making and in the design and delivery of programs.

The study also raised concerns about the approach that Alberta Family and Social Services was taking in delivering child welfare services to the Métis community. They found that Métis children were being apprehended at an alarming rate. The authors recommended that greater community involvement and the use of the least intrusive measures available be encouraged.

The report also outlined a provincial model for the delivery of services, involving a two-phase approach. The first phase would involve a process of consultation with the Métis community on a proposed structure to deliver services. The second phase would be directed at implementing the endorsed structure, as well as developing effective management and administrative controls.

2. Report Based on the Lieutenant Governor's Conference

The second section of the report is based on a joint workshop, held in 1990, and sponsored by the Métis Association of Alberta and the Métis Children's Services. During this workshop, a number of issues affecting Métis families were identified:

(a) the lack of recognition given to the Métis community, entailing a lack of cultural recognition, negative stereotyping, and a lack of positive role models;

(b) the inadequacy of existing programs and services in meeting the needs of Métis children and families, as evidenced, for example, by the non-utilization and/or lack of appropriate health services;

(c) the need for Métis participation in policy development and in the delivery of services, and the lack of accountability to the Métis community; and

(d) the allocation of most resources to intervention and post-intervention services, rather than prevention and early intervention.

3. Report Based on a Workshop Examining the Issues Affecting Métis Families

A research paper constituted the third section of the report. The research was sponsored by the Métis Association of Alberta to outline the global and historical issues affecting Métis families. The following issues were examined in detail:

(a) demographic profiles;

(b) cultural issues, including language, identity, history, discrimination, role models, mobility, and Bill C-31;

(c) economics, including living arrangements, livelihood, income source, education/training, and production/consumption of goods; and

(d) social issues, including leisure time, happiness, the family unit, caring for family members, spirituality/religion, emotional issues, relationships with agencies, the law, family violence, drug/alcohol use, and physical health.

RECOMMENDATIONS

The document presented five recommendations with regard to Métis families:

1. that a conference be organized by the Métis Association of Alberta to more clearly identify the real issues and concerns of Métis families;

2. that the Métis community be given the responsibility to address issues of concern to their families and develop their own approaches to strengthen and support those families;

3. that a representative be recommended by the Métis Association of Alberta for appointment to the Premier's Council in support of Alberta families;

4. that the Premier's Council in support of Alberta families work in consultation with the Métis Association of Alberta Social Services Sub-Committee in identifying issues of concern and in developing strategies affecting the Métis community; and

5. that two more sub-committees be established to enhance services to Métis children and families through the Framework Agreement. These subcommittees would correspond to the government departments of culture and health.

▲ Native Child Care: "The Circle of Care"

AUTHOR: Native Council of Canada
YEAR: 1990
ABORIGINAL GROUP: All Aboriginal Peoples, Urban Aboriginal People
TOPICS: Education, Child Welfare, Social Development, Programs and Services
SUB-TOPICS: pre-school/daycare, child care
SOURCE: National Aboriginal Organization

BACKGROUND

In 1989, the Health and Welfare Canada Special Initiative Fund provided resources to the Native Council of Canada to initiate Native child care research. The objectives of the research were to promote awareness and consideration of the issues surrounding Native child care, and to encourage networking between Native and non-Native peoples, and among organizations operating in the area of Native child care.

PURPOSE

The report was designed to achieve the following purposes:

1. to identify how Native peoples view urban/rural Native child care; and
2. to outline the best way to serve the needs of Native child care.

ISSUES AND FINDINGS

There are two major findings which flow from this report:

1. Euro-Canadian and Native child care beliefs and practices are distinctly different and incompatible;
2. Natives, particularly those living off-reserve, are in desperate need of proper child care in order to help preserve the Native way of life.

The report goes into great detail in order to demonstrate how the Euro-Canadian and Native child care methods are incompatible and how the Euro-Canadian models serve as methods of assimilating Native culture. The report states that Native child care focuses on the community, where all those that come into contact with the child become part of the extended family. In this more holistic approach, the child is reared and taught the Native way of life by the entire community.

The report details the lack of Native child care services in each of the provinces and territories, with great emphasis on the difficulties of the off-reserve Native in urban and rural settings.

RECOMMENDATIONS

The report contains many recommendations, including the following:

1. that Native-run child care centres be accessible to Native people living both on- and off-reserve, and that they be sensitive to the many distinct Native cultures and languages;

2. that financial support to Native peoples be augmented to increase the availability of Native child care; and

3. that legislative and bureaucratic restrictions on daycare facilities be reduced to allow Native child care to be offered in a more suitable atmosphere, specifically, in the home.

▲ Native Peacekeeping: Challenges and Opportunities of the '90s: A Report on the Native Peoples and Policing Symposium

AUTHOR: Ontario Native Council on Justice
YEAR: 1990
ABORIGINAL GROUP: All Aboriginal Peoples
TOPICS: Administration of Justice, Community Institutions, Self-Government
SUB-TOPICS: law enforcement, system, sentencing and remedies, corrections, structures/institutions
SOURCE: Provincial Aboriginal Organization

BACKGROUND

In October 1988, the Ministry of the Solicitor General and the Ontario Association of Chiefs of Police sponsored the Ontario Multicultural Policing

Symposium, at which Native delegates expressed concern over the lack of acknowledgement of the unique position of Native people in Ontario's multicultural society. In response to these concerns, Deputy Solicitor General Stien Lal, with the support of the Solicitor General, proposed that a symposium be held to address the policing-related concerns of Native peoples. Subsequently, the Ontario Native Council on Justice, in consultation with representatives of other Native organizations in the province, developed a proposal for a "Native Peoples and Policing Symposium", held in Thunder Bay on November 19-22, 1990.

The Ontario Native Council on Justice was established to support Aboriginal organizations and their representatives in the development of initiatives to address justice matters for Aboriginal people and to ensure that the existing justice system meets their needs in a culturally-meaningful manner. The Ontario Federation of Indian Friendship Centres, the Ontario Métis and Aboriginal Association, the Ontario Native Women's Association, the Union of Ontario Indians, and the Native Law Students' Association have membership on the Council.

PURPOSE

The objective of the symposium was to address policing issues with regard to Native people in Ontario. In particular, the symposium was expected to promote discussion on present and future directions of Native policing issues and provide ideas and recommendations to be included in an action plan for distribution at the symposium proceedings.

ISSUES AND FINDINGS

There were 258 participants at the symposium, including representatives from First Nations, Native organizations, First Nations Police, Ontario Provincial Police, Royal Canadian Mounted Police, Sureté du Québec, Ontario municipal police forces, and the federal and provincial governments. Fifteen workshops were held over the course of the three-day symposium. The following is a summary of the issues and findings yielded from the workshops:

1. Community-Based Policing – On-Reserve

The workshop emphasized the need to focus on education and community participation in the development of community-based policing. The participants felt that policing must be tailored to each community in order to recognize the diversity of cultures, and that the inherent right of First

Nations to determine and decide on the type of peacekeeping service they require must be recognized.

2. Community-Based Policing – Off-Reserve

Workshop participants discussed the need to establish police/community dispute resolution mechanisms. It was also suggested that Native Liaison Officers be appointed throughout the province.

3. Non-Native Policing of Aboriginal People

This workshop addressed the need to work together in partnership at the community level. According to participants, there must be more emphasis on training and sensitivity. There must also be more interaction between Native and non-Native communities.

4. Recruitment, Hiring and Advancement – On-Reserve

Culturally appropriate training must be provided, with financial support from the federal government. The training program at the Ontario Police College must be made more relevant, Native-specific, and flexible.

5. Recruitment, Hiring and Advancement – Off-Reserve

Workshop participants recommended that more Native awareness and race relations initiatives be undertaken, that policy network with Native organizations to identify possible Native candidates for uniformed and civilian positions, and that police training recognize Aboriginal peoples as a distinct society.

6. Policing in the North

Participants felt that policing in northern regions must be controlled by First Nations. They also found that there was a need for all officers to be provided with cultural training and a history of the area they police. Finally, there was consensus that existing community resources, particularly elders, should be utilized as much as possible, and that issues of jurisdiction should be addressed.

7. Crisis Intervention

The workshop on crisis intervention focused on the lack of resources and programs to address crisis situations, including those that promote prevention, as well as those which provide crisis support and longer-term follow-up services.

8. Traditional Role of Peacekeepers

At this workshop, elders and traditional people reviewed the development of peacekeepers.

9. Police Complaints Process Mechanism – On-Reserve

Workshop participants felt that First Nations peoples should be encouraged to participate in community justice matters and public awareness activities should be enhanced to stimulate Native involvement.

10. Police Complaints Process Mechanics – Off-Reserve

Participants found that there was a need for more interpreters in the justice system, including police forces.

11. First Nations Policing Arrangements, Models and Police Governing Bodies

According to workshop participants, there was a need to develop policing models which would meet the needs of First Nations communities; the use of a community-based teamwork model, for instance, was examined. Participants also felt that jurisdictional issues must be resolved through control of policing by First Nations or through legislation or agreements to enable First Nations to establish and apply their own laws and administer their own justice systems.

12. Policing and Youth

The need to improve the perception of police held by First Nations youth was noted.

13. Local Police Governing Bodies – Off-Reserve

This workshop focused on the importance of communication in educating and sensitizing police commissions, police departments and communities about roles and responsibilities.

14. Policing and Alcohol

Workshop participants discussed the need for a campaign aimed at the Aboriginal community which would highlight alternative and preventive measures.

15. Policing and Victims

Issues discussed included the need for Native resource centres for Native offenders, and the need for victim assistance, including the use of healing lodges and the allocation of training and resources for victim support. Native justice issues must be recognized within the existing justice system.

RECOMMENDATIONS

As a result of the symposium, there were 229 recommendations put forth. These recommendations include the following:

1. that more resource centres, treatment centres, healing lodges, family dispute teams, crisis intervention workers, and sexual assault counsellors be established for Native offenders;

2. that legislation to allow Aboriginal representation on police commissions throughout the province be implemented;

3. that mandatory cross-cultural training be provided to sensitize police and judges to Native cultures, issues and communities;

4. that a special report on the progress and status of past and present recommendations on Native policing be completed by the Ontario Native Council on Justice;

5. that community programs for youth and education programs on alcoholism be implemented;

6. that an Ontario-wide commission of elders, Native health representatives, police and educators be created, whose mandate would include the examination of alcohol-related incarceration and underlying issues; i.e., sexual and physical abuse in residential schools;

7. that First Nations territories be policed by Native people;

8. that a First Nations policing policy centre be established within the Ministry of the Solicitor General;

9. that a Tripartite Task Force be created to study the feasibility of Native justice systems in Ontario;

10. that jurisdictional issues be resolved through control of policing by First Nations or through legislation or agreements to enable First Nations to establish and administer their own laws;

11. that a First Nations Constable Liaison position be defined by the OPP in consultation with the other parties and a wide range of incentives be developed for recruiting and retaining First Nations constables. Native police must have the same status as non-Native police;

12. that Native community committees be established to identify problems and solutions; and

13. that officers assigned to specific zones or areas be assigned for longer periods of time and be more visible in the community.

▲ Le projet de société des Atikamekw et des Montagnais et l'avenir constitutionnel du Québec

AUTHOR: Le Conseil des Atikamekw et des Montagnais
YEAR: 1990
ABORIGINAL GROUP: First Nations
TOPICS: Provincial Government/Aboriginal Relations, Self-Government, Constitution, Claims
SUB-TOPICS: Crown lands, resources, rights, negotiation structure and processes, comprehensive claims
SOURCE: Local Aboriginal Organization

BACKGROUND

This report was prepared for presentation to the National Assembly committee on the constitutional future of Quebec for the purpose of providing general information to committee members.

PURPOSE

The purpose of the report is to summarize the rights of the Atikamekw and Montagnais, to explain the fundamental ideas of their "projet de société", to justify the project using international standards of Native rights recognition, and finally, to express the eleven principles which guide their land claims negotiations with Quebec and the federal government.

ISSUES AND FINDINGS

The report reviews four issues:

1. Native Rights

On March 20, 1985, the Quebec National Assembly adopted a motion recognizing that all First Nations in Quebec have the following rights:

(a) the right to autonomy within Quebec;

(b) the right to their culture, language, and traditions;

(c) the right to own and control lands;

(d) the right to hunt, fish, cultivate and manage animal resources; and

(e) the right to participate in, and benefit from, the economic development of Quebec, in order to allow them to develop as distinct nations and to exercise their rights within Quebec.

This motion was regarded as a very significant step forward given the failure of constitutional negotiations with the federal government and the absence of Quebec at the constitutional negotiating table. The motion guarantees the Native rights outlined, but does not protect the rights afforded First Nations under the Canadian constitution in the advent of Quebec's separation.

2. The "Projet de société" of the Atikamekw and Montagnais

The "projet de société" of the Atikamekw and Montagnais constitutes an effort to express two fundamental ideas: the relationship with ancestral lands, and the persistence of a distinct culture. The report cites the case of low-altitude military flights in Labrador as an example of a threat to a peaceful relationship with their ancestral lands. It is argued that environmental impact assessments, conducted by the Department of National Defence, did not recognize the value of the relationship between Aboriginal people and the land. The Atikamekw and Montagnais also contend that the distinctiveness of their culture is threatened by government assimilationist policies and programs which prevent a proper appreciation of their cultural heritage.

The means which might be used to activate their project are varied. The Atikamekw and Montagnais expressed a desire to take part in major public debates such as the one on energy. Specific efforts to inform and stimulate local discussions about the project at the community level might also be employed to communicate its fundamental ideas. According to the report, however, the most effective means of activating the project is through negotiations with governments. Unfortunately, governments tend to focus negotiations on the present needs of Native groups and not on long-term development objectives. This approach rejects the notion of "dynamic agreements" which may be flexibly interpreted and easily amended, and is identified as a major obstacle to the success of the project.

3. Current International Standards which Recognize Native Rights

Specific rights are granted by the Universal Declaration of Aboriginal Rights of the United Nations:

(a) the right to self-determination;

(b) protection from ethnocide;

(c) the right to use and own existing and traditional lands;

(d) protection from the seizure of lands without clear consent;

(e) the right to claim resources or their value;

(f) the right to participate in all state decisions affecting them;

(g) the right to autonomy in internal affairs;

(h) the right to facilitate international relations with other Native groups; and

(i) the right to fair procedures to resolve conflicts with state authorities.

The implementation of these international standards in negotiations with both federal and Quebec governments has been ongoing since 1979, and particularly since 1986. Three stages were passed:

(a) a Framework Agreement was signed in 1988 and a Provisory Measures Agreement in 1989 to help to structure negotiations and to address present needs (i.e., by creating wild life reserves, and conducting social and economic impacts analyses);

(b) a Memorandum of Understanding was signed in 1990 to delineate the principles to be applied to negotiations in such areas as territory, autonomy, traditional activities, compensation, conflict resolution and amendment mechanisms; and

(c) a Final Agreement or Land Claim Treaty was signed which gives full force to the principles laid down previously.

At the time of this report, negotiations between the Atikamekw and Montagnais and the federal and provincial governments had reached a standstill, partly because the provincial's government was perceived as favouring the interests of the logging industry.

4. Principles Guiding their Negotiations with Quebec

Eleven principles continue to guide the Atikamekw and the Montagnais in their negotiations:

(a) their rights to autonomy as a people;

(b) their rights over all lands on the east peninsula of Quebec-Labrador;

(c) the need to avoid extinction before getting an agreement;

(d) the need for compensation for all past and present violations of their rights;

(e) opposition to all new resource exploitation initiatives until their rights are fully recognized;

(f) exclusive control of resources in the future;

(g) the assumption of responsibility for the development of renewable and non-renewable resources;

(h) the authority to use revenue from resources exploitation for economic planning;

(i) the right to control all aspects of their development;

(j) the need for development priorities to be guided by their traditions; and

(k) equality in negotiations.

RECOMMENDATIONS

No recommendations are provided since the report serves primarily as an information package for Commissioners.

◆ *Report of the Joint National Committee on Aboriginal AIDS Education and Prevention* (1990), see **Reports by Federal Bodies.**

▲ Submission to the Standing Committee on Aboriginal Affairs and Northern Development

AUTHOR: Council for Yukon Indians

YEAR: 1990

ABORIGINAL GROUP: First Nations

TOPICS: Self-Government, Constitution, Claims

SUB-TOPICS: negotiation structures and processes, jurisdiction, comprehensive claims

Source: Territorial Aboriginal Organization

BACKGROUND

Despite the fact that the Indian peoples of the Yukon have never extinguished Aboriginal rights or title to the land, these rights and title have never been defined or recognized by the government of Canada. As a result, resource development and settlement by non-Natives in the Yukon have infringed on these Aboriginal rights and title since the Gold Rush of 1898. The Yukon's Indian peoples have for a long time been attempting to resolve this outstanding issue and clarify their Aboriginal claim to the Yukon.

Beginning in 1973, under the leadership of the Yukon Native Brotherhood, and continuing in the 1980s under the care of the Council for Yukon Indians, Yukon Indians have been actively negotiating a land claim settlement with the government of Canada. This settlement would provide for increased involvement of Yukon Indians in the political, social and economic affairs of the Yukon, and define their role and rights in the use, protection and management of the Yukon's resources. Most importantly, the settlement would clarify the Aboriginal title and rights of Yukon Indians and protect these rights for future generations.

PURPOSE

The purpose of this submission is to express the concerns of the Yukon Indians with respect to Yukon Land Claims negotiations.

ISSUES AND FINDINGS

The submission points out the various obstacles that the Yukon Indians have had to overcome in their 16-year Land Claims negotiations process with the Canadian government. These obstacles include changes in federal government ministers and land claims negotiators, federal land claim polices, funding structures and negotiations processes.

On May 29, 1989, a Framework Agreement was signed clarifying the fundamental principles that would contribute to a final Land Claims Agreement in the Yukon. This Agreement establishes the terms for finalizing a Land Claims Agreement, which will in turn define existing Aboriginal rights currently recognized and protected within sections 25 and 35 of the *Constitution Act, 1982*.

RECOMMENDATIONS

The report makes no formal recommendations. By way of conclusion, the Council of Yukon Indians urges Canada "to recognize that Yukon Land Claims represent an invaluable opportunity for Canada and Northern Canadians to attain in part the objectives which so consistently eluded everyone during the First Ministers' Conference, namely, the achievement of Constitutionally protected, locally appropriate self-government."

▲ Literacy for Métis and Non-Status Indian Peoples: A National Strategy

AUTHOR: The Gabriel Dumont Institute of Native Studies and Applied Research and the Métis National Council
YEAR: 1991
ABORIGINAL GROUP: Métis, Non-Status
TOPICS: Education, Language
SUB-TOPICS: adult, curriculum, protection and preservation
SOURCE: Aboriginal Organizations

BACKGROUND

Literacy campaigns for Métis and non-status Indians have had a mixed reception. The authors assert that their particular needs have not been recognized nor addressed in programming to date; program organizers have not sought the advice of the Métis and non-status Indian organizations and these organizations have not received support for the programs they have designed and proposed. Literacy for Aboriginal peoples is a complex question tightly related to questions of self-identity and cultural tradition.

PURPOSE

The purpose of this research and report was to provide recommendations for action in the areas of policy, programs and strategies to meet the literacy needs of Métis and non-status Indian peoples.

ISSUES AND FINDINGS

The authors identified a number of problems pertaining to literacy programs for Métis and non-status Indians:

1. the lack of knowledge of the Métis and non-status Indian people, particularly relative to Status Indians;
2. the absence of formal structures for involving the Métis and non-status Indian people in the delivery of programs, particularly with regard to contracting program delivery with Métis or non-status Indian organizations;

3. the lack of effective communication links between the literacy units and the Métis and non-status Indian peoples;

4. ineffective policy development with regard to literacy programs;

5. the absence of a fiscal policy for literacy programming for Métis and non-status Indian peoples;

6. the need for structures and procedures for the involvement of Métis and non-status Indian people in the evaluation of programs aimed at Métis and non-status Indian peoples;

7. jurisdictional complications in the delivery of literacy programs;

8. uncertainty over the efficacy of Literacy Councils as a means to meet the needs of Métis and non-status Indian peoples;

9. the absence of philosophical and pedagogical foundations for programming; and

10. the need for some agreement on what is meant by literacy.

The authors examined existing literacy programs for Métis and non-status Indian peoples and identified the following as characteristics of successful programs:

1. control, support, and promotion from the local Aboriginal community;

2. flexibility;

3. curriculum generated by the program itself and geared to the culture, language and interests of the participants;

4. confidence-building activities;

5. support systems geared to student needs, such as Métis counsellors for Métis students;

6. non-traditional teaching approaches;

7. warm, informal learning environments;

8. caring instructors; and

9. the ability and desire to deal with the real life problems of students as they occur.

In addition to these characteristics, the authors listed the following as guiding principles for any literacy campaign involving Aboriginal peoples:

1. recognition of the existence of a variety of different forms of literacy in Aboriginal communities;

2. recognition of English-language literacy programming for Aboriginal peoples as cross-cultural experiences;

3. recognition of the tensions between orality and literacy;

4. recognition that non-literate people have different language usage methods, concepts, and techniques than those literate in English or French;

5. recognition that the teaching of essayist English is a narrow, restricted form of training in English literacy;

6. recognition that literacy is not new to communities and that resistance in the present context is directed at the system which has forced English or French language literacy at the expense of Aboriginal languages;

7. recognition that there is resistance to literacy within Aboriginal communities based on the threat to cultural identity posed by the assumption of the values of an outside culture bound within English or French language literacy;

8. recognition that there are serious differences of opinion within Aboriginal communities concerning the costs and benefits of English or French language literacy;

9. recognition of the rich heritage of language experiences, both oral and literate, that Aboriginal peoples possess; and

10. recognition that issues of English or French language literacy cannot be considered in isolation from issues of Aboriginal language retention, retrieval and renewal.

RECOMMENDATIONS

In order to develop a national strategy for literacy for Métis and non-status Indian peoples, the authors made the following recommendations:

1. that a national forum on issues of literacy for Métis and non-status Indian peoples be held;

2. that the government of Canada and the Métis and non-status Indian peoples develop a literacy campaign specifically designed to meet the needs of the Métis and non-status Indian peoples;

3. that the government of Canada pass a Métis and Non-Status Indian Peoples' Education Act to define the parameters for federal funding of educational programs for Métis and non-status Indian peoples;

4. that the government of Canada adopt the concept of Aboriginal control of Aboriginal education as a framework for the provision of educational services to the Métis and non-status Indian peoples of Canada;

5. that the government of Canada establish support structures (fiscal and cultural) for the education of Métis and non-status Indian peoples;

6. that a national literacy needs assessment of the Métis and non-status Indian peoples be undertaken;

7. that a national literacy coalition for Métis and non-status Indian peoples be formed, made up of representatives of these groups with the mandate to manage the activities of the literacy campaign;

8. that research be undertaken to establish philosophical and pedagogical criteria for the foundation of curriculum and programs for Métis and non-status Indian people; and

9. that a national literacy council for Métis and non-status Indian peoples be established to bring together practitioners working in the literacy campaign for Métis and non-status Indian people.

▲ The Métis Commission on the Canadian Constitution

AUTHOR: Métis Society of Saskatchewan
YEAR: 1991
ABORIGINAL GROUP: Métis
TOPICS: Self-Government, Constitution
SUB-TOPICS: implementation, structures/institutions, development, representation, constituency identification
SOURCE: Provincial Aboriginal Organization

BACKGROUND

The Métis Commission on the Canadian Constitution was established from a federal grant made to the Métis National Council (MNC) designed to enable Aboriginal peoples to participate in constitutional negotiations in a meaningful way. The MNC distributed a portion of these funds to each provincial organization and the Provincial Métis Council in Saskatchewan used the funds to form the Métis Commission on the Constitution in June 1991.

PURPOSE

The Commission was mandated to canvass the views of the Métis in Saskatchewan and prepare a report for the Provincial Métis Council which would facilitate future discussions on Métis rights. The Provincial Métis Council was then to use this report in communicating Saskatchewan's constitutional concerns to the Métis National Council prior to its negotiations with the first ministers and other national Aboriginal organizations.

ISSUES AND FINDINGS

This report accuses the federal government of cultural genocide in its assimilationist practices toward the Métis people. In the opinion of the Commission, the issue of jurisdiction has ensured unfair treatment of the Métis; while the Métis are subject to the same racial discrimination as are other Aboriginal peoples, they do not receive the benefits of federal programs, and they are left out of many provincial programs because they are deemed by their Indian ancestry to be a federal responsibility.

The report is structured in such a way as to enable it to look in detail at the current conditions facing the Métis people in Saskatchewan, examine the operation of Métis-run programs, and then present the results of public consultation and its corresponding recommendations to the Provincial Métis Council.

The report addresses a number of key issues facing the Métis people in Saskatchewan:

1. cultural preservation;
2. social and demographic indicators;
3. education;
4. health and recreation;
5. justice;
6. land and resources; and
7. self-determination.

1. Cultural Preservation

According to the report, the Métis culture is currently being threatened by many factors. The Gabriel Dumont Institute of Native Studies is attempting to revive Métis culture through research, the development of educational programs and the preservation of cultural materials. The right to hunt, trap and fish is also perceived to be critical to the preservation of Métis culture.

2. Social and Demographic Indicators

The report presents a profile of the Métis people. It describes the Métis people as a very young population with 40% under the age of 15 years. It is also a poor population; the Saskatchewan Métis are the poorest Aboriginal people in Canada, with single mothers experiencing particularly difficult economic circumstances. Overcrowding is also presented as a serious problem with many households having six or more residents. The Commission found that increased Métis involvement in social programs such as child care would improve the responsiveness of these programs to the distinct situations present in Aboriginal communities. Furthermore, youth and women must be involved in the political structures which are attempting to negotiate the future of the Métis nation.

3. Education

The report discusses how low levels of education have excluded Métis from employment opportunities in many of the economic growth areas in the province. This situation is exacerbated by the fact that Métis do not receive access to education equal to the Indian and Inuit peoples and must often travel long distances to receive higher levels of education. It is the opinion of the Commission that the Métis need increased control over education, training and employment programs currently administered by governments.

The Commission cites as an example a Métis-owned financial and investment corporation, which provides commercial and business loans to Métis for start-up and expansion and advises them on preparing proposals and on operating businesses.

4. Health and Recreation

The Commission provided health statistics which indicated that rates of infant mortality, suicide, premature death, and accidents are higher among the Métis than among the non-Aboriginal population. In addition, recreational facilities have not grown and matured along with the communities, resulting in problems of personal control, competence and self-esteem within the community, which have in turn led to alcohol and drug problems, especially among the youth. The report notes that current federal programs designed to combat substance abuse in Aboriginal communities do not apply to Métis.

5. Justice

The report argues that the impact of the justice system on the Métis has been crushing, partly because they do not share the cultural values of the dominant society on which theories, policies and procedures of justice are based. The Commission contends that only by placing more Métis in positions of authority in the criminal justice system can the system be more responsive to the needs of the Métis community.

6. Land

According to the Commission, the issue of land continues to be a key concern of Métis people. Land and resources are essential to a nation, yet the land rights of Métis in Saskatchewan have not been recognized since the scrip process which stripped them of this resource long ago. The Métis risk prosecution when they exercise the same hunting, fishing or trapping rights as do Indian people in Saskatchewan, or even the Dene who are permitted to cross the Northwest Territories border. According to the report, the Métis are kept from these practices while their lands are being parcelled out to outsiders for wide scale resource development. The report argues that it is essential to the existence of the Métis nation that the land issue be resolved and that land be provided in order for the Métis to become self-sufficient.

7. Self-Government

The Commission contends that the Métis community has suffered from generations of powerlessness. A political structure has recently been developed to provide the Métis with means of provincial and national representation; however, this organization is currently seen only as a service organization and not as a government. The Commission proposes many changes which would finalize the evolution of the Métis Society of Saskatchewan and the Métis National Council to political governing bodies. The final goal of the Métis nation is self-sufficiency but until that is possible, funding structures, such as those in place for "have not provinces", will have to be used.

RECOMMENDATIONS

In the view of the Commission, the greatest opportunity for the recognition of the Métis nation and rights lies with an amendment to the Canadian Constitution. Such an amendment would be achieved by way of the general amending formula, which would require the consent of seven provinces comprising over 50% of the population, along with the federal government. A constitutional amendment must, at the very least, recognize the Métis right of self-determination, the right to a land base, the right to self-government, the right to determine their own membership, the right to represent themselves, the right to culture, language and heritage, the right to education and health, and the right to equal treatment. If a constitutional amendment is not possible, the Commission believes that entrenchment should be pursued through bilateral agreements with the western provinces and the federal government under section 43 of the Constitution.

In the interim, the Commission concludes that the immediate needs of the Métis people require the following actions:

1. the recognition of the Métis people as Aboriginal people by the federal government with the full rights accorded to other Aboriginal groups throughout the country;

2. the decentralization of programs and services to Métis affiliates in order to increase the responsiveness of such programs to the Métis situation;

3. the direct participation of Métis on boards, commissions and in the delivery of services to Métis people to enhance the responsiveness and the effectiveness of such programs and services; and

4. the legal recognition and expansion of the Métis Society in order to provide for political organization of the Métis people.

▲ National Unity and Constitutional Reform: Report of the Manitoba Métis Senate Commission

AUTHOR: Manitoba Métis Senate Commission
YEAR: 1991
ABORIGINAL GROUP: Métis
TOPICS: Constitution
SUB-TOPICS: development, representation, constituency identification
SOURCE: Provincial Aboriginal Organization

BACKGROUND

The report was financed by a contribution from the Right Honourable Joe Clark, then minister responsible for Canadian Unity and Constitutional Reform. It is based on a consultative process with the Métis people of Manitoba.

PURPOSE

The purpose of the report is to inform the Métis people on issues affecting them, both locally and nationally. It is also intended to provide information on events affecting Métis people and the Métis Nation. This report is based on the second round of constitutional reform issues.

ISSUES AND FINDINGS

The report's discussion focuses on the identity and history of the Métis, issues of self-government, and mechanisms and structures which the Métis can use to further their goals and concerns related to land claims.

The report recounts the emergence of Métis people during the fur trade, as a people distinct from Indian peoples and Inuit. The Commission describes the history of its rights to the land, based on their ancestry, and the provisions of the *Manitoba Act*. The Act set aside land for the Métis, based on a system which the government later changed to the scrip system, thereby disallowing Métis ownership of land, and dissolving most of their land rights.

On July 31, 1991, the Métis Senate Commission (MSC) presented a report to the Manitoba Métis Federation (MMF) indicating that the Métis want change based on achieving practical results. Visits between the Métis, Joe Clark and Prime Minister Mulroney followed. A new initiative, "Canada Watch", was developed by the MSC to encourage all Métis people to keep an eye on the activities of the federal and provincial governments, Indian groups, Inuit groups, special interest groups, and on the Métis themselves.

The report found that the Métis are working toward establishing different forms of government institutions that would give them more control over decisions that affect them. Such forms of government would allow Métis greater responsibility for education, culture, family services, criminal law systems, employment and training, hunting and gathering rights, and over their land base.

The Commission also addressed mechanisms and structures in which the Métis can participate in order to further their positions. There are four mechanisms identified:

(a) the Parliamentary Committee, which provides Canadians with a means by which to participate in the Canadian renewal process, and through which the Métis hope to reinforce the distinction between the Métis and Aboriginal peoples;

(b) the Royal Commission on Aboriginal Peoples, which is examining a broad range of issues concerning Canadian Aboriginal Peoples, and through which the Métis can make their concerns known to all Canadians;

(c) the Electoral Reform Committee, which is discussing the concept of establishing Aboriginal Electoral Districts; and

(d) the Manitoba Constitutional Task Force, which held public hearings, and reviewed the Meech Lake Task Force recommendations to determine those which remain relevant today.

The Commission also examined concerns related to land claims. This section is based on a speech by Thomas Berger, a lawyer representing the Métis people of Manitoba in the land claims case against the Manitoba government. The object of the land claims case was to establish that the Métis are one of Canada's Aboriginal Peoples and are thus entitled to land and to negotiate land claims settlements. According to the speech, Métis rights are guaranteed in the *Manitoba Act* of 1870, which set aside 1.2 million acres of land for Métis people and their children. These rights, however, were undermined by subsequent government actions. The government stalled in distributing the land for seven years, during which time Ontario settlers came, took over the Manitoba Legislature, and kept the land from the Métis. The new Legislature then passed a law stating that the provisions of the *Infant Protection Act* did not apply to Métis children, thus eliminating the authority of the trustee holding the land that was to go to the Métis children, and allowing speculators to get the land from the children. Finally, the Legislature imposed taxes on the land.

Finally, the report recounts the comments and observations made by the Commissioners:

1. future constitutional positions must be generated by a grassroots consultation process, involving more than just the Métis elite;

2. the Métis must become more informed on issues directly affecting their lives; and

3. the strength of the Métis lies at the level of the local community.

RECOMMENDATIONS

The Commission's recommendations emphasize the need to strengthen the local membership. They propose that the MMF implement an appropriate communication network to make information more available, and that they design an awareness program for interested Métis people and for the general public.

◆ *Pathways to Success: Aboriginal Employment and Training Strategy* (1991), see **Reports by Federal Bodies.**

▲ Report of Public Hearings on Constitutional Reform and Canadian Unity

AUTHOR: Métis Nation of Alberta
YEAR: 1991
ABORIGINAL GROUP: Métis
TOPICS: Self-Government, Constitution
SUB-TOPICS: rights, negotiation structures and processes, implementation, structure/institutions, jurisdiction, documents, rights, development
SOURCE: Provincial Aboriginal Organization

BACKGROUND

A Métis Nation of Alberta (MNA) Constitutional Reform and Canadian Unity "Commission" was established for each of the six zones of the MNA. The six Commissions were each composed of six Métis people, including representatives of Métis elders, Métis women, and Métis youth of Alberta. Each Commission conducted open public hearings in selected Métis communities within each of their zones.

PURPOSE

The Commissions' mandate was to solicit the views, opinions, and recommendations of individual Métis people on a wide range of constitutional issues. This exercise was undertaken in response to the federal government's constitutional proposals of October 1991.

ISSUES AND FINDINGS

The major areas of concern included the following:

1. Self-Government

Both land-based and off-land-based forms of self-government were discussed during the Commissions' work. The land-based model was derived from the 1989 land settlement agreement between eight Métis settlements and the Alberta government. In this agreement, the province of Alberta provided the Métis settlements with legislative authority over many local issues for a total of 1.25 million acres of land. The Métis settlements would therefore have quasi-municipal government status over these areas. The land-based government would be elected indirectly, with each settlement electing five counsellors who in turn would elect a chairperson to become the spokesperson for that settlement. The individual chairpersons would then form the Métis Settlements General Council, with a president, vice president, secretary and treasurer.

The off-land-based model would involve the identification of Métis jurisdictions throughout the province and the nation, to be recognized through a constitutional amendment. Each jurisdiction would elect representatives to form a Métis self-governing body responsible for providing programs and services to the Métis people. In these ways, the Métis people, whether with or without a land base, would be able to exercise their inherent right to self-government.

2. Métis Land Base

The Métis in Alberta are in a unique position since they are the only Métis in Canada who do have a land base. In order to treat Métis in other provinces fairly and equitably, their claims for a land base must be addressed. The MNA believes that the federal government has refused to recognize the government of Alberta's settlement agreement with the MNA because it would create a strong precedent that would greatly strengthen future Métis land negotiations.

3. Enumeration and Registration of the Métis Nation

Given that the Métis nation is widely spread out throughout Canada, statistics on its actual size are unknown. As a result, the process of enumeration of all Métis people is important. The completion of this enumeration exercise would provide a better measure of the needs of all Métis people. Financial assistance from the federal government would be necessary in order to accomplish this task.

4. Responses to Selected Federal Constitutional Proposals

In response to the federal constitutional proposals, the Commission addressed a number of specific proposals: property rights, the need for Métis participation in future negotiations, and self-government. Overall, the MNA stressed that property rights should be narrowly defined since broad, vague definitions could potentially affect future land claims. Furthermore, the Métis nation adopted the position that it must negotiate self-government independent of Indian and Inuit negotiations.

RECOMMENDATIONS

The report specifically stated that none of the issues raised were concrete recommendations from the MNA, but rather only ideas generated from the Métis people for further study and for reference in future negotiations with the federal and provincial governments.

◆ *Report of the British Columbia Claims Task Force* (1991), see **Volume 3, British Columbia.**

◆ *Report of the Northern Economic Development Task Force* (1991), see **Volume 3, Saskatchewan.**

▲ Towards Linguistic Justice for First Nations: The Challenge: Report on the Aboriginal Languages and Literacy Conference

AUTHOR: Assembly of First Nations
YEAR: 1991
ABORIGINAL GROUP: First Nations
TOPIC: Language
SUB-TOPICS: protection and preservation, promotion
SOURCE: National Aboriginal Organization

BACKGROUND

The Assembly of First Nations (AFN) has had a longstanding concern over issues related to language and literacy. In 1972, the AFN, together with the National Indian Brotherhood, published the document "Indian Control of Indian Education", which highlighted the need for cultural centres as a basis for the protection of Aboriginal languages. In 1986, the Assembly of First Nations established a Steering Committee on Education to examine the precarious situation of Aboriginal languages and linguistic heritage. Further to the efforts of the Steering Committee, a conference was held in January 1988, which culminated in the development of a language policy based on the needs of First Nations. The struggle to establish the language policy included a private member's bill, Bill C-269, "An Act to Establish An Aboriginal Languages Foundation", which was defeated in the House of Commons in 1989. To augment further lobbying efforts, however, the AFN was asked to develop statistical information to document the extent of Aboriginal language loss. These statistics were presented at the First Nations Languages and Literacy Conference, in the document entitled "Towards Linguistic Justice".

PURPOSE

This report contains documented research intended as a first step toward developing a long term strategy for the revitalization of Aboriginal languages. The conference provided delegates with an opportunity to respond to the recommendations of the report.

ISSUES AND FINDINGS

According to the findings in "Towards Linguistic Justice", 66% of the Aboriginal languages are either in a state of decline, endangered, or at the critical level. Three major problems were identified:

1. lack of funding;
2. lack of curriculum materials; and
3. lack of trained instructors.

In general, the report found that the Euro-Canadian education system does not suit the diverse language needs of First Nations. The report, "Towards Linguistic Justice" recommends:

1. that the Canadian constitution give Aboriginal languages status equal to English and French;
2. that bands pass by-laws in their Aboriginal languages within their communities and establish community or tribal language commissions;
3. that language commissions/councils be established for language planning initiatives and language planning activities;
4. that an Aboriginal language revitalization strategy be established;
5. that an Aboriginal Languages and Literacy Foundation be established as a component of the Aboriginal Languages Act of Canada (a bill introduced by the AFN); and

6. that mechanisms and resources be developed at both national and regional levels to plan for and carry out literacy initiatives.

The Conference also looked at the issue of an Aboriginal Language Bill, a necessary component of the fifth recommendation. Such a bill would support the view of language, literacy and education as a right. Aboriginal languages were seen as the founding languages and it was felt that they should be treated and recognized in this manner. The outcome of this bill would require that all laws, orders, regulations, rules and other legal instruments intended for Aboriginal people be written in their own language.

RECOMMENDATIONS

The conference delegates responded to the recommendations presented in the document "Towards Linguistic Justice" presented above, as well as to a 1990 report of the Standing Committee on Aboriginal Affairs, entitled "You Took My Talk". Their responses are as follows:

1. the delegates unanimously supported giving Aboriginal languages equal status with English and French;

2. some delegates suggested that the federal and provincial governments recognize the use of Aboriginal languages by changing the current names of languages, place names and personal names to ancestral and traditional names;

3. the delegates also supported the recommendation that Aboriginal languages be promoted for internal use within their communities, emphasizing that the push must be from within the community;

4. delegates suggested that Aboriginal languages be used in everyday settings such as band council meetings;

5. support was also given for the establishment of a Language Commission to oversee literacy, language and education initiatives at all levels;

6. the delegates suggested that Indian and Northern Affairs Canada provide the resources for the proposed Aboriginal Language Revitalization Strategy which would promote, preserve and retain Aboriginal languages;

7. delegates suggested that planning and implementation of First Nations instruction start from early childhood and be extended to include post-secondary, continuing, and adult education;

8. all delegates agreed with the establishment of the Aboriginal Languages and Literacy Foundation to co-ordinate initiatives and distribute funding,

and expressed support for the AFN draft of an Aboriginal Languages Bill which would provide for its establishment;

9. the delegates recommended that the Foundation be located and based in Ottawa and begin lobbying Members of Parliament immediately;

10. there was also group support for the need to plan and identify mechanisms to carry out Aboriginal language and literacy initiatives at the local level, with the national level providing support for the elaboration of plans for action; and

11. the delegates agreed that the government of Canada must pass legislation supporting the appropriate implementation of mother tongue literacy as determined by First Nations peoples.

▲ Voices of the Talking Circle

AUTHOR: Yukon Aboriginal Languages Conference
YEAR: 1991
ABORIGINAL GROUP: First Nations
TOPICS: Language, Communications
SUB-TOPICS: protection and preservation, promotion
SOURCE: Bipartite Organization (Territorial/Aboriginal)

BACKGROUND

On April 10-12, 1992, the first Yukon Aboriginal Languages Conference was held at the Council for Yukon Indians (CYI) administration building to celebrate the Aboriginal languages of the Yukon and to honour those who had dedicated themselves over many years to the survival of the Aboriginal languages. More than 200 elders, parents and young people from all over the Yukon and neighbouring areas, gathered in a traditional talking circle to share their ideas.

PURPOSE

This document is a source of wisdom and guidance for First Nations people and others dedicated to the preservation, development and enhancement of the Aboriginal languages of the Yukon.

ISSUES AND FINDINGS

In total, 10 different talking circles were held involving participants from each of the Yukon's language groups. The following list represents the more prominent ideas expressed:

1. there is a need for young people to learn both English and their Native language;
2. communication with the young is important;
3. schools alone cannot save the Native languages, but instead require support from the home and community;
4. elders have to take a lead role in language promotion and protection; and
5. self-determination is integral to the survival of Native languages.

During the talking circles, the elders emphasized five basic points:

1. that language, culture and identity are inseparable;
2. that all language groups are determined to see their Aboriginal language, oral history and traditions survive;
3. that the home and the community must be the primary basis and location for language preservation, development and enhancement efforts;
4. that the elders wish to be actively involved in family, community and formal educational activities in matters of language and culture; and
5. that the knowledge and sharing of one's language and traditions can bring wholeness and fulfilment to Native people.

In addition to the All Language Circle Groups, each language group (i.e., Gwitch'in, Han, Kaska, Northern Tutchone, Southern Tutchone, Tagish, Tlingit, and Upper Tanana) conducted a talking circle of their own and made recommendations specific to their group. In these talking circles, the participants outlined a preservation strategy with goals and objectives, and suggested projects, activities, resources and instructional methods which would enable them to achieves their goals.

RECOMMENDATIONS

A recommended strategy for language preservation was outlined by each of the language groups. Some of the recommendations common to several of the groups include the following:

1. that each language group place a priority in the strengthening of their language;

2. that language training encourage the use of elders as linguists;

3. that various government legislation, land claims agreements and existing programs and services be used to aid in the preservation, development and enhancement of the languages;

4. that the language be taught at the community, family, individual and school levels;

5. that the mass media be more effectively used for language exposure;

6. that programs be developed to teach people to become language instructors;

7. that the recording of the languages and development of language resources continue; and

8. that Aboriginal language phrase books and dictionaries be developed.

1992

▲ Aboriginal Directions for Coexistence in Canada: Native Council of Canada Constitutional Review Commission Working Paper #1

AUTHOR: The First Peoples Constitutional Review Commission, Co-Chairs, Pat Brascoupé and Martin Dunn

YEAR: 1992

ABORIGINAL GROUP: All Aboriginal Peoples

TOPICS: Constitution, Self-Government

SUB-TOPICS: rights, development

SOURCE: National Aboriginal Organization

BACKGROUND

The Native Council of Canada (NCC) Constitutional Review Commission was established to consider constitutional dialogue related to Aboriginal peoples in an effort to work toward a new relationship with neighbouring societies rooted in co-existence and respect. In this report, the Commission offers its first set of suggestions aimed at achieving a new relationship between Aboriginal and non-Aboriginal societies in Canada.

PURPOSE

The purpose of the report is to offer ideas for consideration and discussion. It is designed to stimulate debate and solicit further input concerning the NCC's position and direction on constitutional issues.

ISSUES AND FINDINGS

The report discusses the important role that Aboriginal peoples have played in Canada's evolution and development, and how this role has been forgotten by non-Aboriginal people. The role of Aboriginal peoples as capable and essential participants in the constitutional process, however, has since been recognized by constitutional law, by a series of constitutional conferences on Aboriginal issues, and by growing public support for their positions.

The report emphasizes the exclusion of Aboriginal peoples from the terms of Confederation, and the need for a new relationship by which Canada and Aboriginal peoples can co-exist. According to the Commission, these terms might by expressed through treaties, especially as they are supported by section 35 of the *Constitution Act, 1982* which provides for additional constitutional amendments to be made on the basis of treaties between Canada and Aboriginal peoples. Furthermore, both the NCC and the Assembly of First Nations (AFN) have proposed the establishment of a national treaty to affirm their various roles in major federal institutions. One idea that the Commission offers for discussion is the development of a treaty covenant between Aboriginal people, and French and English Canada to entrench terms of co-existence.

The report emphasizes the need to rank issues within a full package of immediate and future actions. These priorities include the following:

1. the need to ensure equity of access to rights, and mobility of rights;
2. the need to recognize within the Canada Round of constitutional discussions that Aboriginal peoples constitute distinct societies with their own languages, cultures and institutions and that they are a fundamental characteristic of Canada;
3. the need for clear affirmation of the inherent right to self-government, for negotiations of new fiscal arrangements, and for secured access for Aboriginal communities to land and resources;
4. the need for a constitutionally mandated process of dispute resolution which is fair and expeditious;
5. the need to adopt a community-based approach in order to find solutions to national issues;

6. the need to adopt a new treaty process, endorsed by Aboriginal leaders, which features clear dispute resolution mechanisms;

7. the need to ensure unity among Aboriginal peoples, perhaps by re-creating, with modifications, the Aboriginal Summit, as a means of assisting all Aboriginal peoples in reaching common, unified positions on crucial issues; and

8. the need to embrace the principle of securing Aboriginal consent to fundamental changes, and to support this principle by establishing community processes for significant discussion and direction to national leadership.

RECOMMENDATIONS

The report makes no formal recommendations, but rather offers the issues outlined above for future discussion and encourages feedback to the Commission.

▲ The Métis Women's Perspective on National Unity and Constitutional Reform

AUTHOR: The Métis Women of Manitoba
YEAR: 1992
ABORIGINAL GROUP: Métis, Aboriginal Women
TOPICS: Self-Government, Political Participation
SUB-TOPIC: jurisdiction
SOURCE: Provincial Aboriginal Organization

BACKGROUND

This report was made possible through funding from the federal government. It was undertaken as part of the constitutional process to collect the views and opinions of Métis women on the state of the constitutional discussions.

PURPOSE

This report outlines what was heard at a series of meetings held in 1991. It profiles the opinions of Métis women on a series of issues affecting their daily lives, particularly those related to the constitutional negotiations then under way.

ISSUES AND FINDINGS

This report deals with many of the issues under debate in the constitutional negotiations. While Métis women are concerned with many of the same issues as are other Canadian women, they have additional concerns because of their heritage, including concerns over constitutional recognition, self-government, education, identity, child welfare, language, and representation.

While the Métis support their constitutional recognition, it is evident in this report that they feel that being recognized as "Aboriginal" forces them into a definition in which their distinct identities become indistinguishable from the cultures and histories of First Nations. Because of their unique heritage, they embrace both their First Nations and European ancestors and do not support the concept of a divided Canada.

The definition of self-government which has been developed through this consultation is articulated as the "control and administration of programs and services affecting their lives, with the legislative authority to develop and administer these areas." It is believed that self-government would address many inequities in services and programs which currently exist. According to the report, self-government is not the only issue, but until it is resolved, other issues cannot be dealt with effectively.

The report criticizes the federal government for funding the education of registered Indians, but not Métis people. The consultation process found this issue to be great concern to Métis, given that a lack of education or the resources to obtain it causes and prolongs what the report refers to as "economic apartheid". As an uneducated people, the Métis would be unable to develop and staff their own institutions of self-government and service delivery.

The report contends that many Métis can and do pretend to be "white" and that this has caused many problems in the Métis community. Those who do pretend to be white become ashamed of their families and eventually resent the attitudes which made them hide their heritage, and experience pain and guilt because of their actions. Those who do not often resent the part of their heritage which made them outsiders.

Métis women feel that child and family services have too often been willing to apprehend and place Métis children in non-Métis homes. According to the report, the Métis people need the legislative authority to develop their own child welfare systems. The report notes that First Nations child welfare agencies have already taken control over their own children.

Participants in the consultation process felt that the Métis people are not well represented by First Nations groups which purport to represent all Aboriginal peoples. These groups were not seen to be concerned with the serious inequities which exist in funding and programs between First Nations, Inuit groups and the Métis. The report argues that only through Métis organizations, can the Métis have control over their own agenda and represent their own interests.

RECOMMENDATIONS

No specific recommendations are made in this report. In general, the report does, however, call for recognition of the Métis as an Aboriginal people, improved funding, and the transfer of jurisdiction to Métis people to expedite the development of self-government.

▲ National Treaty Conference: Indigenous Treaties – Self-Determination: Past-Present-Future: Final Report

AUTHOR: National Treaty Conference

YEAR: 1992

ABORIGINAL GROUP: First Nations

TOPICS: Self-Government, Constitution, Federal Government/Aboriginal Relations, Treaty Land Entitlement

SUB-TOPICS: rights, negotiation structures and processes, development, treaties, claims

SOURCE: Other Aboriginal Organization

BACKGROUND

The idea of a conference was initiated in November 1991, when a motion was put forward at the Assembly of First Nations to hold a conference to address the urgent concerns and issues affecting First Nations and their treaties. The first National Treaty Conference was held in Edmonton, Alberta, from April 6-9, 1992. Hosted by Treaties 3, 6, 7 and 8, and by the Assembly of First Nations, it brought together an estimated 2,000 First Nations delegates, including chiefs, councillors and elders.

PURPOSE

The purpose of the conference was to review the past, present and future of Indigenous treaties and to consider how these treaties will affect First Nations' inherent right to self-determination and self-government. The intent of the discussions was to reach a consensus respecting treaty rights which would preserve the true spirit of the treaties for future generations and which would serve as the official bargaining position of the Assembly of First Nations during constitutional discussions.

ISSUES AND FINDINGS

Several major issues arose which exemplified the diversity among First Nations yet a consensus emerged derived from common concerns. There was agreement on the need for First Nations to continue to pursue the establishment and implementation of their inherent nation-to-nation treaty rights as agreed upon by the Forefathers of the First Nations and the Crown.

The principles of treaty rights upon which consensus was achieved include the following:

1. First Nations must negotiate with the government of Canada on a nation-to-nation basis;

2. First Nations treaties are sacred agreements that must be protected, upheld and honoured for future generations;

3. the bilateral nature of the treaty relationship between the Treaty First Nations and the Crown must be maintained;

4. only those First Nations party to a particular treaty may consent to any action that may affect that treaty;

5. other Aboriginal groups without treaty rights may not speak on behalf of First Nations; and

6. sovereign treaty rights must attain a higher priority and profile.

RECOMMENDATIONS

The conference delegates unanimously supported the resolution to establish a Sovereign Treaty First Nations Council within the Assembly of First Nations to develop positions and processes on treaties. The Council is to consist of official representatives from each of the treaty areas and is to guided by the following principles intended to maintain the sacred nature and integrity of the treaties:

1. that Treaty First Nations are sovereign nations under their sacred laws;

2. that the nation-to-nation status of the treaties is protected and guaranteed and that the Constitution of Canada respect the sovereign Treaty First Nations;

3. that the Crown in right of Canada recognize, guarantee, and honour inherent and treaty rights of Treaty First Nations;

4. that the Constitution of Canada recognize and respect all differences between sovereign Treaty First Nations and sovereign First Nations which do not at present have rights under treaty;

5. that a complete review of all non-Indigenous laws and agreements which affect the treaty relationship be undertaken;

6. that a complete review of section 91 (24) of the *Constitution Act, 1867* be initiated to deal specifically with the fiscal relationship between the Crown in right of Canada and the sovereign Treaty First Nations; and

7. that any constitutional amendment only occur with the consent of the sovereign Treaty First Nations.

▲ The Report of the Atlantic First People's Constitutional Forum

AUTHOR: Atlantic First People's Constitutional Forum, Atlantic Regional Co-ordinator, Katherine Sorbey

YEAR: 1992

ABORIGINAL GROUP: Métis, Non-Status

TOPICS: Self-Government, Constitution, Federal Government/Aboriginal Relations, Treaty Land Entitlement

SUB-TOPICS: rights, structures/institutions, development, treaties, federal trust responsibilities, commissions/structures/negotiation processes

SOURCE: Regional Aboriginal Organization

BACKGROUND

The Atlantic First People's Constitutional Forum brought together representatives of non-status and Métis advocacy groups from all four Atlantic provinces. The Forum was convened following a series of Community Meetings conducted by provincial facilitators to solicit the opinions of

Atlantic Aboriginal peoples concerning the Canada Clause, and the rights of Aboriginal peoples living off-reserve.

PURPOSE

The Forum was to act as the primary vehicle for off-reserve Aboriginal people in the region to address constitutional priorities. The consultative methods used were designed to improve the ability of Aboriginal leaders to present a strong and united Aboriginal position on the Constitution in future negotiations with the government.

ISSUES AND FINDINGS

The report contains Fact Sheets on each of the five Atlantic Affiliates of the Native Council of Canada: the Native Council of Nova Scotia, the Native Council of Prince Edward Island, the New Brunswick Aboriginal Peoples Council, the Federation of Newfoundland Indians, and the Labrador Métis Association. Each group represents Métis, non-status Indians and/or Status Indians who do not live on reserves. All groups assist off-reserve people of Aboriginal ancestry to form local organizations for the purpose of advancing their general living conditions and achieving a level of self-government.

The issues which were raised in the Community Meetings in each region were very similar across all groups. Concerns were expressed over the following issues:

1. recognition as First Peoples;
2. the proposed Canada Clause;
3. the rights of off-reserve Aboriginal people;
4. the deterioration of language and culture;
5. improved Native education;
6. self-determination and self-government;
7. the mobility of treaty and Aboriginal rights; and
8. economic independence.

The Constitutional Forum also acted as a catalyst for a number of other key discussions with regard to land rights, recognition as First Peoples, treaty rights, and self-government:

1. The Métis expressed considerable anxiety over the government's failure to recognize their land rights, especially in light of the progress being made in the negotiation of other Aboriginal claims. The Métis in Labrador, for

instance, expressed concern that their traditional land is being handed over to sports fishing interests without even consulting the Métis; the lack of understanding of the provincial bureaucracy and the lack of recognition of their Aboriginal status were offered as factors which have contributed to this problem.

2. With regard to the Canada Clause, the participants attached a high level of importance to their recognition as the first peoples of Canada, and as distinct peoples who live throughout the country; this recognition is viewed as vital in their efforts to be considered equals within the federation. In addition, they believe that the constitution should state that it is the duty of all governments to make laws, policies and programs that apply fairly and equally to all Aboriginal peoples and that respect their dignity and their identity.

3. With regard to the treaty rights outlined in section 25 of the Constitution, the Forum participants re-affirmed their belief that the treaty rights of Aboriginal people must be accessible, must not be restricted by modern boundaries, and must not be altered or renegotiated without the consent of the Aboriginal treaty nation or people.

4. With regard to the governance provisions of section 35 of the Constitution, the representatives expressed a desire to re-establish democratic institutions of self-government which are accountable, credible and responsible to their people. Such governments would have powers in such areas as land and resources, economic development, language, culture and education, communication, justice and policing, health care, fiscal management, environment, housing, and the establishment and development of their own constitutions.

RECOMMENDATIONS

The Forum report outlines a number of principles recognizing the dignity and social integrity of Aboriginal People in Canada's Constitution. Specifically, the principles assert that:

1. no law be able to impair the inherent right of self-determination and self-government of the Aboriginal Nations;

2. that no law affecting Aboriginal peoples be enacted without the effective participation of their authorized representatives;

3. that a Schedule be added to the Constitution in not less that one year setting forth the respective authority and jurisdiction of federal, provincial and Aboriginal governments;

4. that a Constitutional Commission on Aboriginal Affairs be established to recommend amendments to this Schedule; and

5. that these principle be entrenched in the Constitution and not subject to further amendments.

◆ *Report of the Saskatchewan Indian Justice Review Committee* (1992), see **Volume 3, Saskatchewan.**

◆ *Report of the Saskatchewan Métis Justice Review Committee* (1992) see **Volume 3, Saskatchewan.**

▲ Response of the New Brunswick Aboriginal Peoples Council to the Report of the Commission on Canadian Federalism

AUTHOR: New Brunswick Aboriginal Peoples Council
YEAR: 1992
ABORIGINAL GROUP: First Nations, Urban Aboriginal People
TOPICS: Self-Government, Constitution, Programs and Services
SUB-TOPICS: rights, development
SOURCE: Provincial Aboriginal Organization

BACKGROUND

The New Brunswick Aboriginal Peoples Council (NBAPC) represents the off-reserve registered and non-registered Aboriginal people of New Brunswick. This report is a response to the Report of the New Brunswick Commission on Canadian Federalism, published in January 1992.

PURPOSE

The purpose of this report is to respond formally to the findings and recommendations prepared by the New Brunswick Commission on Canadian Federalism. The response is generally supportive of the Commission's report.

ISSUES AND FINDINGS

There are five major areas of concern, corresponding to five of the six chapters (there is no response to Chapter 5 on Linguistic Partnership) addressed in the Commission's report.

1. Inclusion of Aboriginal Peoples in Constitutional Discussions

While this practice is supported by both the Commission and the NBAPC, the NBAPC was disappointed that the Commission did not include an Aboriginal distinct society clause, comparable to that of Quebec.

2. National Programs Concerning Off-Reserve Members

The report found that these members use the same programs as non-Aboriginal people, and will continue to do so until self-government is achieved. It was noted that off-reserve members are at the lowest end of the socio-economic ladder and must be compensated.

3. Economic Union

The concern here arises from grouping Aboriginal and non-Aboriginal peoples together in the provincial area of labour market training.

4. Aboriginal People of New Brunswick

The NBAPC expressed concern that the Commission did not directly mention off-reserve Aboriginal people. There is also concern over the Constitution; although the NBAPC supports the removal of section 33 (the notwithstanding clause), they want it to be applicable to self-government arrangements, to avoid being relegated to the level of municipal government.

5. Federal Institutions

The NBAPC asserts that their inherent right to self-government guarantees them participation in these institutions, particularly in Parliament.

In general, the NBAPC support most of the recommendations proposed by the Commission.

RECOMMENDATIONS

The NBAPC has proposed two recommendations. They recommend that off-reserve Aboriginal people be recognized and assured full partnership in negotiations regarding implementation of the Commission's recommendations.

They also recommend that concerns raised by the NBAPC throughout their response be forwarded to the Premier; these concerns relate to the recognition of a distinct Aboriginal society, the opting out clause, labour market training, the specific concerns of off-reserve Aboriginal people, and the inherent right of Aboriginal peoples to participate in Canada's institutions.

▲ Self-Government: Our Past Traditions, Our Present Lives, Our Children's Future

AUTHOR: Métis Nation–Northwest Territories and Council for Yukon Indians

YEAR: 1992

ABORIGINAL GROUP: Métis, First Nations

TOPICS: Self-Government, Constitution, Constitutional Development

SUB-TOPICS: rights, negotiation structures and processes, implementation, development

SOURCE: Territorial Aboriginal Organizations

BACKGROUND

On January 27 and 28, 1992, representatives of both the Métis Nation of the Northwest Territories and the Council for Yukon Indians met at a First Peoples' Forum in Yellowknife to discuss Aboriginal rights and the Constitution of Canada. Representatives included women, men, elders and youth members of the communities. Members of Friendship Centres and the Native Women's Association were also present.

PURPOSE

The forum was organized to meet three goals:

1. to address self-government;

2. to examine initiatives and priorities for the Canadian constitutional negotiations; and

3. to develop a structure that would reflect the region's approach to the decision-making process and future constitutional development.

ISSUES AND FINDINGS

A number of broad issues were discussed over the two-day forum. The predominant issues related to economic needs, future economic changes, and how to achieve the goal of self-sufficiency. The following concerns figured prominently in the forum's discussions:

1. concern that the drive for constitutional change would overtake the important issues of Aboriginal economic, employment, and social problems;

2. the need for employment and education initiatives to overcome obstacles to Aboriginal self-sufficiency stimulated by technological changes;

3. concern about conflicts which might arise between current land claim negotiations and the need to incorporate economic changes into the constitution;

4. concern that self-government be viewed as more than just program delivery;

5. concern that the recognition of the inherent right to self-government through a constitutional amendment not affect the determination of land claims settlements, and that land claims settlements and self-government agreements not set any precedent or have any affect on any other nation's inherent right to exercise self-government;

6. the need for assured participation for Aboriginal women in both the process of achieving self-government and in the exercise of self-government; and

7. the need to acknowledge the importance of elders and youth within self-government.

RECOMMENDATIONS

The report's recommendations were not specific; instead, the forum presented concluding views under the following headings:

1. Inherent Right To Self-Government

Participants reiterated that the inherent right is not negotiable and that the goal of self-government must be achieved through agreement based on community consultation.

2. Values

The forum concluded that values such as healing, sharing, trust, caring, respect for all people, and recognition of diversity are essential to any future agreement. These values should be reflected in all proposals for constitutional amendments.

3. Structure

The forum participants agreed that self-government must be built from the community level upwards, and that elders, women and youth must be fully involved in decision making.

4. Entrenchment of Self-Government

The report asserts that the inherent right to self-government must be entrenched without definition and despite the lack of details on models or process. The onus must be on government to negotiate self-government at the communities' requests.

5. Self-Government in the Territories

There must be a guarantee that Aboriginal people retain effective participation in public government. There should be a mechanism to ensure that any immigration to the North does not adversely affect either Aboriginal self-government or Aboriginal rights.

6. Nationhood and Shared Citizenship

Aboriginal nations and their nationhood should be recognized in the same way as the English and French. Aboriginal peoples see themselves as Aboriginal before Canadian. There should be no conflict or interference resulting from shared citizenship.

7. Land Base

The federal government must ensure an established land base for self-government, to be collectively decided upon.

8. Resources and Financing

A more secure base for the financing of self-government should be established, to be based on an equitable right to land resources, rather than transfer payments.

9. Aboriginal Citizenship and Solidarity

Aboriginal peoples should try to eliminate, as much as possible, the distinctions and labels that are placed on them by others, particularly government. Aboriginal peoples need to decide "who we are", and "who the members of our community are". Members of Aboriginal communities must work together in situations where they share common interests.

10. Social Charter

There should be a social charter to promote and protect cultural and language rights. This charter must incorporate rather than replace the fiduciary responsibility of the federal government for Aboriginal people.

11. Institutional Representation

Guaranteed representation to ensure fair and equal representation should not be necessary when institutions are structured on principles of respect.

12. Amending Formula

Any creation of provincehood or the extension of provincial boundaries into the territories must protect Aboriginal people and self-government. Any changes to the territories should accommodate the concerns of the residing Aboriginal people.

13. Consultation

An ongoing process of Aboriginal discussion and consultation is essential to the resolution of Aboriginal issues. The process should not be dependent upon the timetables of other governments.

▲ To the Source: First Nations Circle on the Constitution: Commissioners' Report

AUTHOR: Assembly of First Nations
YEAR: 1992
ABORIGINAL GROUP: First Nations
TOPICS: Self-Government, Constitution
SUB-TOPICS: right, implementation, structures/institutions
SOURCE: National Aboriginal Organization

BACKGROUND

In August 1991, the Assembly of First Nations (AFN) established the First Nations Circle on the Constitution (FNCC). The Commissioners of the First Nations Circle were instructed to listen to the concerns of the First Nations peoples with respect to self-government, constitutional reform, and other issues of concern to them. The process parallelled the constitutional hearings being held by the Canadian government. The Commissioners held 80 meetings, and four constituent assemblies involving elders, youth, women, and off-reserve Aboriginal people.

PURPOSE

The Commissioners were instructed to gather the concerns of First Nations peoples. The results were then to be used to educate both Aboriginal and non-Aboriginal people about the primary issues facing First Nations. As one means to achieve this purpose, the FNCC findings were used at a one-day session of the Beaudoin-Dobbie Commission that was televised across Canada.

ISSUES AND FINDINGS

All of the primary issues in the report were derived from the actual dialogue of the participants at the meetings and constituent assemblies. These issues may be subdivided into nine primary categories:

1. Social and Economic Issues

The concerns of on-reserve First Nations peoples included high unemployment, substandard housing and services, and hopelessness for the younger generation, while those of off-reserve Indian people included isolation, racism, poverty and cultural alienation. Concerns were also expressed about the impact of residential schools, substance abuse, crime, and AIDS within First Nations communities.

2. Language, Culture and Spirituality

The main concerns expressed concerning language, culture and spirituality, were the loss of language, loss of identity, and the loss of traditional ways of interacting with each other, and the resultant difficulties which are being experienced by many communities. It was generally felt that only by regaining their spiritual balance would First Nations be able to break the cycle of poverty, abuse and despair. Re-establishing language and traditions, and exerting greater control over the justice and education were seen as essential to retrieving this balance.

3. Self-Government

The people felt that they had an inherent right to self-government based on the fact that their ancestors had never consented to be governed by the Europeans. They asserted that the federal government cannot grant self-government because it already exists, and therefore, all the government can do is recognize its existence. The report also noted that there was a general consensus among those consulted that self-government cannot and will not be the same in each community, and that each community must have the freedom, power, and resources to draw on its own strengths and traditions.

4. The Constitutional Process

Reactions to constitutional issues were mixed. Some of the participants called for a boycott of the constitutional process while others simply felt it was irrelevant. The general conclusion, however, was that if another constitutional process was undertaken, it should be inclusive, and First Nations should act in unity.

5. Funding

Frustration was expressed with funding. It was felt that reserves were underfunded and that this problem was worsened by the government's policy of calculating funding based on on-reserve membership; this situation was seen to prevent reserves from delivering services to off-reserve members without shortchanging their on-reserve community. They also felt that government interference could be felt at every level of community management, from choosing leaders to allocating funds.

6. The Indian Act

The participants called for an end to the *Indian Act* because of the ways in which it has interfered in their lives and the divisions within the Aboriginal community that it has caused. They felt that new legislation should be drafted, subject to the consent of those directly affected.

7. Quebec and "Distinct Society"

The issue of Quebec separation and distinct society was also discussed. First Nations people felt that they would be subordinate to the francophone population and last in line for funding and services if Quebec were to separate. There was some consensus that if Quebec were to become an independent nation, the First Nations within the province would opt to remain within Canada.

The people sympathized with Quebec's desire to preserve and transmit what is distinctly Québécois; however, they felt that any definition of a distinct society would identify Aboriginal peoples as more distinct than the Québécois. This is based on the idea that Aboriginal language, traditions and cultures are more different from both French and English than French and English are from each other.

8. Land and Treaties

The loss of their land was another issue discussed in the FNCC's consultations. The people expressed frustration and anger over the federal government's slowness in settling land claims, and the environmental problems posed by mercury pollution and low level training flights in Aboriginal communities.

The non-fulfilment of the promises made to the First Nations by the Crown in treaties was a concern frequently raised by Aboriginal people. They identified provincial hunting and fishing legislation and the narrow interpretation of treaties by the federal government as two of the primary causes of the slow progress in the area.

9. The Concerns of Elders, Women and Youth

Of particular concern to the Elders Assembly were issues relating to Native war veterans and to Aboriginal leadership. They spoke with dissatisfaction about how their reserves and programs were being run, and about how their leaders were paying more attention to government policy than to the advice of elders.

The Women's Assembly felt that First Nations had been influenced by the European view that women are subordinate, largely as a result of the *Indian Act* which tied a woman's rights and identity to her husband. They expressed hope that the Charter would correct this problem, and return First Nations to their traditional respect for women.

The Youth Assembly identified Aboriginal control over Aboriginal education as a major issue. They also noted that there is a clear connection between language and spiritual health.

RECOMMENDATIONS

The recommendations flowed directly from the issues identified in the consultation process. The FNCC put forth several recommendations, categorized as follows:

1. Self-Government

(a) that the Constitution recognize an inherent right to self-government, and view First Nations as separate and distinct societies;

(b) that the pace of self-government be determined by each First Nation;

(c) that fiscal arrangements be based on resource sharing with First Nations governments being on equal footing with federal and provincial counterparts;

(d) that past injustices be acknowledged; and

(e) that First Nations have their own justice systems and that their language and culture be protected and recognized.

2. Intergovernmental Relations

(a) that Quebec and the other provinces recognize the territorial integrity of First Nations and that no mega-projects be constructed in Northern Quebec without the consent of affected Aboriginal communities;

(b) that First Nations peoples be compensated for their loss of hunting and fishing rights as a result of the establishment of parks, game reserves, wildlife areas and private leases of Crown lands;

(c) that treaties cease to be interpreted unilaterally, that oral traditions be recognized, and that any future treaties be written in the appropriate Aboriginal language; and

(d) that there be an immediate moratorium on any provincial laws and policies that impede and violate the full exercise of treaty rights by Aboriginal peoples.

3. Elders, Women and Youth

(a) that elders adopt an greater role in decision-making, especially those related to environmental, educational and healing activities;

(b) that action be taken to meet the special needs of elders;

(c) that women be represented in all decision making and that gender equality be established in the form of an Aboriginal Charter of Rights and Freedoms;

(d) that treaty rights apply without regard to residence;

(e) that Aboriginal students be given the right to be educated in their own language, history and culture; and

(f) that English, French and First Nations work co-operatively to resolve conflicts.

▲ Towards Settlement of Our Rights

AUTHOR: Pacific Métis Federation
YEAR: 1992
ABORIGINAL GROUP: Métis
TOPICS: Self-Government, Constitution, Federal
  Government/Aboriginal Relations
SUB-TOPICS: rights, jurisdiction, documents, rights, development,
  political participation/representation
SOURCE: Provincial Aboriginal Organization

BACKGROUND

This document was prepared by the Pacific Métis Federation (PMF) in
response to the 1992 round of constitutional talks.

PURPOSE

The purpose of the report was to assess the federal government's proposals
for a revitalized Constitution, and to put forth the perspectives of the PMF
on the proposals relating to the Charlottetown Accord.

ISSUES AND FINDINGS

The PMF outlines the history of the Métis people and their historical
significance in the development of the Canadian nation. Their involvement
in past constitutional discussions is also traced.

RECOMMENDATIONS

The PMF presents their recommendations with respect to four specific areas
of the Charlottetown Accord: self-government; the Canada Clause; Quebec;
and participation in federal political institutions.

Self-Government

1. that there be explicit constitutional reaffirmation of the inherent right
   of the Métis nation to self-government in section 35 of the *Constitution
   Act, 1982*, to be judicially enforceable without delay;

2. that the parameters of self-government include the fundamental characteristics of Métis self-government which would include, but would not be limited to democratically elected and functioning Métis governments and institutions, acceptance of the rule of law, and a Métis Charter of Rights and Freedoms to be adopted within section 35;

3. that an alternative dispute resolution mechanism be established to handle disputes over jurisdictions or conflict of laws;

4. that the Constitution provide a legally enforceable commitment to negotiate a land base, jurisdiction and powers of Métis self-government, fiscal relations and resource-sharing agreements;

5. that the *Constitution Act, 1982*, be amended to provide for representation by Métis in the constitutional process;

Canada Clause

6. that the Canada Clause be amended to strengthen the interpretation of Métis rights, including the inherent right to self-government;

7. that the Canada Clause be amended to include the contribution of the Métis people as nation-builders;

8. that one or more constitutional conferences be held to deal with women's rights and women's issues;

Quebec

9. that Quebec be recognized as a distinct society;

10. that with the exception of Quebec, no federal powers be transferred to the provinces until the jurisdictions of Métis self-government are determined;

Participation in Federal Political Institutions

11. that Senate seats be guaranteed in the Métis homeland; and

12. that Métis people be guaranteed representation in Parliament.

In addition to the recommendations outlined above, the PMF also recommends that the federal government assume its primary responsibility for the Métis nation under section91(24). Finally, the PMF stresses the need for a tripartite process which would address constitutional, as well as non-constitutional matters affecting its people.

1993

▲ The Métis Nation On The Move: Report on the Métis Nation's Constitutional Parallel Process

AUTHOR: Métis National Council

YEAR: 1993

ABORIGINAL GROUP: Métis

TOPICS: Self-Government, Constitution, Federal Government/Aboriginal Relations

SUB-TOPICS: rights, jurisdiction, structures/institutions, federal trust responsibilities, political participation/representation

SOURCE: National Aboriginal Organization

BACKGROUND

This paper is the result of community-based consultations with the Métis people on issues pertaining to the constitutional renewal process and how best to entrench Métis rights in the Constitution. The consultations were conducted by member Métis National Council (MNC) organizations in Manitoba (Manitoba Métis Federation), Alberta (Métis Nation of Albert), Saskatchewan (Saskatchewan Métis Society), and British Columbia (Pacific Métis Federation). In addition, the Métis Nation of the Northwest Territories, and the Ontario Métis and Aboriginal Association provided valuable input into the development of the MNC position.

PURPOSE

The purpose of the report was to consolidate the views of each Métis National Council member, of Métis women and of Métis in the Northwest Territories and Ontario, in an effort to present the constitutional aspirations of the Métis nation.

ISSUES AND FINDINGS

The report is divided into seven sections, each describing the history, federal position and consultative findings concerning the issues under examination:

1. Métis Identity, History and Culture

The report presents a history of the Métis in Canada, emphasizing the need for the Métis identity and historical contributions to Canada to be recognized in the Constitution. The landlessness and marginal position of the Métis is viewed largely as the result of a refusal to recognize the Métis as a distinct Aboriginal group. The report illustrates that there is support for the entrenchment of the Canada Clause but only if it done in such a way as to strengthen Métis rights. Many participants also felt that there should be some kind of enumeration/registration process to determine the size of the Métis nation.

2. Métis Land Issue

The report describes the 1981 position of government that the Métis, outside the Northwest Territories, do not possess Aboriginal title. This has generated some tension; the recognition of the Métis as an Aboriginal people has placed their land claims under the umbrella of Aboriginal title, while Ottawa has established a process of implementing the land rights of others but not of the Métis. The consultative process revealed how important the establishment of a land base is to the Métis people.

3. Constitutional Entrenchment of Métis Self-Government

The report describes Métis associations as the starting point for Métis self-governing institutions; however, there is some concern that these associations are seriously undermined by a lack of legal authority and resources. Based on the consultative findings, the report contends that the Métis people want their inherent right to self-government recognized but do not seek sovereignty outside of Canada. These arrangements would govern all Métis without a land base who chose to participate but would only apply to a clearly defined set of matters. In these sense, they view self-government as an expanded form of federalism.

4. Section 91(24) of the *Constitution Act, 1867*

The report found that the federal government has neglected its responsibility for settling land issues and providing distinct services to Métis. There was also frustration expressed over the federal government failure to assume responsibility for Métis services. The resolution of these jurisdictional issue was identified as one of the central constitutional objectives of the Métis Nation.

5. Métis Participation in Parliamentary Institutions

The report concluded that there have only been three Métis people south of the sixtieth parallel who have been elected to the House of Commons since Confederation, and furthermore, that there has never been a Métis person appointed to serve in the Senate. Participants voiced strong support for guaranteed representation for Métis people.

6. The Ongoing Constitutional Process

The participants welcomed Aboriginal representation but felt that only Métis can speak for their people and therefore they must have a voice separate from those of other Aboriginal peoples.

7. Division of Powers

The Métis expressed considerable concern about the decentralization of some powers under the federal constitutional proposals. In the event of the transfer of jurisdiction of administrative responsibility, the Métis would want their interests protected.

RECOMMENDATIONS

The report's recommendations follow the same pattern outlined above:

1. Métis Culture and Identity

The report recommends that the Constitution recognize the contribution of the Métis nation, the Aboriginal inherent right to self-government, and the right of the Métis people to control their own membership.

2. Métis Land Issue

The report recommends that the inherent right of the Métis people to a land and resource base be recognized in the Constitution as a distinct agenda item.

3. Constitutional Entrenchment of Métis Self-Government

The report recommends explicit constitutional reaffirmation of the inherent right of the Métis to self-government, and entrenchment of a list of jurisdictions that Métis governments would exercise. It further recommends that intergovernmental disputes be settled by a alternative dispute resolution tribunal consisting of one Métis, one government official, and a chair chosen by both. While the Métis do not object to the application of the Charter, they report recommends the development of a separate Métis Charter.

4. Section 91(24)

The Métis nation supports the federal assumption of jurisdiction and responsibility for the Métis nation, and recommends that a bilateral process of negotiation be developed to resolve outstanding land claims, enumeration and other issues.

5. Métis Participation in Parliamentary Institutions

The report recommends that the constitution be amended to guarantee the representation of Métis people. It also recommends that Métis electoral districts be capable of crossing provincial boundaries.

6. The Ongoing Constitutional Process

The Métis support an ongoing constitutional process, and recommend that conferences be held annually and include full Métis involvement.

7. Division of Powers

The report recommends that any division of powers recognize a third order of government – Aboriginal self-government – and that any transfer of jurisdiction affecting the Métis nation be, to the extent that it affects Métis, subject to Métis consent.

Author Index

FEDERAL BODIES

ABORIGINAL ORGANIZATIONS

Subject Index

For further information:
Royal Commission on Aboriginal Peoples
P.O. Box 1993, Station B
Ottawa, Ontario
K1P 1B2

Telephone: (613) 943-2075
Facsimile: (613) 943-0304

Toll-free:
1-800-363-8235 (English, French, Chipewyan)
1-800-387-2148 (Cree, Inuktitut, Ojibwa)